1,000 DOLLARS
AND AN IDEA

1,000 DOLLARS AND AN IDEA

Entrepreneur to Billionaire

SAM WYLY

Newmarket Press   New York

This book is published in the United States of America.

First Edition

10 9 8 7 6 5 4 3 2 1

Library of Congress Cataloging-in-Publication Data

Wyly, Sam.
1,000 dollars and an idea : entrepreneur to billionaire / Sam Wyly. – 1st ed.
p. cm.
Includes index.
ISBN 978-1-55704-803-5 (cloth : alk. paper) 1. Wyly, Sam. 2.
Businessmen–United States–Biography. 3. Entrepreneurship–United States–
Biography. 4. Billionaires–United States–Biography. I. Title.
II. Title: One thousand dollars and an idea : entrepreneur to billionaire. III.
Title: entrepreneur to billionaire.
HC102.5.W95W95 2008
338'.04092–dc22
[B]
2008003175

ISBN: 978-1-55704-803-5 hardcover

ISBN: 978-1-55704-825-7 export edition

QUANTITY PURCHASES

Companies, professional groups, clubs, and other organizations
may qualify for special terms when ordering quantities of this title.
For information or a catalog, write Special Sales Department,
Newmarket Press, 18 East 48th Street, New York, NY 10017;
call (212) 832-3575; fax (212) 832-3629; or
e-mail info@newmarketpress.com.

www.newmarketpress.com

Designed by M. J. Di Massi

Manufactured in the United States of America.
This book has been printed on recycled paper.

TO FLORA
... a genuine entrepreneur

Huck explains that *The Adventures of Huckleberry Finn* was written by Mr. Mark Twain, who mostly told the truth.

But Huck was not telling the whole truth because the author was born Samuel Clemens and young Sam Clemens lifted his pen name of Mark Twain from a Mississippi River steamboat pilot who wrote stories for the New Orleans *Times-Picayune.*

So what is here in this book is what I remember.

Some I see with the clear and simple eyes of a child.

Some not.

Others may remember differently.

So be it.

SAM WYLY
Dallas, Texas
October 4, 2007

If you can trust yourself when all men doubt you
But make allowance for their doubting too

      . . .

If you can dream—and not make dreams your master,
If you can think—and not make thoughts your aim;
If you can meet with Triumph and Disaster
And treat those two impostors just the same

      . . .

If you can make one heap of all your winnings
And risk it on one turn of pitch-and-toss,
And lose, and start again at your beginnings
And never breathe a word about your loss

      . . .

Yours is the Earth and everything that's in it.

—From "If"
  Rudyard Kipling (1865–1936)

Contents

CONTENTS

Prologue

I LEARNED SOME real good lessons in the barbershop.

Back in Lake Providence, Louisiana, where I grew up, my family would go to town on Saturday mornings so that Mama could run her errands and Dad could go to the barbershop for his weekly big lather shave. It was a small place with a few chairs and lots of mirrors, and a red-and-white barber pole out front. Dad would lie there in the reclining leather chair as the barber covered his face in hot towels before soaping him up and running a straight razor along a leather strop to sharpen it. While he lay there relaxing—this was a very relaxing way to spend the morning—Dad would talk with our neighbors from the cotton patch who also stopped by the barbershop on Saturday mornings. They would socialize, talk about the price of cotton, soybeans, and corn and about the weather, especially at high-water time. I'd sit there listening to them telling war stories and discussing crop methods and yields. Sometimes they'd debate whether to sell forward their crops just in case the price dropped before harvesttime in the fall.

It was at the barbershop in Lake Providence where I learned the fundamental concept of hedging.

The big dilemma for cotton planters like Dad was that they had to risk money in the spring to plant their cotton without any idea what the price would be after picking it in the fall. If prices went in their favor, they would make enough to get through the winter. If prices went against them, they would either have to convince the local banker to risk his depositors' money to give them another year to try, or pack up and find

1

another way to make a living. So what many farmers did was "sell forward," meaning that they would negotiate a price with the cotton merchants in the spring for all or part of their crop in the fall. By passing the risk of dropping prices onto the merchants, the seller was losing the opportunity that, say, too much rain or not enough rain somewhere in the world would send prices climbing. But selling forward guaranteed there would be more revenue-in than costs-out. That is, as long as they physically brought the crop in; but, considering how they could get slammed by a Mississippi River flood or a plague of Mexican boll weevils, this was not always guaranteed.

One year, when all the barbershop talk was how, come fall, prices were going to rise, Dad felt particularly optimistic and decided to hold on to most of our crop rather than sell it forward. But it turned out to be an awful year and the losses we took were a big part of the reason we had to sell our white painted house with running water in town and move into an unpainted clapboard cabin with no running water or electricity out on the Island Plantation. The cash from the house sale helped pay down our debt on the land and, like Scarlet O'Hara in *Gone with the Wind,* we'd do anything to hold on to the land.

If we had hedged the entire crop, we never would have had to leave Lake Providence, because the hedge would have been like an insurance policy to reduce loss from the manic mood swing of the market. It was a lesson I never forgot.

When I was seven, Mama opened a savings account in my name, made the first deposit of a few dollars, and said that it was for my college education. I did not understand how only a few dollars could pay for college, so Mama explained that if I put money into the account on a regular basis, it would grow in two ways. One, by the sheer fact that I was saving it rather than spending it on Cokes and movies; and, two, because the bank would be paying me to keep my money there. I figured out for myself a third benefit: the more I put into the account, the more I'd get from the bank.

As I got older I poured everything in—the 75 cents an hour I earned working construction and the $1.35 an hour I made lay-ing a pipeline in the oil fields—and even though I can't recall Mama ever using the term "compound interest," I knew what it was by watching my savings grow over the years.

Saving money and preserving interest earnings were fundamental principles that came home to me when I was in high school. I saw in my math book that if the Canarsee Indians who sold Manhattan Island to the Dutch for $24 had invested that money at 6 percent for 300 years, they would have $1.2 billion. If they'd left it invested, today it would be $145 billion.

When Albert Einstein attended a press conference after he won the Nobel Prize, a reporter asked him, "What is the strongest force in the universe?"

He smiled and replied, "Compound interest."

All the journalists laughed.

But as every successful investor from neophyte to hedge fund manager knows, the greatest mind of the twentieth century was only half kidding.

Chapter 1

"Beat Tallulah"

B USINESS IS a lot like football.

You work hard preparing all week to score more touchdowns than the other guy. Sometimes you do that by running the ball better than him, and sometimes you do that by throwing the ball better than him, but sometimes the other guy is just too good and he stops you. Sometimes you come up short of the first down or goal line and have to settle for three points, and sometimes you have to bet the whole game on a "Hail Mary" pass in the very last second, and sometimes if you've prepared better and worked harder, your receiver is in the end zone, unmanned, and he catches the ball. But sometimes the other guy has worked even harder and prepared even better and scouted you so well that all the luck goes his way and you walk away battered and bloodied and think to yourself, "I don't want to do this again next week." But you do, you go through it all over again, because it's playing the game that matters.

And although there's certainly no prerequisite that every entrepreneur should have played football in high school or college or even just in some sandlot league, had I not played in high school, my outlook on entrepreneurship would be very different.

Football taught me about setting goals, coping with fear, using leverage, maximizing assets, and understanding weaknesses. Football also taught me about losing. As an entrepreneur, if you don't know about losing, you can't learn how to win.

When my brother, Charles, and I started high school in

4

Delhi, Louisiana (he was one year older than me), Mama decided we ought to be able to play music, so I took up the drums and Charles took up the trumpet. But·one afternoon I found Mama's scrapbook of newspaper clippings devoted to my Dad's high school football team. There were faded pictures of him and his teammates—their hair parted in the middle, 1920s style—and as I looked at those pictures and read every one of the stories about Dad's games, I found myself feeling immensely proud of him. So he and I started talking football, and when he saw how interested I was, on New Year's Day 1949, he drove Charles, my friend Pat Patterson, and me all the way to New Orleans—528 miles round-trip, which we did in one day—just to see North Carolina play Oklahoma in the Sugar Bowl. North Carolina were the heavy favorites with their star halfback "Choo Choo Charlie" Justice, but Choo Choo had an upset stomach that morning and the Sooners upset the Tar Heels that afternoon, 14–6. It was a great football game and a journey of epic proportions for a bunch of country boys from a town where most people had never been more than 20 miles from where they woke up.

On the drive down and on the way back home, Dad told us great stories about his high school football days, his beloved Louisiana State University Tigers and legends, like Knute Rockne and the Four Horsemen of Notre Dame. He talked about always playing to the best of your ability, about good sportsmanship, and he quoted Grantland Rice's famous lines:

> *For when the One Great Scorer comes*
> *to mark against your name,*
> *He writes—not that you won or lost—*
> *but how you played the game.*

I was thrilled by all this, but Mama was less than thrilled because she knew boys got hurt playing football and she didn't want her sons to have anything to do with it. But, in Delhi, football was hard to avoid.

There are two good movies about what high school sports mean in small towns across America: *Friday Night Lights* about football in Odessa, Texas, and *Hoosiers* about basketball in Milan, Indiana. In Delhi, football was the town religion. Our battles with neighboring towns were won and lost to grand notions of victory and defeat, triumph and humiliation. Every Friday night during the season a lot was at stake. It was something very important, something very tangible.

In my mind, football became a way to be like my dad, to earn respect and to be an important part of the school and the town. So in the summer between my freshman and sophomore years, I exchanged my drums and tasseled marching hat for shoulder pads and a helmet.

I was only 5'7" and 155 pounds, too small to be a noseguard, but that's where the coach put me and I was teeth-gritted determined to make the team. It was the first big goal I ever set for myself.

Setting a goal and then going after it is difficult for some people. For me, it's as natural as waking up in the morning.

You begin by defining what you want. But to decide that, you have to know who you are. I think that's probably the key to getting it right. If you don't know who you are, becoming an entrepreneur can be a very expensive way of finding out. My wife, Cheryl, says: "Be careful what you wish for 'cause you just might get it."

Next, a goal needs to be realistic. Many people yearn for the pot of gold at the end of the rainbow but have no idea how to find a rainbow. Or they aren't willing to put in the time looking for one, or don't have the courage to walk all the way to the end of it.

Everyone needs a mission, no matter what it is: dominating the global marketplace with a product, losing 5 pounds, or just putting money aside to save for something special. The feelings that arise when you think of yourself as being on a mission become the fuel that keeps you moving even when your spirit lags or times get tough. Over the years I've also found that whatever someone's ultimate goal might be, the easiest way to get there is to map out a course with smaller goals along the way. You find one small thing you can do, and you keep on doing it.

Little victories add up.

COACH RAYMOND RICHARDS was a deacon in the Baptist church. His tall, slender appearance and quiet demeanor masked a highly competitive soul. He'd come from Arkansas full of new ideas about training, discipline, and strategy when it came to coaching football. He was demanding and gave his all and expected us to do the same.

We were small and inexperienced but, on the first day, he made it clear that we were going to be in better physical shape than any of our opponents. He taught us to focus on what we could attain, which was superior endurance, rather than worry about what we didn't have, which was size and experience.

He taught me that if you want to win, you have to emphasize what you are and what you can do. He also taught me that before you go into battle you look at your own strengths, then you look at your opponent's strengths, and then you work out how to maximize the first and how to minimize the second. He taught me to study the opportunities and the obstacles until I understood them, and then to boil everything down to just a few key things that needed to fall into place.

August in Louisiana is hot, and doing push-ups, running laps, and doing wind sprints on a dusty field under the burning glare of the afternoon sun were nothing short of brutal. It was so bad one afternoon that, after running sprints for the fourth time, I collapsed in front of Coach Richards and pleaded for mercy. I didn't have another sprint left in me. He wasn't buying it.

He said to me, "There is no limit to the endurance of a sixteen-year-old boy."

He made me get up and keep running. He wasn't being mean; he was teaching me to recognize the huge reservoir of energy, enthusiasm, and strength that we all have within us. He was teaching me that what we perceive as our limitations are often only mental obstacles.

Charles was put at halfback and me at noseguard, and because we both wanted it so bad and worked so hard, we both made the team.

7

I had achieved my goal and could have stopped right there, but in my head that goal was just one milestone on a long trail. Achieving that goal simply meant I could now move on to the next goal, going from benchwarmer to the starting lineup.

Being innately forward-looking and progress-oriented, once one mountaintop is reached, I look over the horizon for the next mountaintop. Just as the pioneers knew how to scout the horizon for the first signs of a rainstorm or daybreak or danger, anyone looking to get ahead in life—especially anyone who wants to be in the business of building companies—needs the ability to spot opportunities, and to do that you keep your eyes on the horizon.

On the most basic level, you learn to see what's there by being engaged with the world, by being in touch with your own internal compass and sense of direction.

When I lined up at noseguard, I was giving away 30 pounds or more to the guy opposite me. But Coach Richards would tell me, "So what if you're small in a big guy's game? You're quick and you're smart and you're tough." And he'd remind me, "It's not the size of the dog in the fight, it's the size of the fight in the dog."

That's why I worked harder than anyone else to build up my strength and to get into better shape. During an average practice, I'd sweat off six pounds. I'd throw myself into those heavy blocking dummies and push them across the field as Coach Richards rode on the back. He worked me on angles of attack and timing. Being small, I could get down real low, and being strong, I could hit the guy real hard, using the power in my legs to lift him up and out of the way. Coach Richards was the one who first told me it was called "leverage."

I was fueled by my belief that there was nothing I couldn't do. Every time I got bashed and ground into the dirt, I got up, dusted off, and headed back for another go. Sure enough, I made the starting lineup. And later, long before the term "leveraged buyout" was invented, I was using the same football techniques in business, going after much larger companies by relying on agility, quickness, smarts, and the leverage of other people's money.

Having made the starting team in my first year, I moved on to my next goal for my second year. This time my new goal wasn't just for me, it was for the team. My battle cry was, "Beat Tallulah!"

They were the Darth Vaders of northeast Louisiana football, thirty minutes east of us down Highway 80, about halfway to Vicksburg. They were also the five-time State Champs. We played them every year on Thanksgiving Day, and every year on Thanksgiving Day they whipped us.

This year, I was determined, would be different.

To begin with, we were now a year older and a year wiser. Also, oil had been discovered in Delhi, and not just a little bit of it, so we were living smack in the middle of a frontier boomtown, which meant all sorts of new people were coming to town. Many of them were oil workers—roughnecks and roustabouts—and they had some good-sized kids who might otherwise have been playing for schools in East Texas or in the rich, natural gas land of south Louisiana. Now they were playing for Delhi. It changed the dynamics of our team, and that is how I started learning about how teams succeed.

Whether you are talking about sports or you are looking at corporate competition, each individual player is essential and yet, oddly enough, winning isn't determined by any one person. In football, if the front line doesn't open up holes, the backs have no place to run. If the backs can't run, the quarterback has fewer options, like no one to pass to. Survival in football, just like survival in business, depends on many varied factors synchronized together to create something much larger that somehow works in unison, each varied factor complementing and expanding the others.

The dictionary word for that is "synergy." If you put an egg, some water, some flour, some sugar, some chocolate, and some pecans on a table, all you have are the ingredients. If you know how to mix them and make them work together, you can wind up with a prize-winning batch of brownies. The result is greater than the sum of its parts.

Understanding that, and with these big kids coming on the team, Coach Richards introduced a new defensive strategy: a five-man line with four linebackers. Being the smallest guy on the field meant that if I was going to play my part, I needed to be the smartest guy on the field. So I memorized what I had to do for each play, and then worked out what everyone else had to do. I neutralized my size disadvantage by maximizing my quickness, instincts, and flexibility. In a game of split-second decisions, playing well meant playing smart. And just like that, we started winning football games.

Then we played Tallulah.

It was Thanksgiving Day, 1950. And it was a brutal game. We came off the field with cleat gashes, bruises, fat lips, and bloodied noses. The begrudgers were sure we'd be beaten, and we were losing 12–7 in the fourth quarter, when my brother, Charles, shot out of the backfield and our quarterback hit him cutting back across the center. Three Tallulah guys had a shot at him, but the first two bounced off and the last dove into empty space just as Charles reached the end zone.

We won 13–12.

I'd never felt better in my life. Beating Tallulah had been so big in my mind, such an enormous mountain to climb, that I could not think of anything beyond that. Then, in the exhilaration of our celebration, I suddenly realized that we were now in the playoffs for the State Championships.

It was the first time in five years that Tallulah would not be playing for the title, which made beating them that much sweeter. As I was walking off the field at the end of the game, though, I felt a tinge of sadness when I saw my Tallulah cousin, Flo Montgomery, crying over their loss.

On a cold and rainy night in Cajun country, we played for all the marbles against Clinton, a town north of Baton Rouge. We were losing 14–7 but, through sheer determination, little by little we brought the ball all the way down to the goal line. We could taste the touchdown coming, which would tie the game, and we knew that if we tied them, we could beat them.

They stopped us four inches short. It was a terrible disappointment, but as I dragged my aching body to the locker room,

I decided this defeat simply meant we had a new goal to set. We'd been whipped by a bigger, more powerful team. The next goal had to be that next time we would not let that happen.

In football, just like in business and just like in life, the best teacher of all is failure.

Charles won himself a football scholarship to Northwestern State in Natchitoches, but there was a funny rule in those days that allowed graduating seniors who were under nineteen years old and had played fewer than four seasons to postpone their college enrollment and stay eligible in high school for one more semester. He was our best running back and, in my mind, keeping him on the team meant that if we really wanted to be State Champions—and believe me, I really wanted that—it was entirely within our reach.

That was another lesson I learned on the gridiron: never let failure predetermine your future.

So Charles signed on for another season, ran riot against our opponents, and halfway through the season we were unbeaten. We'd mauled six teams, outscoring them by a merciless 200–13.

Around town, the begrudgers had faded into the woodwork, and people were telling us the championship title was ours for the taking. Unfortunately, some of us made the mistake of believing that.

The Winnsboro Wildcats came to Delhi after losing to teams we had already trounced, and in our minds we'd whip them without shaking the dust off our boots. But we were so overly impressed with ourselves and so believed our own press clippings that, before we knew what had happened, we were down 14–0.

Confident is good but overconfident can be fatal, and I have seen this same disease of overconfidence afflict more company managers and chief executives than I care to mention. I call it the Terrible P's: Pictures in the newspaper, Perks, Power, and Prestige go straight to their heads. These afflicted managers and CEOs fall under a kind of spell, lulled into a state of inertia by the seduction of so much attention and flattery. When that happens, it is time for those people either to regain their integrity or to move on. If they will not do either, someone had better kick them out.

This is exactly what Coach Richards did to us. He pulled our whole starting lineup off the field and put in the second string. I kept thinking, "Maybe a few guys needed to be pulled, but all of us?"

The Wildcats bullied their way up the field, tearing through the second-stringers even worse than they had blasted through us. They were playing with a fire in their bellies and a gleam in their eyes. They were 100 percent concentrated on winning, no matter what.

We were headed for a very embarrassing defeat.

That's when Coach Richards gave us starters the ultimatum: "One more chance. If you don't turn this game around, I'll put the second-stringers back on the field for the rest of the game, and won't care how bad you get beat!"

The risk of utter humiliation was a reality check. When the final whistle blew, we'd won 24–20.

It was another life lesson: No matter who you are, or what you've achieved in the past, you have to work hard every time in order to win. Lose the fire in your belly and you've opened the door to defeat.

And in 1951, when we played the Donaldsonville Tigers for the State title, we had the fire in our bellies.

A year after losing to Clinton, we knew we were bigger, stronger, faster, and smarter. Today, when I look back on our team, I see that our real strength was unity—the level of oneness we'd achieved. No Delhi squad had ever played for the championship even once. Here we were in the big game for the second year in a row. This confirms to me that some of the most amazing things in life only happen when you establish that unity.

We played them at home, on a muddy field, in a bitter winter wind. Donaldsonville was like us: scrappy, tenacious, and comfortable with sophisticated plays. What's more, they had just beaten Clinton.

My new goal was, "Stop Donaldsonville."

All week on the practice field and that night in the locker room, we told ourselves that defeat was not an option. On the field, every tackle could be heard in every seat in the stands. Even before the first quarter ended, our jersey numbers were obscured by wet, heavy mud. Sixty minutes of battle later, we had amassed 227 yards rushing, and Charles was our leading ground gainer. Our defense held them to 31 yards rushing and a single pass completion of 34 yards.

Donaldsonville was tough, but they didn't want it as bad as we wanted it.

We were State Champs, 26–6.

Great teams do not always win, but without a great team—without synergy and oneness—winning becomes that much tougher. Being a lone gunslinger in team sports or in business will only get you so far. In both fields of endeavor, you need a team playing together and, at the same time, a structure that allows for each player on that team to flourish in his own unique way. Each member of the team has to be empowered with the responsibility and authority to do the job that needs to be done.

That's the game. It's that way in football. It's that way in business. It's that way in life.

Chapter 2

Flora's Boys

T HE STORY OF the entrepreneur is the story of the immigrant, of the pioneer, and of America itself. It is the story of forward progress, of pursuing one's dreams and goals no matter how outlandish they seem to others.

Just like the pioneer pushing for a fresh approach and redemption, the entrepreneur pushes boundaries in search of something new. Sometimes he brings the whole of society with him, rushing forward together into an innovative "next" phase of our communal human existence. Sometimes he runs alone, a single voice shouting into the wind, hoping someone will hear him.

The character of the entrepreneur is central to the story we tell ourselves about who we are as Americans. It is at the heart of our modern-day legends. The story of the entrepreneur weaves through our cultural fabric.

My people first came to this country in 1657—the same year as George Washington's great grandfather—from the lowlands of Scotland and the valleys of Ireland. More of my ancestors crossed the Atlantic in that great wave of Scots-Irish immigration between 1707 and 1776, escaping the tyranny of an English king who thought they ought to be under his rule. They were pioneers, frontiersmen, warriors, generals, explorers, and bare-knuckled fighters. They include Andrew Jackson, Daniel Boone, Davy Crockett, Sam Houston, Lewis and Clark, Ulysses S. Grant, Stonewall Jackson, Mark Twain, Teddy Roosevelt, and Woodrow Wilson. Immigrants from Ireland have produced more American presidents than any other immigrant group, by far.

14

Mel Gibson told stories of my people in the film *Braveheart*, set in the borderlands of Scotland, and in *Patriot*, set in back-country South and North Carolina during the American Revolution. They were familiar stories, similar to the story of Granddad Tom Balch, who sailed back to Bristol to do his part in helping to overthrow the anti-Parliament, anti-Protestant King James II, in what came to be known in England as the Glorious Revolution of 1688. One hundred and ten years later, Grandparents Sam and Mary Sparrow escaped to America from Enniscorthy, Ireland, after the bitter defeat of their United Irish rebels at the Battle of Vinegar Hill.

At Valley Forge, during the darkest and bleakest months for the Patriot cause, when George Washington's army was freezing to death, Granddad Armstrong loyally stuck it out, helping earn the Commander-in-Chief's ultimate tribute, "If I am defeated on all other fronts, I will make my last stand amongst the Scots-Irish."

Uncle Christopher Parker (my great-great-great uncle) was one of the 187 Texas heroes who died with Davy Crockett at the Alamo, and Great-Great-Uncle Alfred Wyly was Captain of a company that fought alongside Sam Houston at the battle of San Jacinto, which created the Lone Star State of Texas and was a vital step in America's fulfillment of its Manifest Destiny to continue growing westward over the continent as an English-speaking people, and the beginning of the end of the long struggle with the Colonial nations of Spain, France, and England for American independence.

Just as his father had joined the United Irish Rebellion of 1798, my great-great-grandfather, General Edward Sparrow, led Louisiana into another rebellion, the one we now call the Civil War. His story reads like that of a character straight out of *Gone with the Wind*. Edward, born in Dublin and educated at the school founded by his older brother, Kenyon College in Ohio, became a Confederate senator, chaired the Military Committee, and lived next door to Jefferson Davis's Presidential mansion in Richmond, Virginia. He also built the family plantation, Arlington—with its beautiful white-columned antebellum house—in Lake Providence, where my cousin Flo Guenard lives today. So my forebears were "rebels" more than once, and more often than not fought on the losing side. Rebel is a role they played for generations and I learned that role from them.

Roots are good.

LAKE PROVIDENCE, Louisiana, where I was born on October 4, 1934, to Charles and Flora Wyly, is so small you will not find it on most maps. It is a place of graceful 300-year-old cypress trees growing on the edge of the Mississippi River and dripping with Spanish moss. And of green fields and lush forests as far as the eye can see. It was a wood stop in the famous steamboat race between the *Natchez* and the *Robert E. Lee,* which Joan Baez made famous in "The Night They Drove Old Dixie Down" and Mark Twain chronicled in *Life on the Mississippi.*

Civil War buffs also know Lake Providence because that is where General Ulysses S. Grant dug "Grant's Canal" to get the Union troops around the Confederate guns at Vicksburg after failing to make it through to the other side of the river.

The only other time Lake Providence made any news was in 1907 when Teddy Roosevelt came to meet Ben Lilly, who was known throughout the United States as the best bear hunter in the country. Teddy got off the train at a railroad siding about 15 miles south of Lake Providence, halfway to Tallulah, and somebody decided they would build a town there called Roosevelt, but it was never built. Even though the railroad siding isn't there anymore, a lone sign there says "Roosevelt." Nothing else, just "Roosevelt." So you have to be there to know that was where Teddy crossed the railroad tracks.

When I was growing up, it was still a conversation point that both armies, Union and Confederate, had been in town during the winter of 1863. Mrs. Newman, my first-grade teacher, took our class over to Arlington Plantation to show us the hoof marks on the floor of a room where the Yankees quartered their horses and the "bloody porch" where the wounded were taken for care. Today, just outside my office, there's a giant 1861 Lake Providence Cadets battle flag. Next to it, I have General Sparrow's final proclamation to the people of Louisiana in 1865 that says, in summary, "The war is over. We lost. Stop fighting."

In the historical process of the birth of our nation, the first big event was the enunciation of the ideals set forth in our Declaration of Independence; the second big event was the trauma and the agony of our Civil War and its long, lingering, and hurtful—both to the North and the South, but especially to the South—aftermath. If you don't understand the Civil War and its painful cataclysms, you don't understand America.

I was born smack in the middle of the Great Depression, when America was struggling economically. For the people of the rural South, it was particularly brutal. In addition to the residual damage of the "War of Northern Aggression"—as some of my Southern cousins still call it—the South had already been experiencing declining agricultural prices since before the Great Mississippi River flood of 1927. Our levees had broken and the flood covered our Louisiana Delta land for miles, except for Lake Providence—which, come to think of it, is something else my hometown is known for. It was the only town in the area not under water and, for years, our license plates proudly read, "Lake Providence—High and Dry."

The stock market crash of 1929, bank failures, and the snowballing destruction that financial panic had on the American economy comprised the final nail in the coffin. Livelihoods were gone and pride was undermined. As President Franklin Roosevelt said, "I see one-third of a nation ill-housed, ill-clad, ill-nourished."

Both my parents had actually come from relatively affluent families. Mama was the daughter of a prominent doctor in town and Dad was the son of a lawyer. Both my parents went to college, but once the Depression hit, they struggled like everyone else. Before the Depression, my mother—who was small, pretty, and tough as nails—had left Sophie Newcomb College and gone up to New York City to study dancing with the group that would later become the Rockettes of Radio City Music Hall. Then she came back to Lake Providence to start her own dancing school.

Dad wanted to be a big-city newspaperman working on the

Baton Rouge Advocate or the New Orleans *Times-Picayune* until the Depression sideswiped him and he had to struggle to try to save the land.

I realize now how hard it must have been for them to see their hopes and ambitions washed away like that, on a tide of bad economic news. But I never heard any woe-is-me talk from either of them. That's how my folks were. That was the ethos they handed down to my brother and me. You do not complain, you do not lament what could have been, you just keep going, taking the bad with the good, dodging and weaving to keep from being knocked over and, ultimately, you move forward.

My parents were driven by a uniquely American frontier spirit, fueled by optimism and an insistent belief that the future would be better. A future that, no matter what the outward circumstances, was theirs for the making. My parents faced life with an attitude that cried out, "Hurl at me what you will, I will not go down." And I simply cannot overstate how much this influenced my life and shaped my attitudes about business.

When I came into this world—known to everybody as "Bubba"—Dad was managing the family cotton plantation. He, my mother, and my brother, Charles Jr., who had arrived twelve months ahead of me, were living in a small painted house on the Tensas Bayou, right as it begins its long, meandering way to the Mississippi River.

Now, a painted house in the cotton South was a sign of distinction. It meant you were affluent enough to afford the paint. But when I was five, my folks could not sustain this lifestyle any longer and we moved into a small cabin on the plantation where Dad was the owner-manager, living and working on the land. Because our place was on a peninsula, when you saw it from town it appeared to be floating, unattached, in the middle of Lake Providence, which is why it used to be called the Island Plantation.

This land came down to Dad from the great plantation that General Sparrow built before the Civil War. My parents had hoped to raise us on this plantation land, but there was nothing left of the family fortune except the land itself and the debt incurred by years of declining cotton prices. My parents had to struggle just to pay the taxes on it. That's another reason they sold the painted house in town.

My earliest memories are of that cabin on the Island, with a rusty corrugated tin roof and a covered wooden porch. The chickens ran around loose and the hogs were in pens. The biggest room in the house was the kitchen, where my mother cooked and heated the water for our weekly baths, and where Mumzell, the black woman who helped Mama with the housework and looked after my brother and me, did the laundry.

We had indoor plumbing when we lived in the painted house in town, but not when we moved out to the cabin on the farm. We had a telephone in town, too, but not on the farm. We had gas heat in town, but when we moved out to the cabin the heat came from logs in the living room fireplace and from the log stove in the kitchen. We had electricity in town, but not out in the clapboard cabin. That's why Dad ran a wire over the slough so we could have lights to read by and could plug in and play our radio, which was important because the radio brought the news of the war. There was no television in 1940.

Listening to that old radio is how I learned geography before I got to school. We would listen to the radio and Mama would spread out the maps and say, "Here's Hitler going into the Netherlands," or "Here's the German army invading France," or "Those arrows mark the path of the German army going into Poland and Norway."

Times were tough and, even in the best of times, farming is always risky. There are always disasters. Sometimes it doesn't rain enough, and other times it rains too much. Sometimes the sun bakes your crops into dust, and sometimes the Mississippi River breaks the levee and floods you out. Farming is basic economics—you always need more land, and that means you always need more equipment, which means you always need more capital. You had that state of affairs going all through the cotton South. The cry of the freed black and the small white yeoman farmer was, "All we need is 40 acres and a mule." When that didn't work, or when disaster struck, or when capital dried up, 40 acres and a mule just wasn't enough to keep you alive.

A few years ago *Time* magazine picked Lake Providence as the poorest town in America. It was a close race against an Indian reservation, but we won. We were Number One. Yet Charles and I never felt poor. We always felt secure, warm, and protected. Cash might have been in short supply, but love was not.

People always commented on how nice our home was, even if it was just a clapboard cabin, because Mama made it nice. I remember that she once drove 6 miles into town to buy fabric and sewing supplies. We could not afford to buy curtains or nice linens, so she made them herself. What she made was so nice that some of the more affluent town women commissioned her to make slipcovers and curtains for them. One Italian woman, Mrs. Vincinci, wanted sofa coverings but did not have any money to pay for them, so Mama traded her for what seemed to be a never-ending supply of homemade spaghetti and meatballs.

I did not realize it then, but in her own way Mama was a good entrepreneur, even though it would not have occurred to her to identify herself as such. Both my parents were (although Dad liked to think of himself as a writer and a scholar), because in those days you had to scramble to survive.

At one point, Dad opened a grocery store in partnership with a local man named Izzy Rozensweig, but even though they both gave it their best shot, it just did not work.

Seeing my father fail like that hurt, but it also taught me at an early age that failure forces you onto another path. It makes a frontiersman out of you because you have to go in search of new opportunities all over again. Failure may not be a fun part of the process, but it's a necessary one.

When I was about eight, my parents were tired of the hard times in cotton farming. So when the Reform Democrats voted out the corrupt remnants of the Huey Long Machine, a neighbor of ours was asked to run the Angola State Prison and implement prison reforms. My mother became "Captain Wyly," head of the women's jail, the first woman in the state of Louisiana to hold that position. Dad became Administrator of Pardons and Paroles. In my parents' minds, this was just an interim stop along the way until they could save enough money to start again, hopefully, in some kind of work where Dad could earn a living by writing, which is what he always wanted to do. For me, and for my brother, Charles, it was a whole series of life lessons.

I watched Mama manage convicts and "free people"—as non-inmates were called—which made me realize that there was no such thing as "woman's work" and "man's work," and that helped me in later life when it came to hiring the best person for a job. I have never suffered macho notions that only a man should manage a workforce.

Our cook and housekeeper was a prisoner named Willy who was in jail for trying to kill his wife and the man she was sleeping with. It is not a pretty story, but then few tales involving two people in bed and a meat cleaver ever are. The way Dad put it was, "Willy's had some bad luck with women and alcohol in his life and is trying to be a better person now."

I have never forgotten how kind Willy was to us—I can still see his huge smile—and through knowing him I learned to always look for the good in people rather than assume the worst.

Dad was convinced that Willy would never do anything violent again, and he never did. But then, with their characteristic optimism, neither Mama nor Dad ever looked at the men and women behind Angola's doors as evil. To my folks, those convicts had simply lost their way. My folks saw bad behavior, not bad people. It's what they learned from the Bible and the writings of Mary Baker Eddy.

At Angola, the inmates worked in the prison itself and on the prison grounds in order to help pay for the cost of their food, clothing, and housing, and there was a palatable sense for every inmate of the possibility of redemption. Good behavior was rewarded. This taught me that change is always possible, that second chances should be everyone's right.

I was eleven when my parents finally saved enough money at Angola to buy the weekly newspaper in Delhi. Along with the *Delhi Dispatch* they also picked up a Western Union franchise and a small insurance agency where Dad sold fire and casualty policies. My parents worked together running the Western

Union and insurance businesses, but the newspaper was truly a family affair. Dad wrote the vast majority of articles in every weekly edition, and many of the ads, too. I can still remember him burning the midnight oil on Monday nights so the paper could be at the printer's next morning. Wednesdays it would go on sale. Mama ran the business side of the paper and was also the photographer and the society columnist. Charles and I set type, cleaned up, sold ads, took subscriptions, mailed out the paper, wrote stories, and edited copy.

It was only natural, then, that when I was ready to head for college, becoming a journalist like Dad was my first choice of career. But in my second year at Louisiana Tech, I asked around about what the toughest courses were and someone said, Accounting and Economics. So I took a couple of those courses, and they opened my eyes to how my dad was earning a living.

The next time I came home for a weekend, I took a good look at our family's business books. The newspaper required a big capital outlay but made only a small profit. The insurance agency was producing almost as much profit but took a lot less of Dad's time and required almost no capital investment. In my mind, Dad should be devoting his time to the insurance business, and I told him so.

He sat me down and said, "You're a sophomore in college and this is as smart as you will ever be. It's downhill from here, as you learn more and more about all the stuff you don't know."

It made me think that all the stuff I didn't know could be a lot.

Then he said, "I happen to like putting out this newspaper. Writing work is all I ever wanted to do. Think about that."

I did think about it, and for the first time I understood that earning money is only part of making a living. Dad lived for the newspaper and wrote nearly every article himself. It made him feel productive and happy. That taught me that you have to love what you do. That earning money is a distant second to loving your work.

Not long ago, *The Christian Science Monitor* published a story about a University of Chicago survey of 50,000 Americans conducted to determine the happiest and most satisfied workers. None at the top were the highest paid. Instead, they were people who help other people and people who do creative work. They were clergy members, firefighters, educators, painters, sculptors, and authors.

My dad was right when he taught us that, in life, it's not the money that counts the most, it's the quality of the journey.

IT TOOK A WOMAN named Mary Baker Eddy to help me understand that.

Born in 1821 into a very literate farm family in New Hampshire, she was raised a Congregationalist in Puritan New England. This was at a time when Emerson and the other Transcendentalists were softening and lifting the stern Calvinism of the founding Puritans. Traditional church teachings were being questioned because of new information coming from researchers such as Darwin and what was coming to be called Science.

Wrestling with health problems all her life, Mrs. Eddy was introduced to the various social, religious, and medical innovations of the era, like spiritualism with its weird séances, homeopathic medicine, and faith healing. Even though she was a devout Christian, her loving faith and radical reliance on the truth—as it came to her from her own study of the Bible—led her on a path of resistance. She boldly refused to join her family congregation until the pastor agreed to drop the requirement of believing that members would burn in hell if they didn't enter a religious profession.

Further defying her upbringing, in 1875, she self-published a book called *Science and Health with Key to the Scriptures,* which explains her own spiritual understanding of a Christian path to the betterment of humanity. Four years later, at the age of fifty-eight, she formed the Church of Christ, Scientist, one of only four American-created major religions.

Based on her writings, Christian Science has always been more than just a religion. It is a method of spiritual healing and, very important, a spiritual philosophy of life. What most people think they know about Christian Scientists is that they don't go to doctors. Which is sort of like saying that every Canadian plays hockey. Mama's father was a doctor and his *New England Journal of Medicine* sat on the coffee table next to Mama's *Christian Science Journal.* Having the two right there like that never struck me as incongruous.

My dad came from a long line of Scots-Irish Presbyterians, which included Sam Y. Wyly, who graduated from Princeton in 1836 and was a preacher who also taught at Tusculum College in Tennessee. My parents were married in an Episcopal Church (nicely enough, one that had been built on land donated by my great-great-grandmother). It was Mama who discovered Mrs. Eddy's teachings, studied them, and oversaw our religious upbringing. That made us a bit different from others in town. Rather than the standard Southern Bible Belt Baptist, Methodist, and Pentecostal faiths of our neighbors, or the big-city Catholic, Jewish, and older mainline Protestant faiths, there were only a very few Christian Scientists in our neck of the northern Louisiana woods. We had to drive 40 miles every Sunday for church and Sunday school, then dinner at an Italian restaurant in Monroe, our big city of about 40,000 people.

What I got from my spiritual training is much more than whether or not to take aspirin, or the arguments of spiritual healing versus surgery. I learned to focus on spirituality, on mental power as opposed to material power, and I developed a philosophy of individual empowerment, as Catherine Albanese describes in *A Republic of Mind & Spirit: A Cultural History of American Metaphysical Religion.* There are many popular spin-offs from Mary Baker Eddy's philosophy, ranging from religious science to the pragmatic Norman Vincent Peale's book, *The Power of Positive Thinking,* to Rick Warren's *The Purpose Driven Life* (both hugely successful). You also find it today for spirituality-seeking young social networkers on Internet sites that focus on spirituality, such as Zaadz.com.

Mrs. Eddy taught me always to be positive. She wrote, "Stand porter at the door of thought," not to accept negative ideas from others. She taught me not to listen to begrudgers, either my own internal voices or the voices of other people who might try to talk me into doing what I knew was wrong or talk me out of doing what I knew was right. She also taught me the importance of thought. If I could see the problem, then substitute a spiritual truth in place of a limiting, unkind, petty, intolerant, or unforgiving material thought, I'd be a part of the creation of whatever good outcome ought to be present. If I could visualize the idea and think it through, then I could figure out anything that ought to be figured out.

Somewhere along the way I also bumped into the works of the poet John Greenleaf Whittier, who wrote: "*Of all sad words of tongue or pen, the saddest are these: It might have been.*"

Right from an early age, I never wanted "might have been" to be my epitaph so, if football taught me that setting goals was like climbing mountaintops, then Mary Baker Eddy taught me not to worry about what might have been. She taught me to look for what is and what can be.

Thanks to Mrs. Eddy, as well, I see problems and solutions as nothing more than opposite sides of the same coin.

I have never spent much time battling my own psychology. If you wallow in your own internal housekeeping—restraining personal demons, comparing yourself to other people, worrying about things you can't change—then you don't have the mental energy left to figure out where you want to go and how to get there.

Chapter 3

Big Blue

IN 1952, after a summer job with the State legislature, I had set my goal to be Governor of Louisiana, started college as a journalism major, and got myself elected Class President and Student Body President as practice for running for Governor when I turned thirty-five, the minimum age. But I was studying business, and I liked it, so the idea of running for governor faded and ultimately disappeared—although my intellectual curiosity with our competitive political process remained, sort of another game to play, noneconomic but meaningful, born and bred into me by my family heritage.

I signed up for an investment class, one of those overview kinds of courses where you learn what a bond is, how savings accounts work, and how the stock market functions. For me, that class was like a whole bunch of dominoes laid out on their ends: You tip over the first one and they all go down. For me, that class started a chain of events that continues to this day.

The professor had us each put together a mock portfolio of five stocks, and we then had to manage it. Of course, managing that mock portfolio was a lot more complicated than just choosing any five companies and hoping their shares went up. We had to do a lot of research and learn everything we could about the companies we were buying. I settled on American Airlines, Bristol-Myers, Stone Container, and Humble Oil (now Exxon).

That was four. My fifth company came to me when I thought back to one afternoon when I was helping my dad at the newspaper and an electric typewriter sales representative came to call on him. The man was well-dressed, in a smart suit with a white shirt and a dark tie; he spoke intelligently and I remember he drove a brand-new Cadillac. I sat there looking at him, thinking to myself how impressive he was and how he projected success. I figured any company that had a quality person like that representing it was worth investing in. So his company, IBM, became the fifth stock in my mock portfolio.

I knew from the numbers I was seeing in my research that the company was a winner, but the more I looked at IBM, the more I thought, "This company represents the very spirit of America."

It began as the Computing Tabulating Recording Corporation (CTR) in 1911, the result of the merger of three companies: the Tabulating Machine Corporation, founded in Washington, D.C., by a man named Herman Hollerith in 1896; the International Time Recording Company, founded in Endicott, New York, in 1900; and the Computing Scale Corporation, founded in Dayton, Ohio, in 1901. The new company, which kept the CTR name, was in the business of manufacturing grocery-store scales and meat slicers, plus all sorts of timekeeping systems for employees, especially systems that used punch cards so that workers could clock in and clock out. Before long, they did away with the scales and meat slicers and concentrated on the punch-card side of their business.

The man who changed the company forever, and who really created IBM, was Thomas J. Watson, Sr. He was a sales representative for the National Cash Register (NCR) Company, who, along with other NCR managers, was indicted in an antitrust lawsuit. Although he claimed to have been too naïve to understand the implications of what those other managers were doing, he was nevertheless sentenced to a year in jail.

As luck would have it for Watson, in March 1913, the Great Miami River flooded downtown Dayton in the country's worst flood in over twenty years. One of the few safe spots was the NCR plant because it was on high ground. Watson was in New York, but he and John Patterson, who ran NCR, personally took charge of the rescue operation. NCR employees built hundreds of flat-bottomed boats so that NCR rescue teams could bring stranded people back to the NCR factory, which was turned into an emergency shelter. Patterson and Watson provided food and medical care, and saved so many people that they became national heroes. This heroic public service was later cited when Watson appealed his jail sentence, and the government dropped the case.

That same year, CTR recruited Watson and he became the company's General Manager in 1914 and its President the year after that. Two years later, he opened a subsidiary in Canada that he decided to call International Business Machines, and that name summed up so well the way he was shaping the company's business that in 1924 he chose that title for the whole enterprise.

A prominent Roosevelt Democrat who wound up supporting the Republican Eisenhower, Watson was a staunch Methodist, a brilliant salesman whose vision of business changed the world. He created a culture at IBM that made it the first truly global enterprise, summed up by the company's slogan: World Peace Through World Trade.

Watson Senior stayed the course even as the Great Depression wiped out businesses left and right. IBM tabulated the 1930 Census and prospered. After Congress passed the Social Security Act of 1935, Watson was able to win the government contract to handle all the employment data for the 26 million Americans covered by the Act—the biggest accounting operation of all time up to that point. For more than a quarter of a century, Watson's IBM increased its product lines and its influence.

As an undergraduate I was impressed with the authority the company seemed to have; the company name was synonymous with quality, integrity, and progress. The clocks on the walls at both Delhi High School and Louisiana Tech had "IBM" stamped on them, as if IBM were the very arbiter of time.

A man who stayed true to his vision of a working world, Watson understood that in order to move the twentieth century forward, the working world needed a new set of tools. I had only seen the IBM clocks and the IBM newspaper equipment, and had not yet seen any of its electric accounting machinery or infant computers, but the importance of good tools was something I understood. Being raised by progressive farmers, I grew up understanding what tools could do. The difference between picking cotton by hand and driving the fields on a mechanical cotton picker was 100-to-1. My instincts told me that in the post–World War II world that lay before me there would be huge changes. America was increasingly coming to define itself as a country of business. Agricultural production was fading. As that was happening, I knew for certain that a whole new set of tools would be needed for a new kind of worker: the knowledge worker. Talk about following the force of change. I admired Tom Watson as much as I did Stonewall Jackson, the genius Civil War general.

So when word reached me on campus in my senior year that IBM was coming to recruit, I immediately signed up for an appointment. But getting a job with IBM was not easy. The company had an esprit de corps exactly like that of the Marines: It was looking for a few good men.

In my mind, becoming an IBM sales rep someday was as close to achieving the American dream as anyone could get. IBM was the best of the best, and becoming the best was a challenge that appealed to me immensely. Just like that, I gave up my goal of becoming Governor of Louisiana and decided to shoot for President of IBM instead.

In the spring of 1956 I sat down for an interview with the two IBM branch managers who came to campus to recruit. Both of them were dressed immaculately in crisp white shirts and navy blue suits. Right away, they did a good cop/bad cop routine on me. One kept telling me how great I was, while the other kept wondering whether I was good enough to make the cut. Was I tough enough to play? Of course, their taunting had the desired effect: It made me even more eager to get an offer from IBM.

The next thing I knew, they sent me a ticket to fly out to Dallas for a follow-up interview. This was an incredibly exciting event for me—not only was it my very first airplane ride, but I did not have to pay for it myself! Coming out of the Love Field Airport exit in Dallas, I saw a billboard that read, "Men Who Get Ahead in Business Read *The Wall Street Journal.* Do you?"

I thought to myself, "No, but I'm going to subscribe!"

IBM put me up at the Plaza Hotel, which made me feel like a big shot, because the room cost $12 a night, which was a lot of money then to someone who was only twenty-one. The next morning, at the IBM school, they gave me a battery of aptitude tests. Then they brought me in to meet Henry Wendler, a man who held legendary status for everyone who worked for, or with, IBM in those days. He had started with the company in 1934, and was generally credited with introducing the Pentagon to the computer age during World War II. He was often referred to, with enormous reverence, as Mr. Dallas.

My interview with him went well enough that I received an offer to join the company upon graduation. I promptly accepted. In my mind, my life's course was set. I even went out and bought myself an "almost" new car, taking out a bank loan to pay for it, based on my future earnings at IBM.

That's when fate intervened. Louisiana Tech was one of the top accounting schools in the country, and the most respected accountant of the day, Dr. W. A. Paton, came to speak to us. The editor of *The Accountant's Manual*—a copy of which sat on the desk of every CPA in America—Dr. Paton was a professor at the University of Michigan Business School. He was a skilled speaker who could boil down complex ideas and tie this otherwise dry field to big national policy issues. He was the first to argue that accountants ought to recognize inflation in their numbers—this was a brand-new idea at the time—and he argued that by failing to do so, accountants, plus the government, were, in effect, putting an invisible tax on their clients.

The head of the accounting department at Tech was Harold Smolinski, called Smokey by all the students, except when he was in the room. Smokey took me aside after the speech and introduced me to the great man. He told Dr. Paton that I was his star pupil and that I was considering going to Harvard for an MBA. This was news to me, of course, but I kept my mouth shut because I realized that Smokey was promoting me on an inside track with Dr. Paton, stirring the Michigan professor's competitive urges. And it worked. Dr. Paton took the bait, saying that anyone who really wanted to get a master's in Accounting needed to go to Michigan, not Harvard. In fact, he said, Michigan was going to offer a new scholarship for MBA students named after him, and he suggested that I apply.

This posed a real dilemma for me, because getting a master's meant not going to work for IBM.

Some people have always known what they wanted to be— like my mother becoming a dancer or my father becoming a journalist—but I never was that way. I was open to opportunities and took a swing at the best ones. Also, I enjoyed being in the company of good scholars, both professors and fellow students. And even though IBM was developing computers, and even though talk was that computers were going to become one of the most important tools for the twentieth century, it occurred to me that by earning a Michigan MBA, there might be something better out there waiting for me.

Anyway, with Smokey egging me on, I figured I could first go to graduate school and then go work for IBM. So I applied for the scholarship, got it, asked IBM if I could defer for a year (they said yes), and became Michigan's first Paton Scholar.

When IBM offered me a job, they offered one to my brother, Charles, too. So he headed off to IBM's training camp in Dallas to learn how to be a salesman, and I began looking for a summer job before reporting to graduate school.

Landing that summer job was a lesson in the importance of personal relationships and in the way anyone can become a good contact. The man who ran the dry cleaners in Delhi had a son working for an accounting firm. My dad mentioned to him that I had a degree in accounting and was looking for summer work. The dry cleaner spoke to his son, who spoke to someone else, and that thread of connections led to an auditing firm in Dallas offering me an internship.

Some people say that life is not about what you know but who you know. I figure that because you never know who knows whom, it always pays to ask. Who you know can get you an audience. What you know and what you make of that audience is strictly up to you.

Chapter 4

Peter Drucker Wrote the Bible

CHARLES HAD MARRIED his college sweetheart, Dee, and I moved in to their guestroom for that summer in Dallas. I reported to work in a nice new white shirt and tie and navy blue suit, and they sent me out to count piles of knives and forks in a tin warehouse. It was 100 degrees outside and much hotter inside. I kept thinking, "This is what I am doing with my college degree?"

After that they sent me to a retail store—at least it was air-conditioned—where I had to take inventory of women's lingerie. I spent a week counting bras and girdles. Next, I helped to audit the Kitchenquip Finance Company, a direct-sales operation to which the Working Girls Club of Houston had sold receivables that turned out to be imaginary.

My parents' newspaper company and insurance firm were "mom-and-pop" or "lifestyle" businesses, aimed at putting food on our table and keeping a roof over our heads. America is made up of millions of mom-and-pops, small lifestyle businesses—dry cleaners, independent insurance offices, dance schools, farms, garages, pizzerias—where hardworking people operate way beneath the business-magazine radar. It is a mistake to underestimate their importance. Since the 1970s, the majority of new jobs in America have come from small business, while jobs at the *Fortune* 500 companies have been steadily declining.

The companies I was visiting in Dallas were a step above mom-and-pops in terms of size, yet still much smaller than any of those Goliath corporations I'd put into my mock portfolio at Louisiana Tech. And the first thing that struck me about them was how they were just bigger models of Mama and Dad's businesses.

Nobody paid much attention to me, because I was only a rookie, which meant I could observe and ask questions and be a fly on the wall. One of our clients was a printing plant. I watched the presses and met the people who sold the printing work that kept the business thriving. I read the accounting reports and met the administrators who put them out. Now I was learning how numbers and personalities interrelated. I could walk right onto the shop floor and ask, "How much more work does it take to accommodate a customer who wants a two-color layout instead of the standard one-color template?; How does that figure into total job cost?; and, What's the real cost if the customer changes his mind halfway through the job?" I was learning to see how manufacturing, financing, accounting, and selling components were locked together like a jigsaw puzzle. I wanted to know how each piece affected the other pieces and how to keep it all running smoothly. It was beautiful.

In my last year at Louisiana Tech, I had bought my car on credit, thinking I would be working for IBM. But now the Paton Scholarship meant I would not be able to make my payments. I went to Dad for advice. He said to me, "You've got a real problem. You have made a deal with your banker, which you are honor-bound to keep. Why don't you go talk with him?"

Feeling trapped by my earlier hasty decision, I walked into the bank with a genuine feeling of trepidation. I was either going to lose the car or lose Michigan. But that banker in Delhi told me something I would never forget. He said there were three things bankers looked for when they lend money, and he called them the three C's.

They were collateral, credit, and character.

I did not have any collateral and I did not have any credit, but the Delhi banker said, this time, character was enough. He knew my family and knew I would pay him back when I could. So my unpaid-for car and I headed out to Michigan.

Those three semesters in Ann Arbor broadened me, put me

in touch with a bunch of smart people, and gave me perspective, but mostly they took me out of my comfortable Southern environment. They also changed my name. For the first time in my life, everybody called me Sam. (Turns out there ain't no Bubbas in Michigan.)

The culture of the Upper Midwest was different from the South. Most of the people I'd known growing up were of Scots-Irish or English descent. Michigan was made up of Germans, Poles, and Scandinavians, and I'll never forget eating sauerbraten for the first time.

One day a professor asked us, "How many different places will you work during your career?" His answer was, "On average, three." That surprised me. I was pretty naïve about the way the world of big business functioned and, until then, it had not dawned on me that I would ever work at more than one place. In retrospect, he was low. This was at a time when nearby Ford and General Motors and the American automotive industry were kings of the world and supplied seemingly lifelong employment to thousands of Detroiters. It was where the sons of sharecroppers from my Appalachian and Dixie roots were moving for good-paying jobs.

Most of what they taught us in those days was functional. This was before they added "entrepreneurship" to business courses. It was all about manufacturing, marketing, and personnel. I found that somewhat boring. I had two favorite courses. The first was Small Business. It was the only course where all the pieces came together. The other was Computing, which was the first computer course that the Michigan Business School had ever taught. I had a feeling that this was the big new thing. But, more important, it was what IBM did. I had never seen a computer lab before. This was soon after Remington Rand made headlines with its UNIVAC I, the world's first commercial computer.

In 1951, that UNIVAC computer could handle an astonishing 1,905 operations per second, which, in those days, made people's jaws drop. It took up an entire room, and was made of vacuum tubes, delay lines, and magnetic tape. Remington Rand sold forty-six of them for about $1 million each. The U.S. Census Bureau bought one. That was a genuine sign of approval, because the Census Bureau had been one of the earliest users of computer-like technology, having bought a mechanical punch-card tabulating machine invented by Herman Hollerith for the 1880 Census.

When the Census Bureau announced that it was going to purchase that first UNIVAC from Remington Rand, Tom Watson of IBM took it as a personal insult. In the industrial marketplace IBM's electricity-driven machines had been the tools for big projects like the Depression era's Social Security and World War II data support for our 16 million troops. Remington Rand was a perpetually frustrated, distant second in the punch-card world.

For the Watsons, and especially for Tom Junior, who was now running the company, this Remington Rand technological breakthrough was a wake-up call, a tough reminder that the last thirty years of having the field of computational devices entirely to themselves was over. What had been a businessman's world of "electric" machines was becoming a world of "electronic" machines. So Watson Junior cracked the whip, and IBM began gearing up for a serious competitive response.

By the time Watson Senior died in 1956, IBM's engineers had done him proud.

No one in the Michigan Business School could teach us about computers, so they brought a guy over from the Engineering School. This was, of course, the dark ages before anyone in the computer business even called it the computer business. First, it was the "electric accounting machine" business. Then IBM called it their "electronic data processing" business.

Because engineers see things differently than business professors, I got a completely different perspective on what computers did, and what they might someday do. The engineers didn't just tell us; they showed us.

Our machine was an IBM 650, history's first mass-produced computer. It was a transistorized machine with a magnetic-drum main memory that spun at 12,500 rpm, producing much faster access to stored material than any previous machine.

The computer itself weighed a ton, and the power supply that you had to attach to it weighed nearly a ton and a half. They came in separate cabinets and together filled a small room.

Using those IBM 650s was no easy feat. You had to take your turn in line with the other students, write your program, keypunch it onto a big stack of cards, do your proofs to make sure it was accurate, and feed it into the computer. If you were lucky and the air-conditioning did not malfunction, you'd get your results back quickly. But there would be errors, which you had to correct, and then you had to repeat the process over and over again until the 650—working on the data with the program that you wrote—came up with the right answers.

We wrote programs in machine language. "Ten" was add and "Eleven" was subtract, and you had about sixty different commands that you could give to the machine and it would do whatever you told it to. I wrote a payroll program and was proud of myself that I got it to do cost allocations. But much of what I came to understand and appreciate about this new tool came from the fact that the teachers were engineers. Looking back, I might never have been so successful in the computer business had I not had the opportunity to experience what programmers and engineers actually did. Maybe it's no accident that when I went into business for myself, engineers—in this case, petroleum engineers—would become my first customers.

As a history buff, I loved learning the history of the development of the stored program concept, the history of all the mechanical, electrical, and electronic advances that had to be made, and the history of the mathematical modeling that had to be done to create those first computer systems. I was fascinated with what the advent of commercial computers seemed to herald.

Having grown up in a farming community, I knew the value of good tools. Every time I looked at this huge, hulking machine with its reels of tape and glowing panels, it gave me the spine-tingling sense that I was learning about something that was destined to become the vital tool of the future, something that could change the world. You could smell the scent of impending change in the air of that computer lab, which only heightened my passion for becoming an IBM-er.

Another exciting thing about graduate school was that it introduced me to the writings of Peter Drucker.

Born in Austria in 1909, Drucker fled the Nazis in 1933, moving first to England and four years later to America. He was a philosopher and a journalist, and taught in London, New York, and as a professor at Claremont University in California. He published thirty-nine books on management, economics, politics, and society.

Drucker was the visionary who coined the term "knowledge worker" because he was fascinated by the growing trend in which work was becoming more mental than manual.

His second book, *Concept of the Corporation,* took a long, hard look at the structure and internal workings of the world's largest corporation, General Motors. He observed that huge corporations were based on "manufacturing efficiencies" and had "managerial hierarchies." But inside those hierarchies, he found executives who too often spent time "keeping" their jobs rather than "doing" their jobs, and the excitement that had originally created their business went stale. When a company got into trouble, it came down to managers sticking to outdated ideas or basing decisions on internal misunderstandings. Drucker could see the problem and explain it in an intelligent and easily understood way.

His *The Practice of Management* was the Bible when I was at the Michigan Business School. In it, Drucker first conceptualized management as a discipline or profession akin to that of a lawyer or doctor.

Two of his ideas in particular struck me.

First, "The only thing that differentiates one business from another in any given field is the quality of its management on all levels."

And second, "The purpose of a business is to create customers."

Many businesspeople do not understand that. In the end you have to put every great idea to that test: Are you really going to be able to create customers with this product or service? Will the dogs eat the dog food?

* * *

THAT FALL, I went to New York to spend Thanksgiving with Charles, who was temporarily in Poughkeepsie, about 80 miles north of New York City, attending the world-renowned IBM Sales training school. The brainchild of Tom Watson, this IBM version of grad school was based on what Watson learned from Mr. Patterson, who had built the first truly professional sales organization at the National Cash Register Company. Watson preached Patterson's sales religion, but made it better, just as Ross Perot later took the IBM sales culture into his new company and made it even more devout.

Over that weekend, Charles and I met in Manhattan and found ourselves walking along Madison Avenue. We stopped in front of IBM's World Headquarters.

In the window was a brand-new IBM 704. It was a second-generation machine, meaning it was based on transistors rather than vacuum tubes and was smaller, faster, had more capacity, and represented such a gigantic leap forward that Charles and I just stood there staring at it for a long time. We were thrilled by the future, not only our own, but the future of a world that would use these machines to change the nature of work.

These were historic times for IBM. Tom Watson, Jr., had just settled a government antitrust lawsuit that had accused IBM of cross-subsidizing its services businesses with monopoly profits from its hardware sales, effectively keeping out any real services competition. For the local independent services companies who were competing against IBM's Service Bureau, this Consent Decree of 1956 would create a level playing field by creating a totally separate Service Bureau Corporation (SBC). Only a small percent of IBM's revenues came from data processing services, so in Watson Junior's mind, the lawsuit settlement merely paid lip service to the government.

This would have a life-altering effect on me, as it set the stage for a great on-the-job training period and then a terrific entrepreneurial opportunity.

That weekend in New York wound up being as much about

IBM as it was about Thanksgiving. Charles was enthusiastic about everything to do with the company. It wasn't Charles's style then (and still isn't) to jump up and down with glee, but I recognized in my low-key, soft-spoken brother exactly that kind of excitement.

Because IBM needed to get SBC staffed as soon as possible, the eighteen months Charles was supposed to spend in training was shortened to six. This meant he would be getting his own sales territory a year earlier than he had expected. It also meant I could look forward to that same fast track when I joined.

There would be other good job offers for me as a Michigan MBA graduate, such as Proctor and Gamble in Cincinnati. But my heart was with IBM.

The University of Michigan is an excellent school. I loved being there and I am proud to have earned an MBA. When I was there, I noticed that the five-and-ten-cents-store founder, Sebastian S. Kresge—the man who invented the Kmart chain— had given them Kresge Hall. When I could afford to, I figured, why not do the same? I have always been so grateful for what I learned there. In 1997 I gave the school funding for a Sam Wyly Hall. (A few years earlier, Charles and I had helped to build Louisiana Tech's 16-story Wyly Tower of Learning.) It's fulfilling to me that today Paton Scholars study at Sam Wyly Hall on the Ann Arbor campus.

My focus as a student was divided between schoolbooks and my ravenous desire to join my brother at IBM. By the time I was ready to graduate, Charles had been assigned a sales territory in New Orleans, his commissions had already tripled his starting pay, and he was earning more than anyone else we knew from Louisiana Tech. I, too, wanted to work at the best company in the world. But before I could start, I had to do my patriotic duty.

Back in the 1950s, military service was compulsory, so I signed up in 1956 with the Michigan Air National Guard and promptly got shipped off by railroad to Lackland Air Force Base in San Antonio, Texas, for basic training. Lights out was at 9:00 p.m. and exactly eight hours later, at 5:00 a.m., they blew a bugle to wake us. The rest of the day was spent at the mercy of a drill sergeant who worked us hard physically and disciplined us mentally to make us good soldiers.

My Michigan Squadron was unusual. Most other units were made up of less educated, younger men. Ours was made up of overeducated young men who had deferred their military service because they were in college. Our drill sergeant almost masochistically delighted in making us soft and self-important young men drop to the ground and pound out fifty push-ups for even the most minor offense.

I didn't mind the push-ups because that was like football training. It was the KP—kitchen patrol—and midnight guard duty that I detested. For KP, they would wake me at 4:00 a.m. to get breakfast ready, and I could not leave until 8:00 p.m., when dinner was done and I had finished mopping the mess hall for the third time that day. For guard duty, they would wake me at midnight, after only three hours of sleep, put a rifle on my shoulder, and make me march up and down outside the barracks. On those October nights, I'd often look up into the clear West Texas sky and think about the beeping I'd heard on the radio—coming from Nikita Khrushchev's Sputnik, the first satellite launched into orbit, which magnified the cold war between the two new world superpowers and accelerated the arms race between Russia and the United States.

I eventually found boot camp to be a nice break from the intense intellectual studying I had been doing. I found it oddly relaxing to focus on staying in step while marching instead of reading and writing about social or economic theories or grand business strategies. Being an optimist, I sometimes think I can learn to enjoy just about anything—which is not a bad life skill to possess—and I actually came to enjoy marching up and down the parade ground for hours on end. It was fun to sing out the cadence counts as a group. And I loved the sturdy boots they gave us.

It was a good experience for me, both humbling and grounding.

* * *

WHEN I HAD first applied for a job at IBM, the company gave me an aptitude test, which, somehow, told them that I had technical talent. Now that I was taking them up on their job offer, they said they wanted me to specialize in analytical and design work. They were replacing their line of "electric accounting machines"—their historic punched-card equipment—with "electronic data processing machines," and I would be an EDPM Systems Engineer.

I found myself sitting again in Mr. Wendler's office. The same man who had interviewed me on that first trip to Dallas was determined to convince me that my future lay in systems. This big guy stared me down from behind his mahogany desk and told me how rosy my future could be.

I kept saying, "No, I'm a salesman," even though I don't know what made me so sure I wanted to be a salesman. A systems engineer sounded noble and intellectual and I had gone to school with engineers, but I had the sales rep job in my head. Burned into my brain was that image of the IBM sales rep who had called on my dad at the newspaper that day. I remembered how intelligently he spoke, how elegantly he was dressed, and that he drove a Cadillac. I kept telling Mr. Wendler, "Sales is where I belong."

We went back and forth for the longest time before he finally agreed. I do not know why he gave in, but I would like to think it was because I had the self-knowledge and confidence to fight him on this. I too am impressed by this stand-your-ground quality when I hire someone. It tells me, "This guy knows who he is."

Too often, people seem willing to let other people or outside institutions place an identity on them. They don't, or simply won't, stand up for themselves. Generally speaking, people who won't stand up for themselves rarely go on to any sort of greatness. Without passion, you will not find much personal fulfillment and are unlikely to do outstanding work. I have found that success stories across all fields share something in common: The person in question is highly motivated. In addition, I am convinced that motivation for success and passion for the work are tightly linked.

When Mr. Wendler gave in, I started on the bottom rung of the sales force. I loved being back in Dallas.

Today, everybody knows something about Texas, but in those days Texas was still like an undiscovered oasis of freethinking, individualistic, action-oriented, business-minded people. It was a place where gut American characteristics were concentrated and magnified. A place where you could taste the frontier spirit that is part of our national heritage. There was a feeling in the air that you could invent yourself as any character you chose, and that your neighbors would leave you alone to be whoever you wanted to be. I liked the aggressiveness of the people in pursuing their goals, and the fact that you could be *poco loco*, as Spanish speakers say: a little crazy. This quality is a big help when you're an entrepreneur. I felt that, in Dallas, there was extra oxygen in the air.

It was February 1958. I got myself a room, not far from the office, in a little house built in the 1920s owned by a seventy-five-year-old woman named Mrs. Thompson. I lived in her "in-law's room," which meant I had my own front door, but I had to share the bathroom with her and, because I did not have a kitchen, I had to eat out. My rent was $10 a week.

I had my car, which meant I could get around, and the training school was air-conditioned, which meant my second summer in Dallas was a lot more pleasant than my first.

Thank you, Willis Haviland Carrier, for inventing air-conditioning. I owe you one. And I'm not the only one. At the height of the dot-com stock market bubble of 1999, Barton Biggs—the wise, graying investments guru at Morgan Stanley—posed this question to seventy-one people: Which invention is more important, the Internet or air-conditioning? Barton was on the losing side of the vote, 70–2.

Obviously, he'd found seventy people who'd never spent an August in Texas.

Chapter 5

Reach for a Star, Not a Handful of Mud

A COMPANY'S CULTURE can be a great asset, and at IBM the culture of the workforce was the company's greatest asset.

Tom Watson, Sr., had always actively sought out "the best of the best" from college campuses around the country. Then he indoctrinated those young men and women with a sense of being part of an elite team. He developed all sorts of techniques to create an esprit de corps that rivaled great military fighting forces like the U.S. Marines. There was that same, visible sense of pride. Every classroom and every branch manager's office had IBM's commandment: "Think."

He had songs written about the company that everyone had to sing in training school, pay was attached to performance with generous bonuses, and he built parks, golf courses, and swimming pools for his workers.

Watson Senior also innovated the 100% Club for salespeople who met their yearly quota, and he fêted them royally once a year at a weekend-long gathering. At the same time, he laid down very strict rules for individual behavior, many of them in line with his austere Methodist upbringing. IBM salespeople were not allowed to drink, not even wine. The company dress code was a dark suit, white shirt, tie—always a tie—and a hat. When I was in training, a cohort was sent home for showing up with a light blue shirt under his dark suit. I complained about the hat and was quickly told, "Businessmen wear hats, so you wear a hat."

I can't tell you how many hats I lost.

You were fired if you lost an account to a competitor, no matter how hard you'd worked or how good your effort had been: Lose to a competitor of IBM and you lose your job.

Today, Watson's rules look draconian. Today, punishing employees for personal behavior on their own time is an invasion of privacy. Nevertheless, Watson managed to create among IBM employees a sense of "being in this together." This feeling helped drive the company to unparalleled excellence and market dominance.

Tom Watson, Jr., took over in the midst of an American cultural shift that questioned the Marine-like dedication his dad had put in place. By the time I got there, Watson Junior was fully in command and the company culture was changing. Eventually he even liberated IBM-ers from the hat rule. In 1960, the country elected the hatless, vigorous, stylish young John F. Kennedy as President. Watson Junior had the guts to lead the company's transition to the computer age, a bet-the-company move that demanded both courage and vision. He also maintained the integrity of IBM's culture, while simultaneously, and with a gentle sense of humor, making modifications to fit the changing times.

He kept hosting the 100% Club gatherings, which reminded me of religious revival meetings where people were not ashamed to be swept up in enthusiasm and faith. I remember Watson Junior at my first 100% Club gathering at the Beverly Hilton in Los Angeles. Under the old rules, if you were caught drinking during working hours, you were fired. It did not matter to IBM if your customers were swigging back three martinis over lunch or not, you had to stay dry. At that meeting, though, he relaxed the rule, saying, "If you're going to have a drink, at least make sure it's gin, so our customers will smell it on your breath. I'd rather they think you're drunk than stupid."

He made a speech at that meeting that thrilled me, and really summed up the enthusiasm he wanted us all to share. "You have to reach for a star," he said. "You may not get a star, nor will you get a handful of mud."

I loved it.

Jack Welch, who ran General Electric, likes to point out, "It's important to celebrate." He's right. And that's another thing I like. When someone achieves a goal, you celebrate it with him or her in some way because that's a motivation to achieve the next goal. When people don't feel that they're accomplishing anything, they get demoralized. People need to feel proud of their efforts, need to feel that what they're attempting is actually possible, and need to feel that their managers are behind them. The best celebrator I ever knew was Carole Morton, who managed our Sterling Software team in the San Fernando Valley of California. Every time a sale was made, Carole rang a bell.

Work and joy are not mutually exclusive.

On my first or second day at IBM training school, I met a guy with a military crew cut and an East Texas twang, whose father was a cotton trader in Texarkana, the last town on the border, 40 miles before you get to Hope, Arkansas, Bill Clinton's hometown. It was "Bubba country," and it still is. The really big things created there and given to America and the world since I grew up there are Wal-Mart and the presidency of Bill Clinton.

This man I met was carrying a plug board panel for an IBM 407 printer on his back with red, green, and white wires sticking out at all kinds of crazy angles. Instead of just learning how to sell the computer, we also learned how it worked as a tool. Not that, as a salesman, you were going to personally make it work, but you had to know how it worked.

This was complicated stuff, and because we were all in this together, the fellow with the twang and I started talking. He told me he went to the U.S. Naval Academy, and had just finished his tour of duty as a Navy officer. Maybe because he was a little older, maybe because of his years in the Navy, or maybe just because he was who he was, this guy was different, a cut above.

We were told if you wanted to be a successful IBM salesman, you had to make forty calls a week, but this guy saw it differently. He said, "I don't need to make forty calls a week. I only need to make one if it's a good one, but I always make more than forty."

He would become the first IBM-er in Dallas, maybe even the world, to earn his entire year's quota by the end of January.

There was never any doubt that this guy was something special, and that he was going to be a winner. I had no idea how our paths would run in uncannily parallel lines for many years. How, as two of the most devout converts to IBM's corporate faith, we would leave and battle IBM. How he'd wind up as one of my oldest and best friends. How thirty-five years after that first meeting, I would have to choose between him and another very good friend, George Herbert Walker Bush, when both ran for President of the United States, along with my fellow Bubba country boy Bill Clinton, in 1992.

His name was Ross Perot.

I MOVED INTO a nice garden apartment on Abbott Street, just on the edge of Highland Park, splitting the $130-a-month rent with Remmington Johnston III, a Yankee immigrant from Fort Wayne, Indiana, who worked for Pollock. In the 1960s, this was a paper company. We had a swimming pool filled with American Airlines stewardesses, making it a pleasant place to hang around. In quieter moments, when the pool was empty, I got to know some of my neighbors. The fellow next door, Jack, was a chubby, middle-aged guy from Chicago who took off his tie in the afternoons but still wore his suit coat and white shirt hanging out by the pool and walking his dogs. He had dachshunds and sometimes after he walked them, we'd chat. He told me he owned a jazz club on Oak Lawn Avenue, and when I told him I had a clarinet-playing friend from Louisiana who was looking for a job, he hired him.

Dallas was a good, friendly place to live and I felt like I was on top of the world, with my future at IBM looking brighter than ever before. But about six months later, my boss, a tall, redheaded fellow with a Philadelphia accent named Bill Glavin, called me into his office with bad news. "We're terminating your training program."

I couldn't believe it.

He explained that a drop in the price of oil was causing a Texas recession and IBM was missing its quotas. The company needed to cut the budget, and the first thing that would have to go was sales training. He told me, "You're not going into sales. You're going to be a machine operator in Fort Worth."

I was aghast. I had this nice apartment with this nice swimming pool in cosmopolitan Dallas. But most of all, I didn't want to be a machine operator.

I wanted to be a sales rep.

Bill said, "There are four people in your job, and we're firing two of you to get our expenses down. We're keeping two of you, and those two are both going to be machine operators."

When life throws you a curve ball, you have to be flexible, so I told Bill, "Well, when you put it like that, Fort Worth is sounding better all the time."

A few days later, I walked into my new workplace, thinking to myself, "This is not what I signed up for." But the unexpected led me to the best thing that could have happened.

I actually had to make stuff work. I had to run jobs for real customers, and it was a very good learning experience. I had the chance to study different businesses by being able to look deep inside those companies.

One of those jobs, straight out of the West Texas oil fields, was processing the oil royalties for the Lamar Hunt Trust. I remember going over all the printouts and saying out loud, "Wow."

Growing up in the Delhi Oil Patch, I had seen some folks stop farming to live off their oil royalty money. I remember my dad laughing when he read in *Time* about two Texas oilmen named Sid Richardson and Clint Murchison funding a guy who tried to take over a railroad. When they happened to win it, Sid called Clint and asked, "What's the name of that railroad?" (It was New York Central.)

So I was very aware of the oil business and had seen the issue of *Life* magazine that called somebody named H. L. Hunt the richest man in the world. The checks I was processing, for huge sums, were made out to his son Lamar, who'd only just graduated from Southern Methodist University a couple of years before.

I was running jobs that needed to be done. People were

counting on me to get these jobs right and get them out on time. I was in the engine room learning new things every day from systems guys and operations managers.

Six months later the Texas oil patch recession was over, and I returned to Dallas full-time. Now I was where I wanted to be, a salesman for IBM's Service Bureau Corporation (SBC) with my very own "territory" of customers and prospective customers.

I was economically responsible for any net change in my sales. It didn't matter whether I personally did anything smart to warrant a positive outcome or whether I was at fault in a negative outcome; the buck stopped with me. I'd earn commissions on my territory's increase in revenues and I'd be docked for any shortfall. Whatever happened hit my paycheck. It was IBM's way of ensuring focus. It was Peter Drucker's "managing for results."

Looking back, if my work as a machine operator in Fort Worth was the best training for an IBM salesman, then being an IBM salesman with an SBC territory was the best training any entrepreneur could ask for, because it was a lot like running my own business. My job was to approach small and mid-sized companies and convince them that they could save money, time, and headaches if they outsourced their data processing services to us, replacing their NCR or Burroughs bookkeeping machines. To create a customized proposal, I needed to understand exactly how the present system worked. That meant going over everything with our systems analysts, then figuring out the cost of every single step. I had to get the customers to focus on improvements in speed, accuracy, and flexibility, which would make their enterprise more productive and profitable.

I could hear Drucker saying, "The purpose of a business is to create customers," which is exactly what I was doing for the Sam Wyly corner of IBM. It was a lesson in that link between feelings of ownership and motivation. I not only had a profit-and-loss statement for each of my customers, I also had one for my territory and myself because my list of customers was my business.

After three years at IBM, during which I became a member

of the 100% Club every year, I began to feel restless. I began to think that there was something else out there for me. In turn, that made me feel a little guilty, because in my heart I knew my restlessness meant I was no longer 100 percent dedicated to my job. And if I couldn't be a true-blue IBM-er, I ought not to be on their team at all.

At first, I tried to guide my internal restlessness by looking elsewhere within IBM, trying to land a job selling the largest mainframes on the hardware sales side. But IBM's hardware managers could not recruit salesmen for the Big Iron from SBC.

One of the reasons this great opportunity of working for SBC was available to Charles and me was that the company couldn't get old-timers to go to SBC because the old-timers didn't think of SBC in the same way they did IBM. They didn't know that, ultimately, services and software would become bigger than hardware at IBM. They'd have to learn that from me and Charles and Ross and others. We were the poor cousins on the wrong side of the tracks. The company's history and culture was hardware, and everything else that anyone in the company did was aimed at increasing the hardware revenue. To become a top manager, then—much less President of IBM—you had to have been a hardware sales rep. This held true right up until the 1990s, when an outsider named Louis Gerstner had to be brought in to rescue the company from the deep trouble they got into because of their hardware-only mentality. Hardware became a commodity and big profits turned to big losses. Then they had to learn to earn most of IBM's profit from the contract services and software businesses they had looked down their noses at. That's IBM today, prospering from businesses they didn't care about until they learned how by watching me and Ross Perot go do it and make the *Forbes* 400.

Another problem to me was the system that IBM had for promotion. That was based on a willingness to move anywhere in the country, or anywhere in the world, should the company decide to send you. Guys at the 100% Club joked, "IBM means 'I've Been Moved!'"

Bill Glavin was moved to California. My next boss, Bill Grubbs, was moved to France. And hey, maybe they liked it better elsewhere, but not me. I had my own set of priorities. I'd fallen in love with Texas and Dallas, and I'd begun to put down some roots.

Little by little, I felt the time approaching when I would have to leave IBM. I'd had a couple of brief conversations with other companies, but there weren't any offers on the table. The longer I stayed, the more uncomfortable I felt. It came to me that the only right thing for me to do was to quit, even if I didn't have another job. I walked in, told my boss I was leaving, and went home, knowing that the real source of supply for me and mine was spiritual, not dependent on any particular human organization or set of circumstances, and that I would be in my right place, wherever that was.

At this point I was twenty-six years old, married, with a young son and no back-up plan. Quitting was something that met no pragmatic test of rational human planning. But deep down, I knew something better was waiting for me.

I left the office that morning and drove back to our little one-story house on Marquette Avenue in North Dallas. It was a highly unusual time for me to be home and, since no one was expecting me, my wife, Rosemary, was out with our baby, Evan.

As I looked around the kitchen, with the sun pouring in through the window and Evan's crayons and paper and a cup of water on the table, I was filled with an inner peace. I knew there was nothing to fear. I stood there confident that something good would happen, even though I didn't know just what or when. At that moment the phone rang.

The man on the other end said he was calling from Honeywell and wanted to make me an offer to manage the start-up of their computer mainframe business in Dallas.

It was a powerful moment. I found myself having the conversation, but it was as if I wasn't in the room. I felt that God was present. I was relaxed, and even though I didn't yet know the specifics of the future, I trusted that it would be okay. I felt utterly serene.

Honeywell was a thermostat company that had gotten into the computer business. In the computer market there was

IBM and then there was everybody else. *Fortune* magazine described the market as IBM and the Seven Dwarfs. Honeywell was one of the dwarfs.

I flew up to Wellesley Hills, Massachusetts, where Honeywell was based, and took a tour of their plant. I saw their new computer, the Honeywell 800, which they'd designed to compete with IBM's big 7000 series. Right away, it struck me that this company had actually come up with a better product, a 48-bit machine that was designed for both the scientific and business markets. They were betting that computers could turn out to be a strong leg of the company, even if developing and building them cost hundreds of millions to get going, and I liked the idea of being part of such an audacious bet.

They would make me a manager and wanted me to stay in Dallas with an 80 percent salary increase. I'd get to hire my own team of technical and sales people, and they'd even build me a new office out of a corner of the big space that housed their thermostat and aerospace engineers.

Instead of just having a slice of one city, my territory would be two and a half states: Oklahoma, Arkansas, and the northern half of Texas. I really liked the idea that my boss would be based in Chicago; he'd be too far away and too busy to spend much time meddling with my team and me. In fact, it turned out that his oversight would be limited to only four meetings over two years, which was a huge move toward independence for me.

Joining Honeywell also meant a move away from a punch-card world to a real computing world. They had a great electronics business serving the military and the aviation industry. Honeywell was clearly a quality company, and I would be in on the ground floor of their bet on the company's new strategy.

Going with Honeywell after being with IBM was like quitting an NFL Championship team and joining a start-up team. On the other hand, this was the little guy going after the big guy, David versus Goliath. And in the back of my mind, I could still see that 155-pound noseguard, leveraging his quickness and agility to help his team of small-town country boys win the State Championship.

51

Honeywell was offering me the chance to help create a winning team, and suddenly that seemed like the most exciting, rewarding thing I could do.

In the back of my mind I could still hear the crowd shouting, "Beat Tallulah!" Now I set a new goal. And in the back of my mind, I was shouting, "Beat IBM!"

I was starting from scratch, one of the Seven Dwarfs. I didn't have any customers and I didn't have any staff. I was supposed to find customers, find programmers, hire salespeople, and end up with a team. There wasn't any particular timetable, mainly because the bosses at Honeywell didn't know what anybody ought to do. They never laid out a plan. Coming from IBM, where everything was set out for you, I found the level of anarchy amazing. And I loved it.

Selling really big-ticket items like those computers when your company was better known as a manufacturer of thermostats wasn't easy—especially when the competitor is IBM, the best-known data processing company in the world.

I was naïve in my estimation of how IBM would react to real competition. The world wasn't defined as IBM and the Seven Dwarfs just because it sounded nice. Beating them in a market where they had many years of being all-powerful, even with a superior product, turned out to be much tougher than I thought. I'd go to prospective customers and say, "I'm Sam Wyly, and I'm from Honeywell, and we sell computers," and they'd laugh and say, "Nah, Honeywell sells thermostats, IBM sells computers." It wasn't easy.

I WAS TRYING to get through the door at Republic Insurance Company but they'd always been an IBM shop. When a committee of all six vice presidents finally took a vote on their IT future, they came down 4 to 2 on the side of IBM. But when the customer says no, that's where the selling begins.

During one of several meetings with the president of the company, Russell Perry, he told me a story about dealing with IBM. A few years back, he'd bought some hardware from IBM and grew frustrated with the long delivery schedule. So he worked out a deal with another insurance company president to swap delivery slots. As long as the other company was willing to wait, Russell figured he would get his machine faster. This went against IBM's policy of total account control, however, and IBM did everything in their power to thwart Russell's deal. In the end, they couldn't stop it and had to deliver the other company's machines to Russell. But by playing the tough guy and claiming they owned the rulebook, by rubbing Russell's face in a contract that said he didn't own the machine or his own account, IBM made Russell feel as if they thought they owned him.

They'd infuriated Russell, so when Republic's committee voted against the Honeywell sale, I went over their heads. I don't recommend it every time you are turned down, but in this case I figured I had nothing to lose.

I went to see Russell and quietly reminded him of the way IBM had treated him. He looked at IBM and saw arrogance, looked at a lean and hungry Honeywell and saw a company that would value him as a customer and, just like that, he announced, "I'm overriding the committee."

So, after losing the committee vote 4–2, I got the contract by the chief executive officer's veto vote of 1–0.

That was a big boost for me and for Honeywell, especially because Republic was right next door to IBM's Dallas headquarters. Every day on their way to work, my former colleagues had to look at the first account in town they'd lost to Honeywell, one of those puny Seven Dwarfs.

Off and running, I felt real good about the way things were going. Before long, my five-man office in Dallas was outselling Honeywell's bigger offices, where they had thirty people. And I was making $30,000, triple my IBM earnings. By 1962 I had a two-story house on a tree-lined street in a good school district and two cars.

What else did I need? I certainly didn't need to start a new business just to have more income. I was fine the way I was. Except I wasn't. I was getting restless again.

I knew that to make it to the top at Honeywell—just like at IBM or, for that matter, at any established company—I'd have to uproot my family and go wherever in the world they needed my skills. And I'd have to do it over and over again as I climbed the ladder. Maybe that sounds exciting to some, but not to me. The fact is I liked the tree-lined street where I lived. My in-laws were nearby, and my own parents had moved to Houston to be near Charles and his family. I didn't want to leave Texas, and I didn't want to spend my life in transit.

My restlessness was forcing me to face up to this single truth: I was not at heart a big company man. I didn't want to be under anyone else's authority. I wanted to call the shots for myself.

I was rereading Ralph Waldo Emerson at the time, and kept going back to his quote, "A great institution is the lengthening shadow of a man." Tom Watson, Sr., had achieved this with IBM. Now I was wondering what kind of shadow would follow me. Could I create and build an enterprise?

Since childhood, I had had a sense of destiny and thought about what was waiting for me. There was nothing wrong with my job at Honeywell. Nor, for that matter, had there been anything awful about my job at IBM, and both paid me generously. But something inside me was crying out for change.

By allowing moments of quiet reflection, I gave myself the mental space to realize what was most important to me. I wanted to be captain of my own boat. I didn't need to make all the money I'd been bringing in from Honeywell, but I wanted independence.

Those years at IBM and Honeywell were important for me and for the career I was about to start building as an entrepreneur. I will always be grateful to IBM and to Honeywell for the experiences and the opportunities they gave me. They are really good companies.

An entrepreneur knows when to move on. And that time had come for me.

Chapter 6

Me and Ross Perot

Ross Perot spent some time at Texarkana Junior College awaiting his appointment to the Naval Academy. He loved both Annapolis and his years of active duty. In a way, joining IBM was a lot like being in the Army or Navy. He traded in his Navy uniform for Watson's white shirts and navy blue suits. He was a perfect fit.

And even today, he'd still be a perfect fit because he's never taken off those white shirts and navy blue suits. I have a picture of us together back in the late '60s when he's wearing a sports shirt, but that's only because we were at a conference where suits and ties were outlawed; he had to wear a sports shirt, and that might be the last time he ever did. Today, he shows up at Dallas Mavericks basketball games in a suit and tie. He comes to the games with Ross Junior and Ross III and all of them are wearing suits and ties, and they are the only ones in the whole crowd dressed like that, other than the coaches. So the spirit of the U.S. Navy and Tom Watson's IBM lives on with the Perots in Dallas. I love it!

IBM blue was coursing through Ross's veins. Mine, too. We were true believers. The world was divided into two classes. There were those of us who worked for IBM, and then there were all the other unfortunate people in the rest of the world. Our punch cards had square holes and Univac's punch cards had round holes, and round holes don't work. We had 90 percent of the market, they had 10 percent, and that's how God intended it to be.

Ross and I were IBM culture blood brothers. We were drinking the Kool-Aid. Then I left to join Honeywell, which was high treason. Personally, he and I would always be friends. But in his business mind, I was now his competitor. In mine, he was the same.

I zeroed in on Texas Blue Cross, which just happened to have been one of Ross's accounts. Getting a non-IBM computer into Blue Cross was a serious competitive process, convincing IT managers of your service, quality, and price.

My new Honeywell 400 had his IBM 1401 beat on every aspect. Mine was faster, better, and cheaper. Mine had better software, the machine was easier to program, and early customers loved the Honeywell service. The only place where we tied was in delivery times (more than a year). And at IBM, delivery schedules were sacred. There is no exception. This is discipline. This is IBM.

To show the Texas Blue Cross guys just how great Honeywell was, I flew them to New York City to watch one at work at Metropolitan Life Insurance. I flew another group to Cleveland to see the machine at work in a department store there. It was six months of hard work, but I knew we were going to win.

But Ross could not let that happen, so by internally selling IBM on making an exception to their delivery rules, he got Texas Blue Cross instant delivery.

He went straight to the CEO and sold him on this big thing IBM would do for Dallas Blue Cross. The chief overruled everyone else down the chain of command who had decided for Honeywell and gave IBM the order.

IBM knew if we got our foot in that door, they were vulnerable in other accounts. Nothing personal, but Ross was not going to let me and Honeywell have it. So he broke IBM discipline, and to do that he had to go all the way to the top because nothing short of a papal dispensation was going to break the ironclad eighteen-month delivery schedule. I hate losing, but I admire the work of a genius.

Ross was the world's greatest computer salesman. The year he beat me at Texas Blue Cross, he made his annual sales quota in January. He had tripled his quota by March. Ross was earning huge commissions; he was an IBM hero.

And then, one day, a year after I walked out, Ross walked out.

He left IBM to found a company of his own, Electronic Data Systems (EDS).

Ross was Tom Watson, Sr.'s, greatest disciple. When he created EDS, he copied Watson Senior's style verbatim: exact uniform, exact military discipline, exact focus on account control and selling at the top.

SOON AFTER Ross left IBM, he and I brainstormed a way to help me get a Honeywell customer. We published a newspaper ad offering immediate delivery of an IBM 1401, at a discount. Republic Insurance had ordered this machine eighteen months earlier, prior to IBM's 15 percent price increase. We were offering to resell it.

The controversy stirred up by this ad greatly amused IBM's customers and helped me and Honeywell win. With Ross's help I had weakened IBM's strategy of value through scarcity. Competitors and customer IT managers had been battered by IBM's tight control and their use of the "FUD" factor: fear, uncertainty, and doubt about any decision other than buying from IBM. Our ad and the big stewing process it created made it clear that you didn't have to deal with IBM exclusively. What IBM was selling was now illusion.

We had exposed the Wizard of Oz.

The ad gave Ross's tiny start-up company, whose greatest strength was his own powerful personality, the attention of company presidents who were trying to figure out what was going on in their own information technology shops. It also helped me nail down that Republic Insurance Company order for Honeywell, which turned out to be the first sale of a non-IBM computer in Dallas. I quickly followed it with a bigger sale to another local company and a third sale to a military base in Oklahoma.

We were off and running.

Chapter 7

The Birth of a Company

SHORTLY AFTER my little adventure with Republic and Ross, I came across an IBM study making the rounds of local customers that tried to justify a $3 million IBM 7090 computer center in North Texas. The study, along with conventional wisdom in Dallas at the time, concluded that it couldn't be done, that there was not enough market. At least, that's what IBM's survey concluded.

But it triggered a thought for a similar but different business that might work. I didn't have $3 million, but I had $1,000 and an idea.

Initially, when I have an idea, I tend to be protective of it. Sure, there comes a time when you need to brainstorm with trusted advisers—whether it's a spouse, a close friend, a business associate, or a board member—because eventually you need to get other people's insights. But in the beginning, you need to be self-reliant and to nurture and safeguard your idea. As Mary Baker Eddy teaches, you need to protect your good idea from other people's negativity until it's out of its infancy.

So I didn't talk to anyone about my new idea, I just kept going to work at Honeywell, managing myself and my staff, and making sure we did our job. But I never stopped looking at this new opportunity and never stopped trying to figure out how I could make it happen.

Peter Drucker says that entrepreneurs need to spot "fault lines" in order to recognize when times of change are occurring, and that it's in times of change that the greatest opportunities arise.

I also knew I was observing this "fault line" within the background of huge future productivity for the knowledge worker to come from content software. This would be as great a leap forward as the revolution in hybrid corn and wheat seeds, productivity tools coming from America's research and scholarship that were lifting hundreds of millions of people in the world out of starvation and poverty.

In 1963 Dallas, there was so much change going on that sometimes it seemed as if the ground beneath my feet was nothing but zigzagged fault lines. Wherever I looked, I could see discrepancies between what people expected the world to be and the way it really was. Dealing with Russell Perry at Republic Insurance, for example, I witnessed firsthand IBM's failure to notice—let alone respond to—changing customer demands. It was as if they were unable to accept that they suddenly had genuine competition.

These disconnects, or "incongruities," as Drucker calls them, happen during times of great change, and IBM's attitude bears this out. They were still the biggest player on the field, by far. But being arrogant when you have a monopoly is one thing. Being arrogant when you have real competition is reckless.

Years later, George Soros was explaining to someone why he was so amazingly successful as a hedge fund investor. He spoke about "the bias." He was pretty much referring to the same thing as Drucker, pointing out that there's often a gap between market perception and reality.

It's in those gaps that the clear thinker makes his way. To accomplish this, however, you must be willing and able to conceive of things that, to most people, seem inconceivable. It gets back to that old expression, "Ask yourself what isn't, then ask yourself why not?"

A feeling of omnipotence was blinding IBM to the changes that were taking place. They discounted the importance and the realities of the changing marketplace. Their assumption that they would always dominate and control the computer marketplace, just as they had dominated the punch-card equipment marketplace, struck me as nothing short of hubris. And, just as I'd learned on a muddy Louisiana football field that hubris leads to mental lethargy and defeat, I also learned that mental lethargy leads directly to opportunities for your competitors.

It was clear to me that the stored program computer was going to change the world. It was also clear to me that, even though IBM would probably continue to be dominant in this brave new world, there was room for more than one successful player.

I knew there were a whole lot of people out there who wanted the power and productivity that a big computer system offered, but who couldn't afford a multimillion-dollar mainframe.

So how could I create a company to fill that gap?

I knew some engineers at Sun Oil and at Texas Instruments, and had been talking to them long enough to know that they clearly had a need for a mainframe. The guys at Sun Oil, for instance, were driving more than an hour to Vought Aerospace, in Grand Prairie, just to use a big computer there. They were driving out there on weekends or late at night, whenever they could get access, only to find that they were regularly being bumped because some Vought engineer was still working on his military wind-tunnel research.

I also knew some engineers at Southern Methodist University (SMU) who were gnashing their teeth in frustration at the old vacuum-tube warhorse of a computer they were forced to use because there was no budget for a newer, more powerful, semiconductor-based machine.

It all added up to convince me that there was a big void in the market. I could see a customer base—whose language I spoke and who would understand and value what I wanted to offer— just waiting to be scooped up. I also knew, with the total conviction of a revival preacher, that if I could get my hands on one of the new, lower-cost, higher-powered supercomputers coming from Control Data, I could sell computing services on it and make a profit.

My plan was to do with big computers what real estate developers did with land: Buy it by the acre, then resell it by the square foot.

I'd originally called on J. B. Harville, head of SMU's computing lab, when I was looking for Honeywell customers. It turned out that SMU had no money for a new computer, but I liked JB and every now and then we'd get together to talk about computers. He was the fellow who first tipped me off to the work of some Texas Instruments engineers, led by a genius named Jack Kilby, who were trying to solder lots of transistors onto one surface, something they were calling an "integrated circuit." JB explained to me how it would work and promised, "It will be smaller than a refrigerator. Maybe as small as a bread box."

JB was talking about the development of the microchip, which is at the heart of today's personal computers, cell phones, and video games, as well as Toyota's 50-mile-per-gallon Prius hybrid car. Ultimately, Jack Kilby of Texas Instruments shared the Nobel Prize with Robert Noyce of Intel for this invention.

Anyway, JB's problem was that UNIVAC had given SMU an aging, vacuum-tube 1103, which meant they were stuck with a computer that took up a huge amount of room, needed a lot of air-conditioning, and offered very little in terms of calculating abilities. I remember to this day JB moaning, "Transistors! Transistors!"—which had replaced vacuum tubes, marking the second generation of computing. The third generation would start when the microchip was in production. The fourth generation arrived when the telephone married the computer and PCs became affordable and ubiquitous and a lot of software was developed, and we called all this the Internet.

Since this computer had been a donation, the school's administrators refused to acknowledge the need for funds for a better computer. Their attitude was, "Why won't UNIVAC or some other manufacturer just give us another, more modern gift?" What an incongruity. SMU, where knowledge workers are schooled, was stuck with a completely out-of-date machine at a time when computers were becoming vital to both industry and education.

For an engineer like JB, being left in the dust by schools like my alma mater, the University of Michigan, was head-bangingly irritating. As an entrepreneur, I saw this problem at SMU as a golden opportunity for me. All I needed to do was merge JB's dilemma with my ambition. SMU had real estate. In other words, they were already paying for the space in which to put a machine and the electricity to power it. My thought was that if I could figure out how to buy the next-generation machine, I could install it there and, in exchange for allowing SMU's professors and students access to it on nights and weekends, I could rent it out during the day to cash-paying commercial customers.

The first step was getting an affordable computer. Control Data was founded by former UNIVAC denizen Bill Norris with Seymour Cray. These mathematical geniuses had built a powerful machine, the CDC 1604, that could compete with IBM's new 7090. It wasn't cheap at $1.5 million (that would be something like $10 million today), but it had the capability to take on IBM at half the cost and it had the critical software I needed for engineering customers: a good Fortran compiler.

Interestingly enough, Bill and Seymour had arrived at the name for their computer, CDC 1604, by adding the St. Paul, Minnesota, street address of their new company, which was 501, to the number of the last machine they'd done for UNIVAC, which was the 1103. This playfulness gives you a sense of the changes taking place in computer culture. Such a whimsical decision would never have occurred at straitlaced IBM.

I took a long look at what the CDC 1604 had to offer and filled yellow notepads with my calculations, but no matter how hard I crunched the numbers, I couldn't come up with a profitable business model based on a $1.5-million machine.

And yet, here were all those Texas Instruments and Sun Oil programmers driving night after night to Grand Prairie.

STARTING A BUSINESS from scratch is like which comes first, the chicken or the egg? Since I had potential customers, I knew that there must be a way to get a machine. I had an intelligent way to cut expenses, by housing the machine at SMU and paying the rent and electricity bills with part of the machine's capacity. But I had no $1.5 million (down from $3 million), and without that, I had no way to buy a machine.

It was very disappointing.

I knew it was crucial to keep a clear head. You set your goal—"Beat Tallulah!"—and no matter what, you keep your eye on the prize. Sure, everyone feels discouraged when progress grinds to a halt, but you can't let frustration take over and control you. Rational problem solving is essential to company building.

Building successful economic models is hard, but they're part of the game. More often than not, if it's too easy, somebody else did it already. So you have to expect obstacles. If you let frustration take control, your precious infant idea won't mature. When you're knocked down, don't give up, get up. If you can't be creative, disciplined, persistent, and rationally optimistic in the face of repeated failure, you need to consider a different line of work.

Everybody faces frustration, obstacles, and failure differently, so there is no one right approach. What works for me is to stop, step back, take a deep breath, and seek to get to the most spiritual perspective. To think about where we are and what we are trying to achieve and try to see the problem from all sides. It's funny, but when you take the time to let the well fill up like that, you sometimes discover there's a solution that's actually better than your original idea.

Back in Louisiana, when my parents were getting started in the newspaper business with the *Delhi Dispatch*, they needed a printing press but couldn't afford a new one. So Dad started wondering aloud if there was such a thing as a secondhand printing press.

He started calling around, and, sure enough, he found a secondhand press up for sale cheap. I remember driving with him to Jacksonville, Texas, for a look. He bought it on the spot and it met the needs of the *Dispatch* just fine.

As I was mulling over my own dilemma, I thought about my dad and said to myself, "If it worked for him, it could work for me." There was no secondhand computer market, but that didn't mean I couldn't find somebody who wanted to sell one.

IBM had seen to it that there was no secondhand market for their equipment. They did this originally with a rent-only policy. Customers paid a monthly rent and IBM eventually replaced the older equipment. When their settlement of the government's first anti-monopoly lawsuit required them to sell also, they simply made the sale price so high that everybody rented. But then came the Seven Dwarfs, who were happy to sell so as not to have a huge pot of cash in a rental portfolio. So like my dad had done, I started calling around and, sure enough, I discovered a company in Washington, D.C., called CEIR that wanted to sell one of theirs.

They were a professional services company, set up like a firm of accountants or lawyers, except that they were staffed with computer analysts and programmers. They'd bought some computers during a brief boom in military contracting, but suddenly found themselves at the bottom of an equally tremendous bust and they were eager to sell one of their machines. They offered me a used CDC 1604 for $600,000 cash, which was less than half the cost of a new one. It was a great price and being able to cut my capital cost from $3 million to $600,000 was definitely a step in the right direction. There was still a small problem, however. Their asking price of $600,000 was exactly $599,000 more than I had. Ever the optimist, I didn't see that as an insurmountable obstacle, I only saw a challenge. My company wasn't based on a complicated business model. I wasn't trying to come up with rocket science. But building an entity of any kind is a process, one that requires balancing your hunger for achievement with your patience and perseverance.

At the time I found that used CDC 1604, I was still in the very creative first stage of entrepreneurship. Our culture doesn't place enough emphasis on creativity. We're so focused on *doing* that we neglect the mental work that comes first.

When I was at IBM, the signs on the wall said: "Think."

And that's as good a piece of advice as I ever got. Whenever I find myself faced with a seemingly insurmountable problem, I remind myself that I cannot let fear or gloom take hold, and I think it through. Albert Einstein said that the most important part of the human mind is its ability to imagine. Mary Baker Eddy said we must form perfect models of thought, and look at them continuously, or we shall never carve them out in grand and noble lives. Creative thinking is at the entrepreneur's core.

First, I took stock of my strengths and weaknesses. I believed my greatest strengths were that I understood my customer and my product, and that I possessed the entrepreneur's determination to turn my idea into a reality.

As for weaknesses, there were three big ones glaring back at me: I had no customers, I had no track record as an independent businessman, and I had no capital.

SMU was ready whenever I was, so for the moment I had the luxury of being able to approach a potential client who could be both a customer and a supplier of capital, sort of. I thought about those Sun Oil engineers who were regularly making the long haul out to Grand Prairie, and went to see John Rice, who ran Sun Oil's production and exploration lab in Richardson, Texas. In my briefcase I had a contract with me, just in case he was ready to sign up with a business that existed only in my twenty-eight-year-old head. My opening gambit was, "How'd you like a shorter drive?" We both knew what his answer would be. I told him about my plan to house the CDC 1604 at SMU and explained how we could cut his costs while at the same time increasing his productivity. Rice said he and his engineers would like all those things just fine and, what's more, Sun would be helping SMU get low-cost computing. I almost reached for my briefcase. But then he said that liking my idea didn't mean he was ready to sign up.

Next step was to hit the bankers, starting with the biggest in town: Republic Bank. I had an account there and had once borrowed $10,000 from them to be a Saturday-morning investor in growth stocks. I'd paid it all back on time, so I expected the welcome mat to be out for me. But when I told my banker, "I want to borrow $600,000," he burst out laughing. I mean a real old-fashioned belly laugh.

My thoughts flashed back to the banker in Delhi who lent me the money to buy my car and his talk about the three C's: collateral, credit, and character. In Delhi, character was enough. In Dallas, I didn't have collateral, didn't have credit, and even if this banker thought I possessed good character, he couldn't conceive of a set of circumstances where he would hand me $600 for every $1 of my own.

But again, obstacles are only challenges. For every brick wall you come up against, you have to figure there's something on the other side. You don't despair that there's a brick wall in your way, you go through it, over it, or around it. This is what I did. I went to the second biggest bank in town, First National, armed with my facts and figures, my committed expense levels, my list of prospective customers, plus the unshakable confidence that we'd have revenue sources pouring in the moment we opened. I told that banker, "Call the folks at Sun Oil and Southern Methodist University, and they'll tell you they'll sign contracts the minute the computer system is financed."

He wasn't terribly impressed. We talked for a while and, listening to him, I began to understand what that brick wall was. In Dallas, bankers were used to making loans against residential property, commercial real estate, or oil property. Of course, it's easy to make a loan when the guy borrowing the money is putting up a pumping well! The banker can see a revenue stream and knows that there are reserves in the ground because those are certified by professional petroleum engineers, professionals like the guys at Sun Oil. But when those same bankers looked at me, they saw someone asking them to finance a wildcat well, which could possibly turn out to be a gusher but was far more likely to be a dry hole in the ground, and a loss for the bank.

"Okay," I said when he stopped laughing, and I took another shove at the brick wall. "What's the worst that can happen to your bank? If you give me this loan, I'll have enough cash in your bank to stay afloat for twenty-three months. You've got to believe I can drum up at least enough business to be operating above my breakeven point in twenty-three months."

"I do," the banker said, "but if your interesting theory doesn't work, how are you going to pay me back?"

Interesting theory? This guy had the nerve to call my rock-solid business plan an interesting theory? In no time, I was heading for the Mercantile Bank, brick wall #3.

Getting my third "no" of the morning didn't take long, and I found myself back on the street just before noon. I had set the bank meeting at 11:00 a.m. because I wanted to watch the parade.

President Kennedy was coming to Dallas.

Although the 1964 election was a year away, John and Jackie Kennedy were launching the campaign for reelection with a stomp through Texas, paying homage to the home state of Vice President Lyndon Johnson. The Democrats needed to nail down Texas because the Republicans were beginning to show signs of challenging the Democrats' 100-year-old monopoly in the state.

So after leaving the Mercantile Bank, I tried to find a spot from which to watch the motorcade, but it was too crowded. Instead, I darted into Neiman Marcus, the big department store just a block away, ran up three flights of stairs to the men's department, and found a window with a view looking onto Main Street. The motorcade approached from my right. The President was waving from the back seat of the big Lincoln convertible, with Jackie sitting next to him wearing that pink suit and matching pillbox hat. Smiling, handsome, and silver-haired, Governor John Connally, as big a hero in Texas as the President was in Washington, was sitting on the jump seat with his wife, Nelly, just in front of the Kennedys. Main Street was mobbed on both sides with people waving little American flags. I have always been a presidential electoral contest fan, and I was caught up in the same enthusiasm that so many Americans shared for our vigorous young president.

During the Cuban Missile Crisis, I watched Kennedy go eyeball to eyeball with a powerful and belligerent Nikita Khrushchev—at a time when each had his hand on the nuclear trigger and the destruction of Dallas and Moscow could potentially be only twenty minutes away—and then the other guy blinked. I had memorized big chunks of Kennedy's famous inaugural address—"Ask not what your country can do for you, ask what you can do for your country..."—because, like Abraham Lincoln's Gettysburg Address, I found the same Shakespearean cadence that I loved in my King James Bible. Seeing him in person, right there, so young and so handsome with his beautiful First Lady, was a very exciting moment, even after my third "no" from the banks. I left Neiman Marcus elated.

I crossed the street to the parking garage where I'd left my car and went to pay for my ticket. But the cashier had her ear pressed up to the radio on her desk and a look of utter horror on her face. She gave me a blank stare and announced, "The President's been shot." Her voice sounded tinny and small in the vastness of the parking garage, and I didn't believe her at first. Then, all of a sudden, police cars started pouring out of the police station next door, one after another, with sirens blaring and red lights flashing.

It was a shocking and sick feeling. Utter disbelief and total anguish swept through me. I felt numb, and didn't know what to do. I was supposed to meet JB and his lawyer at SMU. I drove over there, but we could not think, we could not talk, we were all numb. So I made my way home, turned on the television, and just sat there, in a daze, forgetting about everything except the tragedy that had happened right here in my backyard and almost in front of my own eyes. I felt violated by some evil that I could not understand.

Two days later, I was still sitting in front of my television, as I had never done before. I watched, bewildered, unbelieving as the police began to transfer the assassin, Lee Harvey Oswald, out of the station where they'd been holding him. They were taking him out of the basement right next door to the parking garage where I'd heard the awful news. It was eerie. Then, as I and tens of millions watched on TV, a short, chubby man in a dark suit and brimmed hat with a pistol in his hand stepped into the picture and shot Oswald right in the belly.

My eyes almost popped out of my head.

I watched the replay again and again, almost as if I were in a trance, then suddenly jumped out of my chair and screamed, "That's Jack Ruby!" He was the neighbor with the dachshunds who'd lived next door to me at the garden apartment with the stewardesses and the swimming pool. The guy who had given a job to Lacy Stinson, my clarinet-playing friend from Ruston, Louisiana. It was, without a doubt, one of the strangest moments in my life.

There had been so much hope with the vigorous, bright, and young Kennedys; it was destroyed in a flash. Like the Japanese attack on Pearl Harbor, and the terror of 9/11, what happened on November 22, 1963, in Dallas was a watershed moment in the lives of every one of us who lived through it. Coming to grips with such a sudden and tragic intrusion of history took time.

We all deal with these things in different ways, coping as best we can. I remember thinking to myself, at one point, how that fateful parade in downtown Dallas was an incredibly sobering reminder that, in the grand scheme of things, my entrepreneurial risk was really not so important.

EVENTUALLY, I set up another meeting with John Rice at Sun Oil. The only way I was going to make any banker understand that this was for real, and actually get one of them to come on board, was with a signed contract in my hands from Sun Oil prepaying part of a five-year commitment, along with my SMU deal. I'd already convinced John and his engineers that having a CDC 1604 so conveniently at their disposal would be helpful, and that my plan would greatly reduce their costs. So, finally, he agreed to back my proposal with a $250,000 contract.

I kept telling myself that the chicken and egg problem was solved. That is, up until the moment when John and I met with the controllers at Sun Oil. They said Sun takes risks on oil wells, not on whether or not some young entrepreneur will survive to meet his obligations to Sun, and refused flat out to sign off on the deal we'd negotiated. They demanded more security in case I went belly-up before their five years were done.

I was rudely shoved back to square one. But while nothing is ever as simple as you think it will be, few things are really ever too complicated to work out. For me, that means trial and error. But I was in a bit of a spot. After all, I was going around telling everybody involved not to worry, that things were just about to fall into place. I was telling CEIR it was okay to ship the machine, even though I couldn't tell them for sure how they'd get paid. I was telling SMU to get the space ready. I was telling my prospective customers that they'd soon have a better choice.

Sometimes, while you're trying to untangle those knots, what you've been waiting for just walks through the door not looking at all like what you thought you were waiting for. You just have to have your eyes open wide enough to see it, and recognize what you're seeing.

An agent from New Hampshire Insurance came to sell me a policy. He'd heard about my venture and wanted to know if I was interested in property insurance for "my" computer. He was selling a good product, and I said I'd be happy to buy his property insurance, but first I had to get into business. He asked me why I wasn't yet in business, and I explained my situation.

He smiled. "What you need is a performance bond. We do that for construction contractors all the time."

A performance bond would mean a promise from a big insurance company that if I went bust in less than five years, they'd pay back what was not yet earned from Sun Oil's cash deposit. In other words, the insurance company would guarantee my performance of our contract. I asked how much it cost; he said 2 percent of the original amount and 1 percent of the declining balance. I told him if he got me the bond, I'd buy his insurance, too. He did, and then I did; and after SMU and Sun Oil, the New Hampshire Insurance Company bond became the third piece of the puzzle to click into place.

Chapter 8
A Thousand Dollars and an Idea

I HAD ALWAYS believed that three pieces of the puzzle would be enough. But now I needed another piece—I hoped it would be the last—but I didn't know where I was going to get it. That is, until I opened my eyes and realized it had been sitting right under my nose all the time.

My father-in-law, Len Acton, had come to America in the 1920s from Manchester, England, with his mother when he was nineteen, took a job with a ladies' clothing distributor out of Kansas City, and made his way to Texas. There, he met up with a lawyer named Guy Mann and the two of them became "deal men," buying and selling companies, working for the legendary Texas oil wildcatter Clint Murchison.

Clint also backed Guy's brother Jerry, which was no surprise because Jerry was sharp, very sharp. Jerry was a genuine local hero, called the Little Red Arrow, who had put SMU football on the map in the mid- to late 1920s as one of their all-time great All-American quarterbacks. He got the nickname because of his accurate passing and, in the Texas Sports Hall of Fame, he is up there with the other SMU greats: Don Meredith, Kyle Rote, and Doak Walker.

From SMU, Jerry went on to Harvard Law School, where he served as a part-time evangelical preacher in local congregations. Then he came back to serve as Texas Attorney General. In 1941, he ran for the U.S. Senate as a Franklin Roosevelt Democrat, along with Lyndon Johnson. But they both lost to the Governor, W. Lee "Pass the Biscuits, Pappy" O'Daniel, a passionate, charismatic Texan, who regularly toured the state with

71

his Hillbilly Band and won over audiences with a song he wrote called "Beautiful Texas." Jerry and Lyndon just couldn't compete. Pappy's constant radio play got him elected.

Fifteen years after Jerry had thrown his last football, *Time* magazine described him as a man who "doesn't cuss, doesn't drink, is slight, quick, deep-eyed, and keeps his weight down to his quarterback's 150 pounds."

By the time I met him, he hadn't thrown a football in nearly thirty years, and had long since given up politics. He had set up a conglomerate in Dallas called Diversa, which owned, among other things, a dog food company, some oil rigs, and some real estate.

Diversa bought almost anything they could, as long as they could use cash. So I asked my father-in-law and Guy to set up a meeting for me with Jerry Mann. He listened to my proposal, went over my business plan, and we worked out a deal. Diversa would guarantee my monthly payments to the bank in exchange for 49 percent of my company.

Some people might think it was a hefty chunk to give up, but I was the one who offered them 49 percent and was more than willing to do so. I never considered offering less. As far as I was concerned, the difference between their half and my half was all the difference in the world. Maintaining control is often hard for entrepreneurs, unless you're already wealthy and happy to risk your own money. As a young and decidedly not wealthy entrepreneur, I felt that as long as I still had 51 percent—which meant I controlled my own company—they were more than entitled to their half.

So that was our deal, and Jerry and I shook hands on it. I now had Diversa's guarantee, plus the performance bond, two five-year customer contracts, Sun Oil's cash prepayment, and a machine that I was buying for 60 percent less than market value. I told myself that would be enough for some banker, somewhere. To see if the addition of the Diversa guarantee made us a good enough credit, I went back to the fourth bank that had rejected me. Its vice chairman went to my church and had become sort of a cheerleader for my efforts, even though I had only $1,000 of the $600,000 I needed. When I went back to the bankers who had already turned me down, Jack Garrett studied my deal, looked at all the components I had been juggling for months, saw that everything had fallen into place, recommended it to the Texas Bank Loan Committee, and they said yes.

Feeling like the king of the world, I hurried over to Diversa's offices to close the deal. I sat down with their lawyers and accountants at the big boardroom table, and everything was going fine until one of the lawyers brought up, in a casual way, that Diversa's "half" of my company really meant 51 percent.

This stopped me in my tracks. "That's not the deal we agreed to. That's a different deal."

They refused to budge.

I demanded to talk to Jerry. After all, he and I had shaken hands on this. The lawyers warned me that Jerry would not budge, either. When Jerry came in, I asked the lawyers and accountants to leave. I reminded him we had shaken hands on the 51–49 percent split in my favor. He waved away my concerns, saying that it was not him; it was the lawyers and the accountants who were insisting that Diversa would be foolish to assume the risk without that extra 2 percent, and that he could not disregard his lawyers.

I felt deceived. I felt betrayed. Their 51 percent control could be like working for IBM or Honeywell again. I felt a threat to the most important value I was seeking: independence. I had to ask myself, "Do I say no? Or do I say yes and accept their contract, even though it isn't what we shook hands on and it makes me uncomfortable?" This was a major difficulty for me. The 51 percent issue is at the very core of what every entrepreneur is trying to do: control his own destiny.

We were talking about my company. I dreamed it up. I put it together. And I was going to run it. I was not going to hand it over to some committee of lawyers and accountants. But neither could I let anger get hold of me.

I knew that "those whom the gods would destroy, they first make angry." That said, not getting angry does not mean not being firm. So I firmly told Jerry, "I want to run this company. I don't have time to sit around and explain to your staff what I'm doing. No offense, but they don't know beans about what I'm trying to do, and neither do you, for that matter. I've got to be able to run this business. I can't explain strategy at the same time that I'm inventing it."

They were sort of a mini-General Electric conglomerate—"our business is businesses": Everything was for sale at a good price, and Diversa had a continuing need to cash out assets to pay off debt. I looked him straight in the eye and said, "I'll go ahead and do this, if you will agree that I can come back to you later and offer you a fair market price for your 51 percent, and that you'll take it." It was one of those life-altering moments, a fraction in time, when you have to make an instantaneous decision, knowing that neither of two possible outcomes is ideal.

Cashing out as soon as possible at a good profit was at the heart of what Jerry was trying to do with his company, so he agreed. We did not put this in writing. On this point, I knew I could trust him. The lawyers and accountants returned to the table, and I signed on the dotted line.

I was finally an entrepreneur.

MY FIRST THOUGHT was to name the company Mustang Computing, after Southern Methodist University's football team, but my wife felt it put regional limits on the company. I had big plans, so I called it University Computing. If UCC took off at SMU for North Texas engineers, I could put the same operation in place with other universities in other cities. Make it work once, then "add zeroes."

If it works in one place, it can work in ten places; and if it works in ten places, it can work in a hundred places. You just keep adding zeroes to the right side until you are everywhere in the world.

Our office on the SMU campus was an unobtrusive one-story brick building. Our Control Data 1604 computer was so large and generated so much heat that we had to tear up the floor and raise it so that we had room underneath for all the cables and air-conditioning components. The system was transistorized, which was a big step up from vacuum tubes, but we were still fifteen years away from the days of affordable microchips, the building blocks of today's personal computers with which almost a billion people now use the Internet. It would be a while before Sun Microsystems' chant, "The network is the computer," would become reality.

Once we got our equipment up and running, I remember walking around looking at it, with its big rotating wheels of magnetic black tape on the front—much like an oversized reel-to-reel tape recorder—then peeking under floorboards to see all the wires and feel cool air blowing through, and thinking, "This is a powerful machine." It was more than a 100–1 improvement in speed, memory, storage, and programming ease over the IBM 650 I had used at Michigan only seven years earlier.

I was proud of myself for spotting a hole in the market and then creating an enterprise to fill it, but I knew that this was not the finish line. I had not yet won anything.

To carry this venture to its maximum potential, we needed skilled operators and programmers, so we trained some SMU students and hired additional staff. We also needed to put the right management in place, and when I asked J. B. Harville for advice, he said, "The most important thing in a partner is someone you can trust." I told him the man I trust most is my brother.

Charles was down in Houston at the time, working hard as an IBM salesman. He, too, was an annual member of the 100% Club, and doing just fine for himself and his family. He had been with IBM for eight years at this point as their top sales-man in New Orleans and one of their top guys in Houston. Charles does not have the natural-born entrepreneur's restless-ness for change, and if I had never called him, he might have happily filled out his days as a lifetime IBM-er. But he answered the call at a moment's notice, moved his family up to Dallas, and joined me in University Computing. Another big blessing was that my parents, who had sold their newspaper in Louisiana and moved to Houston to be near their grandkids, picked up stakes and came to Dallas, too.

Bringing Charles in was the best decision I ever made. Together, we started convincing customers, one by one, that we were the outfit to do their scientific and engineering computing. In addition to Sun Oil and SMU, we landed Texas

Instruments, some oil reservoir consultants, and a number of smaller companies with programs to run.

Those first few years were a blur of activity—I was out of the starting blocks and tearing down the track for all I was worth. By the time I looked up to get my bearings, it was 1964 and we'd been in business a full year. We had revenues of $700,000 and earnings of $100,000.

Charles had his hands full minding the fort, making everything work in Dallas, while I was the company's ambassador, traveling around, drumming up business, and always thinking about adding zeroes. I could have stayed behind, but expanding aggressively and quickly was the right thing to do. I was convinced that we were early riders on what would become a massive wave.

We had to expand into new cities or someone else would get there first. So I focused my attention on oil patch towns. In Tulsa, our prize was Sunray DX Oil, a company with engineers by the bushel. They had just built themselves a new headquarters, and needed access to a nearby mainframe with big memory, high speed, and good engineering software—a system exactly like the one we were running in Dallas. The closest I could get was directly across the street.

I met a retired insurance guy named Ben Voth, because he owned that building. When I explained to him what we were doing at UCC, he said he was bored silly with all the free time on his hands, and wanted to buy into our fledgling company and help in any way he could. We were not looking for capital, but with more capital, we could grow faster. I knew we could not expand as we hoped without a lot of equity capital, and Ben's investment could be our first step. Diversa's lease guarantee had made the initial debt leverage work, but they had not invested any cash equity for their half ownership.

I also thought Ben could be a big help. Charles and I were in our early thirties and looked young. Ben was in his mid-sixties and looked the elder statesman part. So he bought in, and we made him chairman; having some gray hair on the board is always a good thing.

My offer was $50,000 for 5 percent of the company, but then

Ben proposed $100,000 for 10 percent and I said, "Why not?" Years later, he loved telling people that he was the man who capitalized Sam Wyly at $1 million, even wrote a book about it called *A Piece of Computer Pie.*

When I took that investment course at Louisiana Tech, the rule they taught was that you needed five years of revenue and profit history before going public. We generated a little revenue in late 1963, and then quickly showed a profit in 1964. In the first half of 1965 we made as much as we had in all of 1964. We decided to go public in September 1965, after only two years in business, three years short of the five-year benchmark.

We were only the second initial public offering that our broker, A. G. Edwards, had ever done. Young Ben Edwards and a college buddy he had brought in were the underwriting department. The key guy in making it happen was Till Petrocchi, their Dallas broker. Our timing was good.

If you study the public markets historically, you find that there are times when the window is open wide and cash flows like the mighty Mississippi. Then there are times when the window slams shut and suddenly it is as dry as a West Texas canyon littered with the white bones of cows that died of thirst. You also find that particular moments in time tend to favor or disfavor particular kinds of companies or products.

Once upon a time, it was tulips. In the first half of the seventeenth century, as Dutch traders sailed from Holland to explore new worlds, tulips became a kind of currency. People in various parts of the world saw them as both a luxury item and a status symbol, and the price for tulip bulbs shot up. Traders exploited the situation to the point where a single bulb sold for as much as the average Dutchman's annual salary. People were buying bulbs not to grow tulips, but for the profit they could make buying and selling them. In fact, tulip bulbs were traded on the Dutch stock exchange.

It is basic economics: When speculation gets out of hand, prices cannot be sustained. Fortunes were made on the way up, but with so many people willing to buy, the sellers arrived. The bubble burst, prices hurtled down, and tens of thousands of people lost their life savings.

It was the same kind of Tulipmania that led to the Great Crash of 1929, and then spiked again in the late 1950s and early 1960s when any company with the suffix "tronics" in its name could do no wrong. Buying frenzies made prices skyrocket until someone realized that many of these companies had no intrinsic value, and just like that, the bottom fell out.

In the late 1990s, it was the dot-com bubble, a mania for technology and telecommunications companies that would benefit from the Internet. Web-based companies were hailed as the new saviors, able to solve all the world's problems. Then one day someone noticed that most of these dot-com emperors had no clothes. In the Great Crash of 2000 and 2001, the technology- and telecommunications-heavy NASDAQ stock index dropped 70 percent.

Fortunately, just as we went into the market looking for capital to expand University Computing, the word du jour was "computer." Everybody wanted to get on that bandwagon. We sold 40 percent of the company for $1,000,000, opened on September 9, 1965, at $4.50 a share, and instantly doubled to $9. In the four years that followed, investors got as much as a 100–1 return from a split adjusted $1.50 IPO price to a peak of $157. Yet, at the same time, the Dow had declined and long-term government bonds were earning a real rate of return of minus 5 percent a year. A. G. Edwards sold the warrants that we gave them as an underwriting sweetener for enough to double their net worth.

It was a good time to remember the people who'd helped me get to this point. So I gave 100 UCC shares to each of about fifty people: relatives, my Sunday school teacher, my Scout Master, teachers in high school, my debate coach in college, my first customer at Honeywell, and a few friends, including Ross Perot. In September 1968, when Ross took EDS public, he sent me a gift of shares. I still have that certificate at home, hanging on an upstairs wall, framed in a little glass box with a hammer and a sign that says, "In case of emergency, break glass."

We held our first annual UCC stockholder meeting in Dallas in 1966—by then we were doing business in twenty-three states—and 200 people made their way through torrential rain to attend.

Not bad, I thought, for a too-small noseguard from Delhi High School.

One of our first employees used to say that working for University Computing was like riding the nose cone of a rocket. Back then, most public companies were low-risk, low-reward affairs, run by Depression-era boys all grown up: folks with dark suits and silver-gray hair who were intent on achieving stability. We had a very different idea about how to build a company. We set out to grow University Computing by 100 percent a year. Some people looked at me like I was crazy. But we did it, five years in a row.

In expanding, my intention was to stick to computer technology, so I searched for small, undervalued companies that provided niche services within my larger field. We bought D. R. McCord and Associates, a company that used software models to simulate oil reservoirs.

McCord had already invested in computer software and employed some top-notch programmers. Geologists would collect raw data in the oil fields and bring it back to Dallas, where the same programmers refined the data to provide McCord's customers with invaluable information on how to get the most production out of a given oil reservoir. A lot of oil has been left underground for one reason or another. Those customers were the majors—the biggest names in the oil business—and McCord advised them on problems such as how to suck oil out from underneath Long Beach, California, without Long Beach sinking into the sea. They also had some government customers, like Abu Dhabi, a Persian Gulf emirate. What came with McCord was an income stream from petroleum engineering expertise and software they had designed. On top of that, we got paid for computer time. That's "synergy."

TECHNOLOGY WAS changing at a breakneck pace. Just to stay afloat we had to keep moving forward. Many others were doing start-up software and service businesses. Every year I'd check the Yellow Pages in different cities, to see who the competition was and, each year, a third of the names would have disappeared. They had gone out of business. It was survival of the fittest. Playing in a high-mortality-rate game like that, survival is not just about having a good idea. It is also about how well you execute.

Our dream was to be a computer utility service, to make access to computers as easy as it was to heat, light, and water. The biggest piece of that puzzle fell into place in Los Angeles. Setting up our center there, we purchased a UNIVAC 1107, which had the best ability to do computing and storage and to transmit data from one computer to another over the phone lines. UNIVAC 1107 technology was the best fit in the space where the computer met the telephone, which today we call the Internet.

For UCC, the UNIVAC 1107 made geographic distances meaningless. It represented our best opportunity to grow from a small regional player to a major nationwide business and then to a multinational company.

By the time I wrote our annual report in 1966, we had gone from a single center to a group of independent computer centers, each run by local managers with programmers, operators, and salespeople reporting to them, to a national business. We bought a home office building from Trammell Crow right off Stemmons Expressway near downtown Dallas. Remembering seeing "IBM World Headquarters" on their Madison Avenue building in New York City, we wrote, "University Computing World Headquarters" in giant letters on the freeway side of ours.

I particularly liked the word "World."

Chapter 9

Multinational Entrepreneur

IN 1965, when our little company was two years old, I said that by 1975 computers and information technology would be a multibillion-dollar industry and that half its value would derive from software and services. I wrote in the company's 1966 annual report, "We intend that UCC shall have a leading position in this market."

Some people think of an entrepreneur as someone running his own "small" business.

Not me.

One week before taking UCC public, our investment bankers said they could not sell the shares and the offering would fail. I refused to believe them and phoned people who knew us and our company to ask them to think about buying some stock. Not only did those people buy, they also spread the word to their friends and family, and we proved the bankers wrong. The same stock that "would not sell" doubled on the first day of trading and began a long climb upward over the next four years, such as has seldom been seen in history.

During 1966, we tripled our share price from $9 to $27, and then dropped to half that during a tight money squeeze. I was walking down the Bahnhofstrasse in Zürich when I spotted the stock quotes in the windows of the Union Bank of Switzerland. I thought prices were dropping because I wasn't in Dallas minding the store. But everybody else's stock was dropping, too.

In 1967 the American Stock Exchange, the speculative forerunner of NASDAQ, doubled. The Dow Jones, composed of the biggest, oldest, safest stocks, hardly moved. Our shares were up by a factor of seven. It was a good year for our team of software and hybrid hardware pioneers. Yet everything I had learned about valuations and the rules on multiples in my investment course at Louisiana Tech seemed to be out of sync. I could see that other companies were being bid up the same way, and I imagined it was because people suddenly liked small, fast-growing companies better than the old Dow smokestack companies. We were in. They were out. The markets were hungry for fast growth.

We expanded aggressively, but in so doing created employee scarcity. There were not enough men and women out there who understood what we were doing or who could do the jobs that UCC needed. To bring new talent into the company, I took another page out of Tom Watson, Sr.'s, playbook: Hire the best people, link pay to performance, and when they perform, pay them handsomely. You want employees who are knowledgeable in their fields, willing to work until the job is done—whether that's 5:00 p.m. or 5:00 a.m.—and who understand that their own personal success is directly linked to the company's success. So early on at UCC we granted employee stock options, not just to a favored few but also deep down in our organization. Sharing the wealth multiplies the wealth. A lot of people at UCC were soon making a lot of money. As I write, I laugh at a newspaper story about an early Google employee who was hired as a masseuse for the forty employees who were working very long days. She's now a millionaire traveling the world. Same story as our University Computing.

A company built around people who have a stake in its future has a greater chance of success. This was one of the reasons that UCC continued to grow, while one out of every three companies in this new industry were falling by the wayside every year.

CREATING AN ENVIRONMENT to attract and hold able people was the easy part. The hard part was learning how to be a good manager. Right after we started, when I was spending a lot of time setting up in Tulsa, I could not figure out why some employees were not doing what I wanted them to do. Then it hit me that I had never told them exactly what I wanted them to do. I was just expecting them to know, as if they could read my mind. So I had to find ways to set goals with a two-way feedback.

I realized I did not know how to be the president of a company. So when I heard that the American Management Association had a course for presidents that summer at a lake in upstate New York, I signed up. And who did I find also taking the course? Ross Perot. I didn't know he was going to be there, and he was just as surprised to see me, but seeing him confirmed to me—because Ross is not one to suffer fools gladly—that I had come to the right place.

This was a good place to be. I learned how to reach agreements with managers in setting goals and achieving results. I learned that these mutual understandings need continual revising to deal with changed circumstances. Sometimes things don't work out. Sometimes there are positive surprises.

It also reconfirmed for me what Peter Drucker was teaching in his books. Management by objectives. And managing for results.

Early on, I had tried to figure it all out myself. Now I was happy to accept that none of us is that smart—there is just too much to know, there are only so many hours in a day, and there are many ways to do everything. You have to agree on the objectives and delegate both responsibility and authority. You cannot hold people responsible if you don't give them authority. Responsibility without authority is managerial hell.

Being a maverick by spirit means that I am not a happy committee guy. Actually, I'm mostly a "conceptor." That's a term used by Marlene Miller in her excellent book *Brainstyles: Change Your Life Without Changing Who You Are*. Marlene creates four buckets, or styles of brain, based on how you react to new information, new circumstances: conceptors, knowers, deliberators, and conciliators. Conceptors are creative people who rely on both right-brain intuition and left-brain judgment and switch back and forth, sometimes to the confusion of their fellow workers or family members. The conceptor style manifests itself through an ability to see the big picture, to see things not as they are but as they ought to be.

Conceptors can get bogged down with the day-to-day running of a business; we need to be teamed up with conciliators, who are comfortable in the intangible and emotional face-to-face world, with the logical and practical knowers, and especially with natural deliberators, who bring order out of chaos. They plan their work, and then work their plan.

And it really is true; the devil is in the details.

To get the best out of people who have the front-line responsibility for making the business work day to day, you need to be confident in their abilities. Moreover, you need to show them that you are confident, knowing what's going on but not meddling.

You hold managers responsible for results, as opposed to trying to control how they get those results, and then you reward them for their successes. You give them a chance to create wealth for themselves and for other investors while making the company a good place to work for everyone.

The Management Course for Presidents and Drucker's books taught me the language of managers, and I combined that with the language of programmers and engineers that I knew. This helped make University Computing a good place to work.

Outstanding people were coming to us from IBM, UNIVAC, and the aerospace think tanks like Vought and Lockheed. Among them was Mac McCain, a Southern-born and -bred Georgia native with a ready smile. He was also a fellow history buff, who had named his boys after Henry Clay and John Calhoun. He was interested in us and we were interested in him, so I offered him a good salary and the possibility of a handsome bonus. It was the stock options, the culture of the place, and "the chance to change the wide world with digital" that really won him over. When UNIVAC's chief, James Rand, heard that we were hiring Mac away, he offered to make Mac President of UNIVAC. Mac refused and came with us.

To HAVE THE MOST productive team, there has to be room for individual creative work within the structure of the company. For the most part, I believe in a decentralized structure to foster that level of creativity: It allows for personal knowledge, instinct, and decision making. Dean Thornton, our CFO, said it had once been his mission to treat his people in such a way as to keep them "sullen but not mutinous."

That's outrageous. The best work does not come out of sullen people! The best work comes from highly motivated, richly rewarded, happy-to-come-in-every-morning people. Being a spiritual man and a student of Mary Baker Eddy, it's natural that these transcendental values found their way into my corporate world. Looking for the good in other people came naturally.

Looking back at published articles and interviews during that time, I see that I had the same thoughts then as I do today. When the trade journal *Texas Business & Industry* asked me about UCC's meteoric rise, I said, "The key was to provide a place where highly talented people can work comfortably and productively. Since we have great faith in the individual, we seek capable technical people, then give them goals and plenty of freedom."

I searched for the managers who had done the best job of developing software at IBM and the Seven Dwarfs. From my tour at Honeywell, I was convinced that Eugene Debs Scott—named by his parents after their hero, Eugene Debs, the perennial Socialist party candidate for president—had done the best work at General Electric.

Gene had spent many early years of his career working for IBM as a lowly technical maintenance guy, basically unknown and unloved by the salesmen who ran the company, until the big boss himself, Tom Watson, Sr., showed up at Gene's shop one day on an inspection visit. Watson complained about the messiness around one piece of equipment—little chips from the holes punched into the IBM cards. Gene told him it was because of a flaw in the manufacturing process. Right then and there Watson said, "Come to the engineering lab and fix it." Gene was instantly promoted from an hourly paid job to engineering designer, a huge career jump.

GE stole him from IBM and we stole him from GE, but it was all the more personally satisfying to me that he had once been a Watson favorite.

The structure I built at UCC was the model for the structure I have built at other companies. Each manager understands what we are trying to accomplish, has his own set of specific goals to meet, and needs to keep his eye on patterns that allow him to see red flags.

We also required routine audits, with the chief financial officer reporting to both the chief executive officer and the board. The same with division CFOs and presidents. That reporting was transparent, so that everybody understands the process.

That has the added benefit of monitoring, say, a manager or sales rep who is overly interested in getting his current bonus. In a decentralized structure, it is vital to have routine audits in place and a method for the financial officers to tell the board the truth without having to go through the line managers. President Reagan used to tell his nuclear aides dealing with the Soviet Union, "Trust but verify." The same applies in a company. Trust but have solid auditing.

SHORTLY AFTER ACQUIRING D. R. McCord in 1966, I went to England, a country I love. I was thrilled to ride the rails from London to Birmingham. As a history buff, I loved visiting the Tower of London and Westminster Abbey and seeing the history-soaked countryside with barnhouses and buildings that were hundreds of years old. I loved taking in the roots of the culture that we English-speaking peoples call our own. I went to the Wylye River and the tiny town of Wylye, even though I cannot trace my own Wylys (there are different spellings) back to any particular spot in Scotland, Ireland, or England. I can trace one set of multi-great-grandparents to Enniscorthy, Ireland—they were rebels in the United Irish Rebellion of 1798 and chose to come to America as opposed to being thrown in the dungeon by the English king—and on Mama's side, to Tom Evans, who sailed from Rhydwilym, Wales, in 1710 with family and friends from their Welsh Baptist Church. I even loved the newspapers and the word choices used in British English.

This was a bizarre time in their history. Harold Wilson's Labor government was still pushing Socialism and making a mess of it. The United Kingdom was not entrepreneurial and there were few homegrown business success stories. For the most part, business there was traditionally staid and hierarchical. The spirit of entrepreneurship would not come until the 1980s, when Margaret Thatcher forced Britain away from command and control and toward free markets.

With trains, planes, telephones, gas, electricity, doctors, dentists, and hospitals already nationalized, Wilson added to the collection of government-mismanaged industries by nationalizing the steel industry. (Lenin would have been proud.) He was then forced into devaluing the pound, against the dollar.

That actually happened during my flight to London. When I got on the plane in New York, the pound was worth $2.80. When I got off, the pound was worth $2.40. The United Kingdom suffered crippling strikes on a regular basis from unions demanding more protection from the wicked capitalists. Yet they wrote newspaper articles about me, the bayou rebel capitalist, as an "American Success Story."

We bought a company just like ours from a woman in Birmingham—she was the only other one with a UNIVAC 1107. We started a computer services company in Shannon, Ireland. In one deal with Walter Haefner, a Swiss entrepreneur born in 1910 whose father was a Presbyterian missionary to Tibet, and who himself was the owner of one of Ireland's most successful thoroughbred stud farms—one year, his horse won the Belmont Stakes—we moved UCC into ten European cities including Zürich, Vienna, and Frankfurt. Walter had built great businesses in car dealerships and real estate. He was the only non-German on the Volkswagen board. Walter had owned these "computer centres" for several years, but he was tired of what seemed to him like a continual start-up. Besides, he was sixty-five, and maybe it was time for him to tidy up his affairs. (He's ninety-seven and healthy as I write.)

So we made a verbal deal at the Waldorf-Astoria Hotel in New York City, where he had an apartment. The next day, the General Electric CEO said they wanted to be the buyer, but Walter honored his handshake deal with me.

We used the new multinational businesses to demonstrate the feasibility of a worldwide network of computer centers and telephone lines. We hosted an exchange of greetings between the mayor of Dallas, Erik Jonsson, and the Lord Mayor of London, Sir Gilbert Inglefield. Using UCC computers, we transmitted via ground lines in each country and then by satellite across the ocean. I bought a full-page ad in *The Wall Street Journal*, with pictures of each mayor beside our Cope 45 terminals.

Data messages like this had never been sent before by civilians. The military, of course, was electronically more advanced. For those of us outside the military, this new method of transmitting data was a big deal.

Our UCC's board doubled my salary to $48,000 and granted me a stock option bonus of $1.2 million, which made me one of the highest-paid chiefs of a public company in 1969. When a reporter asked why, I gave him Babe Ruth's answer after he signed an $80,000 contract in 1930. When asked why he was paid more than the President of the United States, Babe smiled and said, "I had a better year than the President."

In addition to offices in New York, New Jersey, Louisiana, Illinois, Missouri, Kansas, Oklahoma, California, the U.K., and Ireland, we had expanded UCC into the Netherlands, Venezuela, and Australia. Wherever I traveled, I would painstakingly describe to people I met the concept of a digitally connected computer network. I compared it to electricity: power available in the exact place you need it. Just like you plug in your electric toaster. "We believe," I wrote in the 1966 annual report, "that in the future many corporations will no more own a large computer than they would their own generating plant."

It was clear to me from the start that this would work. But when we would meet with corporate execs to sell our computer processing services, their response was: "We don't send our work out." Our answer was, "You don't have to. You can do it right here in your own offices. You just link over the phone lines to our large-scale computing center, maybe to Dallas, maybe to London. All you need is a batch processor to come in over the phone lines to our central computing system."

Whether we were trying to sell it to the company controller, the manufacturing department, or the engineering department, whoever it was, they could see how we saved them money and made their knowledge workers more productive. After we gave demonstrations on test data, they understood our concept of a "computer utility."

We were selling our computer utility and making real advances in technology. This was what I came to see as our sweet spot, that imaginary place where the new digital computer was married to Alexander Graham Bell's old analog telephone lines. Of course, Bell's analog technology would first have to become digital. We tied our future to that digital world.

For many people, the idea of computers talking to each other over phone lines seemed too much like science fiction. But not to me. It was going to happen, just like Huey Long building roads and bridges to pull Louisiana up out of the mud when horses and wagons were replaced by Henry Ford's Model T. This, too, would change the world. Ford could not have done it without Long's roads. Similarly, we needed to build a digital highway for digital computers.

Chapter 10

If You Can't Join 'em, Beat 'em

COMPUTERS TALK to one another with all the ease of flipping the light switch. It is instantaneous. But it's also a relatively recent phenomenon. In the 1980s, if you were using a computer in one part of the country and needed to get information to or from another computer across the country, you had to send your data over the voice telephone lines, analog as opposed to digital lines.

But what's okay for voice is not okay for data, because computers speak an entirely different digital language. As keynote speaker at the annual industry conference around that time, I told the assembled American Information Technology managers, "The computer industry has dialed into a busy signal." I went on to say that you won't get what you need from the AT&T monopoly, and IBM considers this AT&T's domain, so we will bring you the solution.

They stood up and cheered.

Gene Bylinsky, a senior editor at *Fortune* magazine, wrote a book called *The Innovation Millionaires.* In it, he titled the chapter about me "Sam Wyly Builds a Highway for Computers." He described how I had 300 of the best and brightest engineers building the U.S.'s first nationwide digital highway, routed on digital microwave towers built 20 miles apart. Today, 14 fiber optics–based backbones carry the data traffic of the World Wide Web from Tulsa to Tokyo to Tangiers. We blazed that trail but, unfortunately, ended up facedown in the creek. It's a tough lesson to learn, but sometimes when you're charting a path through enemy territory, the other guys shoot back.

Working through the analog phone lines meant, in the 1970s, having to deal with AT&T. There was no other choice. AT&T was the only game in town. They were the biggest monopoly ever, the baddest, meanest dog in town—with no leash. Anyone who came close got bit, while the government looked the other way.

I spent some time in Italy, where the government owned the phone company, and it took the average citizen two years to get a phone installed at home. A friend of mine lived in France and told me how the post office there owned the phone company and that the waiting list for him to get a phone was five years. The official excuse was that they had to wait for new lines to go up. That turned out not to be true because when my friend finally got his phone, all they did was split a nearby line in two and hook it up to a new number at the exchange. It took all of fifteen minutes. Back then, inefficiency from the centralized command and control meant that the French Post Office took five years to do fifteen minutes of work. These days there are several French phone companies. They are private and they compete, and if you want a phone, you can have it in a day. What's more, in monopolies, not just in France or Italy but wherever you find them, inefficiency breeds apathy. Managers and workers lose sight of customer needs because there is no reason for them to care. There is no incentive for the monopoly to do anything more than the bare minimum that they are required to do.

In contrast, when you break up a monopoly you create competition, and competition creates choices for citizens, who then get better service, better products, innovation, and lower prices. AT&T was living proof of this. They thought in terms of forty years to write off their equipment investment, which was a disincentive to innovation. Without competition, customers had no choice but to accept whatever AT&T told them was good for them. The consequence of federal and state lawmakers' regulations intended to keep the phone company from gouging the public ultimately resulted in exactly the opposite: price gouging.

God had not given AT&T the monopoly. Governments

endowed it and protected it, and it would take governments to change it. For that reason, monopolies spend time and money (that could otherwise be put into innovation) lobbying the lawmakers to maintain the monopoly. For each Texas state senator in Austin, we had at least ten Bell employees and lobbyists working to prevent change. The same was true of the electricity monopolies, but we will get to that story later.

To understand what we faced in the late 1960s with AT&T's monopoly, you have to go back to what happened after Alexander Graham Bell patented the telephone. He looked around, saw Western Union telegraph poles up alongside the railroads' rights-of-way, realized that those poles could also carry phone lines, and offered to sell his patent to Western Union for $100,000. But the telegraph people said, "Why would someone want to talk to somebody else when they can send a telegram?" so they turned him down, believing that phones were nothing more than toys. Within a few years, Bell's original company merged with some other phone companies to become American Telephone & Telegraph Company (AT&T).

They claimed "natural monopoly" status, as did electricity utilities, which meant AT&T wanted to be the only phone company in the United States. In 1913, the Feds struck a deal with AT&T known as the Kingsbury Commitment. It allowed AT&T to work out deals with smaller independents that now had geographical monopolies on local lines, while AT&T carried the "indies'" long-distance calls as well as AT&T's own long-distance calls. Their power to dictate how many pennies per call the locals would get—that is, after AT&T took its own self-determined share—gave AT&T effective control everywhere. AT&T's managers probably had benevolent intentions, and were honest, but they didn't foresee how power would corrupt.

After World War I, the Feds took control of the telecommunications industry, claiming it was a matter of national security. They set regulated rates and then—in a classic screwup, handing the game warden's badge to the biggest poacher in town—the Feds appointed the president of AT&T to oversee the national phone system. Simultaneously, as states began regulating local phone companies, AT&T brought together twenty-two of those companies under the umbrella of the Bell System. Competition was dead. By the end of World War II, AT&T had moved into every aspect of telephone service, including the manufacturing of phones. They decided whose hand phones could be connected to their network, meaning you had to use their phones on their network, which was the only network. This completely eliminated consumer choice.

In 1970, what few private phone lines were available from AT&T to handle computer traffic were costing something like $3,000 a month, plus usage costs. At those prices (obviously much more in today's dollars) there would never be an Internet. Compounding the problem, analog transmissions of digital data were full of errors.

We needed a line for $300 a month or less that would transmit digital, flawlessly. But AT&T had no interest. They were even less interested in our idea of a dedicated digital network because they were making plenty with analog lines.

So I went back to Alexander Graham Bell's original notion: telegraph poles and wires.

Telegraphy, the way we knew it in America, was invented in Germany and perfected in England. By 1839, the first commercial telegraph system followed the tracks of the Great Western Railway for 13 miles from London's Paddington Station to West Drayton. At the same time, Samuel F. B. Morse, of Morse code fame, was working on the American version of telegraphy, and sent his first message along 2 miles of wire on January 6, 1838: "A patient waiter is no loser." It was nearly six years later that he sent his now famous "first" message from Washington to Baltimore ("What hath God wrought?"), staged for congressmen, press people, and historians.

As the railroads pushed west, telegraph poles went up alongside the track and, by 1902, the nation was wired, coast to coast. Sixty-five years later, there were telegraph poles everywhere. This I saw as the physical assets for an instant national data network. What's more, the telegraph franchise was a legal loophole to AT&T's telephone monopoly. The way the body of

93

law had developed for more than a century, telegraph law and telephone law were completely separate. This gave us plenty of room for an end run around AT&T's telephone monopoly.

The more I looked at telegraph poles, the better I liked them. The closer I looked at the company who owned those telegraph poles, plus a lot of wire in the ground in all the big cities—the Western Union Company—the more I became convinced that they were just sitting on a mother lode of rights-of-way and copper wire connections.

The way to get our hands on that mother lode was to buy it. But in 1968, our UCC assets were $42 million and Western Union's assets were $741 million. Most people would say, "You've got to be crazy to even think about buying Western Union." So we went to them with our vision of the future growth opportunity and proposed a friendly merger. We were told not just no but "Hell, no!"

Remember Coach Richards telling me, "It's not the size of the dog in the fight, but the size of the fight in the dog?"

In April that year we made a cash tender offer for control of Western Union, managed by André Meyer at Lazard Frères. Absolutely nobody believed the daring of that move. Not in the computer industry. Not on Wall Street. And especially not at Western Union. They saw us as pipsqueaks from Texas who had the audacity to think about taking on a great national institution that, along with the railroads, had done much to create today's America by connecting the West to the East and the South to the North just after the Civil War.

We pipsqueaks from Texas almost pulled it off. Unfortunately, we were done in by some small print 1,500 miles away.

Western Union's lawyers came up with a dusty old New York State law, dated 1905, that said no one could buy more than 10 percent of a telegraph company chartered in that state without the approval of Albany lawmakers. Hard to believe, but it was right there in black and white and there was no possibility of getting the New York State legislature to understand why it was vital to build digital highways.

Talk about unintended consequences!

Originally, the law was written to stop Western Union from monopolizing the telegram business, but the law backfired and was used by the monopolist for its own protection. I didn't understand how Western Union executives could be so blind, and frozen in a time warp, until I spent part of a day riding the elevators and walking the halls at their New York City head-quarters (nobody knew who I was and nobody asked). I could actually feel the lack of life in that company. Of course, it also occurred to me that I had come a long way from my high school job of typing telegrams in our small-town newspaper office.

Saying no to us, Western Union lost a fabulous opportunity that, arguably, would have enabled their survival. Having lost their telegraph, telex, and private line businesses to competi-tors, they were going out of business. We would have trans-formed them into a phone company for computers and moved them into the digital age. They could have been a key part of the digital infrastructure of Tom Friedman's flat world. But their myopic CEO and board could not see where the markets and technology were going, and their egos got in the way.

Years before, Western Union could not understand why any-one would rather make a phone call than send a telegram. Now they were turning their backs on their one and only chance to be an important part of what became the Internet. They had the local rights-of-way into every city and town in America, which at that moment in history represented enormous value. They wasted every last penny of it. But if you can't join 'em, beat 'em!

Chapter 11

Monopoly Buster:
Datran, or Die Trying

According to the Oxford English Dictionary, the word "Internet" was introduced around 1974 and, even then it only appeared in a few technical journals. The same is true for the expression "Information Superhighway." The word "cyberspace" came even later, making its first appearance in a science fiction novel in the 1980s. Finally, "World Wide Web" has been with us only since 1991, when Sir Tim Berners-Lee, a U.K.-born MIT professor, coined it.

Computers originally had the sound of science fiction. I read Norbert Wiener's *Cybernetics* (subtitled *Control and Communication in the Animal and the Machine*) in the college computer lab at Ann Arbor. It was groundbreaking mathematical thinking and it underlined the concept of the stored program computer whose feedback mechanisms enabled the machine itself, once carefully taught, to recall both data and programmer instructions and then make decisions.

By 1966, I understood that wherever computers eventually took us, it would not happen until computers could talk to one another quickly, efficiently, and cheaply. We were moving into a digital world and my instincts moved me to lead the charge.

Once the Western Union episode was behind me, I thought about how to move forward, knowing I'd still face a number of obstacles. An enormous amount of capital would be needed. Then there was the monopoly power of the telephone company with the protection of lawmakers in Washington and in every state capital in America. And we'd need to engineer a technology solution that really worked and that the prospective customer would love.

So the very first thing I did was bring in a UNIVAC guy from Houston named Sy Joffe. He said that the smartest telecommunications engineer at UNIVAC was an ex-Navy man named Ed Berg, who had floated around on a rubber raft for two days during the Battle of Midway after Japanese dive-bombers and torpedo planes sank his aircraft carrier, the *Hornet*. Ed was the brains behind the UNIVAC 1107s and 1108s, particularly the part of them that married computing and telecommunications. A brilliant engineer, he told me that computers were destined to shift from being giant calculators to a means of communication, and that he could engineer it all like a beautiful digital symphony. Ed became our architect-in-chief for America's first nationwide digital network, what we envisioned as a highway for computers.

It wasn't such a crazy dream. After all, it had been years since the Russians launched Sputnik and President Eisenhower decided that the only way to fight Russian science was with American science. He created a new office inside the Pentagon called the Advanced Research Projects Agency (ARPA).

Their mission was to make sure that the United States developed state-of-the-art technology for our military. What made ARPA unique was that it operated independent of traditional military research and development. Over the years, they developed unmanned aircraft, virtual reality, infrared sensing, X-ray/gamma ray detection, artificial intelligence, Star Wars technology, and global positioning systems. By the beginning of the 1970s, they were working on a digital network so that defense forces could communicate during a nuclear attack, even after the United States had absorbed several nuclear hits.

This marked the military birth of the Internet. Our opportunity was to deliver its private-sector sibling. We decided to call it Data Transmission Company—Datran for short—and started building a phone company exclusively for computers.

Ed explained to me that, in his design engineering ideal world, we would need to transmit data at the speed of 25,000 words per second. That doesn't sound fast today when we talk about nanoseconds and terabits per second, but it was lightning compared with AT&T's analog phone system. And we believed that if we could send data that fast, our project might develop into a low-cost system for electronic mail so that people could send written messages back and forth over distances more quickly and more clearly than by U.S. mail or by telegram, just as the telegram had beat out the Pony Express horseback riders. The problem was that you couldn't efficiently accomplish what we wanted to do utilizing an analog plant from a phone company.

We studied satellites and fiber optics, but they were too far into the dim and distant future. So like ARPA, we decided that the best available technology was digital microwave. Ed promised that we could make the first digital switch work.

Our plan called for building transmitters right across the country, spaced 20 to 30 miles apart. We scouted land for towers, negotiated permission from farmers, got all our permits in order, and started building towers.

The folks at AT&T, meanwhile, were doing their best to get our dream tossed into the garbage. That's the reason we headquartered Datran in Washington, D.C. If we were going to make this happen, we wanted our senior managers in the FCC offices ten times a day and camped on their doorstep at night. We would get in the FCC's face and make them understand that we were never going away.

The telephone monopoly couldn't make our docket completely disappear, so they got the process slowed to a snail's pace. They were so powerful that our stuff stayed on the FCC's shelf, unread, for two years.

Of course, I understand why they were so belligerent. We were threatening their very existence. We were planning to move the same amount of data on $1 of digital capital investment that otherwise required $10 of analog capital. We were going to offer higher-quality, lower-cost, and better customer service than they could. We were going to give people a choice, not just what the phone monopoly said was good for them but what the consumers themselves wanted. If we got the FCC's permission, they were in serious trouble.

Our original cost estimate for Datran was $375 million, which put us in the same cost neighborhood as Comsat, the company that launched the Early Bird communications satellite in 1965 and took telephone and television traffic into space. But Comsat was a creature of Congress and enjoyed regulatory protection, had a public stock, and, most important, didn't threaten AT&T.

We were going to have to do it the hard way.

This was doubly true when you factored in that the government hadn't given any indication they would welcome competition against the Bell System, which meant that we could lose. AT&T argued there was no need for a separate digital network because there was no demand for one. We proved there was. Well, they said, there might be some demand, but not for the data-transmission services that Datran wanted to do. We proved there was. Okay, they said, even if there was a little demand for what Datran wanted to do, AT&T could meet that minor demand in the command-and-control way, so there was absolutely no need for Datran and this free-market heresy.

They never stopped thinking like the telephone monopoly they were. "Bell heads," we used to call them. They cast doubt on our competence to do what we said we could do, on our technical abilities, and on our financial resources. Both voice and data ultimately would travel digitally with efficiency thanks to microchips, although that was a long way in the future. Yet we knew back then during our initial challenge to the Bell monopoly that this technological breakthrough had to happen. We knew it from thinking through the existing technology and extrapolating forward. But regulated monopolies have little or no interest in innovation; change threatens their long-term write-offs of whatever equipment they've already installed.

When the "it's not necessary" argument didn't fly, AT&T came up with the old wives' tale that monopoly status assures good service and if you open up the market to competition, some customers will be left out. They erroneously argued that the free market is free to disregard customers when the cost of doing business cuts too deeply into profit.

You hear that all the time with monopolies: If you privatize the post office, then mail carriers won't deliver letters to rural North Wherever because it's too far out of the way and therefore unprofitable. Except FedEx and UPS are in effect private post offices and they'll deliver anywhere. Anyway, as soon as they came along, offering a better service than the U.S. Post Office, what did the USPS do? They came right back at FedEx and UPS to compete by offering overnight priority mail.

Of course the market was big enough for all of us, but AT&T was arrogant, genetically incapable of accepting a competitive market. When they were finally forced to move out of the monopoly, they just didn't know anything else. They tried to be IBM and got killed.

We had to spend almost as much money fighting the regulatory battle as we did creating the technology. We had run headfirst into a clash of cultures. Computer people were in a hurry to get things working. Phone company people were in a hurry not to miss the carpool at four o'clock. How else could anyone explain why, in those days, it took two months just to get a telephone line installed?

The man I brought in to run Datran was a young electronics engineer from Texas Instruments (TI) named Glenn Penisten. He had been in charge of new businesses and the semiconductor research laboratories at TI and understood that getting this new network on line wasn't like lighting up a Christmas tree. You didn't just throw a switch and be in business. Glenn saw this ultimate goal as a series of smaller, intermediate goals, which was right in line with the way I've always set goals. We'd have to build this thing one step at a time.

Standing in our way was the Chairman of AT&T, a tough old South Carolina codger named John DeButts. He was completely imbued with the idea of monopoly as the only right religion. He had long ago bought into the concept that by sacrificing some profit for the sake of owning a monopoly, he was doing the right thing and no one should dare question him on that, especially when he was providing the best telephone service in the world at a reasonable price. The fact that he was dead wrong didn't change his mindset. He said there was nothing broken, so there was no need to fix it.

He was stunned that we were brazen enough to challenge his authority. He believed that our digital network was just another kind of phone call, and he was convinced that God had decided no one else was going to offer phone calls to America. I also think he was insulted when we said straight out, "You guys don't know what you're doing and we do."

Glenn got in to see DeButts, hoping to convince him that digital data transmission was a new field and that there was plenty of POTS (Plain Old Telephone Service) that would always be available to him. Glenn wanted DeButts to understand why he should let us little guys go ahead and make this data world happen. Monopolies are never strategically oriented—they don't need to be—and DeButts just kept walking around the mulberry bush. He didn't want to hear what we had to say.

I never had any direct interaction with DeButts, but in my mind the two of us were talking all the time. I kept saying, "John, I'm gonna whip you in Washington," and I could hear DeButts saying, "Sam, ultimately you might, but it'll take you thirty years to whip me in every Statehouse."

He was right. But that wasn't stopping me.

We needed more than better technology to build a nationwide network; we needed a lot of capital. I decided to look for a cash-cow company that had "really safe" written all over it. I wanted to have a rock-solid financial base, and saw that in a property and casualty insurance company owning triple-A stocks and bonds.

Gulf Insurance Company was run by a classmate from the Management Course for Presidents, August Buchel, and it was exactly what I was looking for. It had a very strong investment-grade portfolio of blue chips and a lucrative fire and casualty business. We could invest the dividends out of Gulf to help build Datran. So we merged Gulf into University Computing in an exchange of stock. Having a high multiple on our stock, we could give the Gulf shareholders a big premium over their market value, just as America Online paid the Time Warner owners in 2001.

August became our partner and joined the UCC board while continuing to run Gulf. But just as we upgraded Gulf's stock and bond portfolio so that it paid higher dividends, we ran headfirst into major disasters.

The 1970s economic crunch began in 1969, and by 1970 the United States had hit a real inflationary recession. I found out the hard way that not only UCC and Datran, but also Gulf was vulnerable. Everything came crashing down. In 1969, UCC made a $17 million profit. In 1970, we had an $18 million loss. Very bad news.

The economy started looking up in 1971. Gulf Insurance generated around $8.5 million and University Computing earned a $2.6 million profit on $128 million of sales. I concluded optimistically, as ever, that we could put another $5 million in Datran.

But all our markets downturned against us sharply in 1972, and we lost a staggering $83 million on sales of $101 million. We were taught to worry about either inflation or depression. In the '70s, we got both. Both bond and stock markets crashed. And liquidity for smaller companies disappeared.

Wall Street can be fickle. The capital markets no longer wanted to hear about my plans for a digital future. Earlier, I'd get 100 brokers and bankers calling us. Suddenly, my phone stopped ringing.

You couldn't give tech stocks away. And safe blue chips dropped to five-times earnings. Treasury bonds dropped 50 percent. People were pulling whatever was left of their savings out of their mutual funds and depositing their remaining cash in bank deposits. Fear ran high. Those bankers and brokers who had once adored us computer-age dreamers were now gone from Wall Street and out selling cars and houses and teaching school.

During those times, when the public scorecard wasn't good, it didn't burden me more than I could bear because I kept my own scorecard. I knew that the public scorecard would one day catch up. Eventually, if you're doing the right thing, it will be there. We simply needed to survive long enough to keep our dream alive. We had to cut back and pay off debt, sell parts of the company, and seek fresh capital.

Our Swiss friend Walter Haefner had come on the UCC board and saw the promise in a digital future, so I turned to him and he came through for us. He liked the idea of Datran enough to make an entrepreneurial bet and, over the next five years, invested $40 million.

Without Walter, Datran would never have stood a chance. But inflation was raging and even though Gulf's portfolio was blue chip, the oil shock drove interest rates through the roof. High interest rates and inflation forced up the cost of repairing cars and houses and the cost of insurance claims. Then came the fierce April and May winds of West Texas and the Gulf Coast. They blew the roofs off buildings and smashed cars. A hurricane ripped into Corpus Christi and a tornado leveled a part of Lubbock. Gulf Insurance took its biggest-ever underwriting losses. In just one weekend we lost 12 million bucks. It was unbelievable. Of all the risks I worried about, Texas weather was not among them. It was the Mississippi River Flood of 1927 all over again.

I had seen Gulf Insurance as a safe haven, but it turns out that Bobby Kennedy was right when he said, "There are no safe havens."

Times were tough—the worst decade in my business life. I had to mortgage our stock in Gulf Insurance to secure a $30 million loan, and Walter invested another $20 million.

But the good news was that after five very long and expensive years, the FCC had finally made its decision.

It was yes.

They ruled that competition in the area of data transmission was both practical and desirable. They didn't have the power to bust up AT&T—their monopoly over voice transmission remained in place—but they said that Datran could transmit data over private lines.

We won.

Unfortunately, that didn't mean AT&T was going to accept defeat gracefully. They hunkered down for a long war of attrition. They shifted to street fighting in the capital markets and in Congress.

We were negotiating a $50 million private placement and it looked like everything was all set to go, but then our banks told us that "calls had been made"—AT&T had threatened them—and they were pulling out of the deal.

We were close to a deal with United Telecom, a Kansas City–based independent telephone company. Their CEO, Paul Henson, advocated the deal. Again, United's board backed out, saying, "We have to live with AT&T." AT&T had the power to cut United Telecom's revenue by reducing United's share of long-distance fees on calls into and out of United Telecom's local territories. AT&T had monopoly power and they were making predatory use of it.

As the battle heated up, the Bell monopoly ruthlessly used their power in Congress. With one-third of the House of Representatives in their pocket, they introduced the Bell Bill, which would overturn the FCC's decision for competition.

I walked into the office of the congressman from Plain Dealing, Louisiana, a fellow Louisiana Tech grad, and said, "You're a free-market guy, an Adam Smith guy—how can your name be on this?"

To him it was simple: "I've got a plant with five thousand Bell employees and it's got a plant manager and it's got a union leader. And in the past I've been refereeing between the plant manager and the union leader and now, with this Bell Bill, I've got both of them in here saying, Sign it."

The Bell Bill did not get passed. This marked the beginning of the end of the telephone monopoly. But a free market would be a long time in coming and we'd have a lot more pain to endure.

We were working with the Bank of Boston to syndicate a $50 million credit for us, with First National Bank of Dallas and Philadelphia National Bank each committed to $5 million of the $50 million. But even though the Bell Bill ultimately didn't pass, it sent a signal to bankers that AT&T and the lawmakers in their pockets would not tolerate competition, and that was the end of our bank syndicate.

In 1974, Americans watched an agonizing presidential impeachment process that ended with President Nixon's resignation, a first ever in American history. That same year saw the market crash and widespread financial crises.

Still, I felt Datran could be recapitalized—that is, until the interest rates hit 12 percent and another big loan fell through. Glen Peniston and his team of managers came up with a two-year "Hold the Line" plan. I sold some assets, Walter invested more, and we limped through another year. In 1975, Gulf Insurance fell victim to inflation, which was skyrocketing its costs of paying damage claims for houses and cars, and posted huge losses again. We had to suspend its dividends and lose this source of funding for our big idea.

If I'd had five hundred million bucks of my own money to bet, I would have put it on the table and waited AT&T out. But I didn't have it. Even Walter didn't have that much. And I couldn't find anyone else who would put that kind of money up to back my dream.

We built that part of the network that could be built with the capital we had, from Houston to Chicago. When we switched it on—fifty-nine microwave towers connecting those two cities—it worked. It was fast, error-free, much less expensive than AT&T, and praised as a technical marvel. The begrudgers could no longer say, "It won't work." We started signing up new customers, and even the begrudgers had to admit that we'd been right all along. Chief among them was AT&T, which now came into our market with a data service. They raised prices on local and long-distance phone calls to cross-subsidize the battle with us and undercut our price by 40 percent.

My dream wasn't to be.

Datran made so much sense to me that I thought everyone else should be able to see it just as plainly. I thought we could go out and just get it done. But I'd been optimistic about how quickly we could bust the Bell monopoly. More important, the capital markets had disappeared—not just the stock market but the venture capital markets, the bank debt markets, the bond markets, everything. New investments by venture capitalists dropped 95 percent.

In August 1976, after investing eight years and 100 million bucks, I pulled the plug, turned off the lights, and shut down Datran.

I was beaten. And I felt beaten.

Most entrepreneurs, at least when starting out, get emotionally attached to a company. UCC and Datran were my babies. Those companies and I were one. There's some good in thinking that way, in identifying so closely with your creation, but it can ultimately give you a lot of misery. That's how I was feeling then—devastated.

This was a difficult time for me personally, not just because of seeing 90 percent of my wealth disappear during the 1970s. After all, one house and one car were still all I needed; but for eight years, through the disasters and the disappointments, I never stopped believing that having a competitive alternative to the telephone monopoly—giving customers a choice—was good for Americans and that ultimately it would be done. Datran was the biggest and toughest thing I'd ever tried. It was the future, but I was there too early and the capital markets had gone away for the entrepreneur.

When someone beats me in a fair fight, I can accept it and forget it. But being done in by a state-granted and state-protected monopoly was different. I decided that I was going to litigate this case even if it took forever, so we made a deal with two law firms. I said, "I'll spend $200,000 a year forever to get economic justice, and you'll get 28 percent of whatever we win."

So they bet their lawyer time, while I paid the expense budget. We slapped an anti-monopoly suit on AT&T and dragged them kicking and screaming into court.

It took four years but when the smoke cleared, UCC recovered $50 million and set the stage for the end of AT&T's monopoly power. That made me, along with two other American entrepreneurs, Bill McGowan and Tom Carter, a footnote in entrepreneurial history for busting up the telephone monopoly.

* * *

TEXAS INVENTOR Tom Carter petitioned the FCC in 1968 for the right to hook his "CarterPhone"—a two-way radio system that was the original wireless phone—to the telephone network. He was in the offshore oil business and needed a way to communicate from rig to rig out at sea. Until he came along, AT&T categorically refused to allow any non-AT&T equipment to be used, because that's how they protected their monopoly rights to sell only their own equipment. But the FCC sided with Carter. As a direct result, innovation flourished, creating markets for answering machines, fax machines, cordless phones, cell phones, and computer modems. Hundreds of millions of cell phones are being bought every year now. Thank you, Tom Carter!

Then Bill McGowan petitioned the FCC to allow his Microwave Communications of America to sell "private line" phone service to businesses. The FCC and the courts sided with McGowan. Today, thanks to him, there are dozens of long-distance carriers, giving the customer real choice in the marketplace, and the price of long-distance calls has dropped to the point where some companies no longer even charge for them.

And then there was Datran, the third FCC filing.

It took the Justice Department eight years, but once Carter, McGowan, and I had paved the way, U.S. District Court Judge Harold Greene agreed and ruled in 1982 that those three FCC decisions created competition and that was the right thing to do. He busted up AT&T and the Bell System into eight different companies.

Within three years of the settlement, not only had prices dropped and service improved, but those eight new "Baby Bells" were among the top sixteen most valuable market cap companies in the whole world.

Clearly, what was good for the public customers was also good for the public owners of the former protected monopoly.

Chapter 12

Before There Was Software, There Was Don Thomson

DON THOMSON was the best there ever was.

I was looking for somebody exactly like Don to run Datran, and when we found him, I offered him that job. He turned me down. I asked why. He answered, "Because you don't understand how hard it is to whip AT&T."

I told him I knew very well how hard it was, and wanted him because he'd already been successfully doing just that at International Telephone and Telegraph (ITT).

He still said no. Then he told me, "The job I would like to have is running University Computing."

So I hired him to run UCC.

This was at a point when the markets had turned against us and we were in trouble. Maybe that's what really attracted Don. He sought big challenges. Before he arrived, we'd gone through five presidents at UCC.

A tall, good-looking guy who was prematurely silver-gray, Don was funny and the ladies loved him. But there are seven things you can do to get a heart attack and Don did them all. He once told me there hadn't been a male in his family who'd survived much beyond fifty. He made it, but only just.

Working with him, no matter the context, there was always the feel of high jinks in the air. It was as if we'd both run away from school and were on an adventure, like Tom Sawyer and Huckleberry Finn floating down the Mississippi. He had a unique enthusiasm for what was new, tough, challenging, and fun. He possessed a bristling intelligence and was full of vinegar. We shared the same tenacious love of a good fight and a kind of joy in taking on the powers-that-be.

Don had grown up in a big Irish family in the Bronx. One brother was earmarked for the priesthood, and his sisters were supposed to have ten children each. But Don was dyslexic (although he didn't know it at the time) and dropped out of school after the ninth grade. His family basically thought he was retarded. It was only when he joined the Army in 1948 and they gave him the usual battery of intelligence tests that he discovered his dyslexia. Still, he would read three books over a weekend—he absorbed knowledge, just soaked it up—and quickly became an expert on running the IBM punch-card machines.

I could tell right away that Don wasn't like any of the other guys I'd hired to run the company because he showed up with only one sidekick. Very often, executives bring an entire team with them. That may be understandable, but it isn't always good because they're not necessarily bringing the best of their former company with them. If it's just their two dozen closest chums, it can lead to problems large and small. Also, even when the two dozen are good people, integrating the boss's pals into a new company can be more complicated than it's worth. After all, moving in new faces usually means moving out friendly old faces, and that can upset the people who are staying. But Don showed up with only one of his pals, and that guy's job was to encourage employees to complain about what wasn't working.

That's just the way Don was. So is this story.

Don, as it happens, was an extremely good baseball player and could really pitch. He had been stationed in Japan and his colonel, who ran a ball team, wanted so badly to beat the other colonels and their teams that, in June 1950, just as Don's two years were up and he was getting ready to come home, his colonel pleaded with him to pitch one final game.

"No way," he said. "I catch the boat tomorrow and then I'm out of the Army. I'm going home."

"I'll make a deal with you," the colonel said. "Stay and pitch and I'll send you home on a *plane*."

That sounded good to Don and he agreed. But the very next day, hordes of North Korean troops rolled into South Korea and President Truman signed a freeze on the release of all soldiers in Japan.

Don went running to his colonel. "You said I could go home. I'd be home already if I hadn't stayed to pitch."

"What do you want me to do?" the colonel shrugged. "This is a presidential decree."

Pretty furious about the wrong done to him, this naturally rebellious Irishman went out and got gloriously drunk, then weaved his way through the streets of Tokyo to General MacArthur's headquarters at the Dai-Ichi Seimei Building. Still there today, this is a majestic office tower with huge columns going up five or six stories at the front. Overlooking the Imperial Palace, it had become symbolic of the imperial MacArthur's power and personality in postwar Japan. Don was going to tell MacArthur exactly what he thought of Truman's presidential decree, so he peed on one of the columns.

Of course the MPs grabbed him and tossed him in the stockade. His colonel came to visit him and warned, "There's no way you're going home now. You're going to be court-martialed. You're going to end up doing time."

In the cold hard sober light of the next morning, Don started looking for a way out of this mess. He reminded the colonel of his knowledge of IBM's plug board computers. The colonel decided there was something in this and cut a deal. He told Don, "Because of the North Korean invasion, we've got to expand and support our front-line troops quickly. If you agree to go to Okinawa and make those damn IBM machines work, I'll get the charges against you dropped."

So Don spent his unexpected third year in the Army setting up a new computer system in Okinawa.

When he got out, he took a job with ITT, working for the controller and doing the IBM stuff. He stayed there for the next ten years.

This was a staid old business, staffed with guys who had been there forever, running phone companies in different parts of the world, like Cuba. They had that same telegraph-company mentality I found at Western Union—that is, until the board decided to bring in fresh blood and turned to a guy named Harold Geneen.

He had been very successful running the defense contractor Raytheon. When he took over, ITT was a $760 million telephone company. By the time he left in 1972, he'd overseen 350 acquisitions and mergers, ITT had a presence in 80 countries, and was a $17 billion conglomerate with interests in insurance, hotels, and even Madison Square Garden. Along the way he spotted Don running the IBM machines, realized how sharp he was, and sent him to the Harvard Advanced Management Course. When Don came back to ITT, Geneen gave him a division to run and Don promptly made a lot of money for ITT. So Geneen gave him another division to run and he made even more money.

In Geneen's eyes, Don was a star.

THE MINUTE DON moved to UCC, he took a look around, saw eight UNIVAC computers scattered across the country, and brought them all to Dallas headquarters. He quickly determined that our biggest moneymaker customers were banks, so he sent the sales staff out to sign up more banks. He turned chaos into discipline and made work exhilarating for people on his team. He set a new standard with his bold vision for growth and how to implement that vision. Thanks to him, by 1972 UCC was making money again. We reduced long-term bank debt by $62 million and had another $18 million to invest in Datran.

More important, it was Don who spotted a great growth opportunity in a new business they used to call "software products."

In 1967, "software" was barely a word.

I was walking down the hallway of a company in California one morning and spotted a sign on a door that said, "Software Products." I remember stopping and staring at it and thinking to myself, how can software be a product?

To me, as it was then to most people in the computing business, software was a set of instructions that you wrote to tell a computer what to do. Each company had its own staff to write programs to do their own unique jobs. But it made sense that many things could be done the same way in multiple companies, with lower cost to all.

The notion that software could be a product intrigued me and, when Don came on board, we talked about that a lot. What I found particularly appealing was owning intellectual property that was not capital-intensive like our computer utility business, and developing something proprietary to sell through a nationwide or worldwide sales team.

Make it once, profit off it forever.

We looked around to see what was already out there, trying to figure out how to get into software, and discovered there was good news and bad news. The good news was that there were some independent software products available. The first one we spotted was a mathematical program created by some small company for use on an IBM 7044. So a market did exist. The bad news was that, though there clearly was a market, it wasn't a very good one because often within a few months of an innovative software product coming to market, IBM developed and offered the same thing for free and boom!—that developer's company was finished.

IBM's long shadow looming on the horizon didn't bode well for anyone thinking of investing in stand-alone software. Not as long as IBM could imitate it, bundle it with their machines, and thus stamp out unwelcome competition. Making this game even more difficult, we noticed that those few folks who somehow slipped under IBM's radar found themselves fighting a public that didn't exactly understand the concept of software as a stand-alone product.

Don Thomson remained convinced that software was the future and that that's where we needed to focus UCC's energies. Soon software revenue was growing 30 percent a year and making 30 percent margins. We were paying for the sales organization and still making 30 percent margins.

Our sweet spot, where the computer met the telephone, created software compatibility problems. So we'd started to write our own software using Digital Equipment's (DEC) new minicomputer as front-ends. Hardware costs had come down a lot. We'd gone from a $3 million IBM 7090 computer to a $1.5 million CDC 1604 computer and then to a $600,000 secondhand computer. But here was Ken Olsen at DEC making a $100,000 computer that promised tremendous speed and capacity. This was Moore's Law in action, which says that every two years a dollar will buy you twice as much computing power.

I'd always seen the computer as a tool, exactly as the plow is a tool and the tractor is a tool, and the mechanical cotton picker is a tool that does the work of a hundred people. Better tools are the reason that when I started school, there were thirteen and a half million farming jobs in the states of the Old South and today there are only 200,000.

I saw the same thing happening with the stored-program computer and all the digital possibilities that it opened up, leading to innovations like the Nokia cell phone. I had a sense that at some fundamental level, it was the same as with all those earlier tools, from the plow to the steam engine, that helped man do manual labor. Here was something that helped man do mental labor, a tool for thinkers.

I especially liked the idea of being able to provide our oil company customers with the model for petroleum reservoir software. This was something they could all use, and the McCord software was a pretty good model to draw on. So with a healthy respect for IBM's wrath—I was especially worried that somewhere in their corporate mind they thought of me as unfinished business—we started a small independent software business in 1970. Our first product was an IBM-compatible tape management system.

Of all the great things Thomas Watson, Sr., did, I continued to be enchanted with his use of the word "Think" and the way he posted it all around IBM.

It connoted a lot. Work was becoming less and less manual labor and more and more analytical work. With the introduction of the PC, computers would soon be moving from business to home, from corporate to personal. And businesses would soon be moving from the office to everywhere else, wherever

113

the individual user of the laptop happened to be. Before long, the boys from Apple would bring out a $5,000 computer that (thanks to Moore's Law) would fall rapidly below $500.

I couldn't see all this coming back in the sluggish '70s, but I felt it. I didn't know it then, but affordable computers would eventually be the death of UCC's original online computing business, as well as our computer leasing and manufacturing business. Only our software products would survive long-term. But their success would be huge.

As it turned out, our worries about IBM were overblown. Once again, times were changing.

Reminiscent of IBM's 1956 battle with the government that had brought forth the Consent Decree, by 1968 they were locking horns again with the antitrust guys at the Justice Department, this time over bundled software. In order to settle that litigation, they had to agree to stop bundling, to price IBM software separate from IBM hardware. That suddenly leveled the playing field.

Our tape management system quickly became the industry standard. We called it UCC-1, and followed it with a pair of even more successful systems of software programs, UCC-7 and UCC-11.

Little did I know at the time just what we had.

Chapter 13

Earth Resources

B ACK IN THE LATE 1960s, UCC was being hailed as one of America's fastest-growing companies. But I'd sometimes ask myself, "How could we possibly be worth so much?" Then I'd look around and see some junky company in our industry and tell myself, "They're a weak company but look at how much the market is valuing them, and we're worth more than they are, so maybe we really are worth 80 times earnings."

I saw this as a window of opportunity and decided to take advantage of the share price to diversify our personal assets. I would cash out a small percentage of my stock every year, selling some at $2, some at $30, and some at $155. But I held on to a good-sized chunk because my own identity and the company were bonded in my mind.

Listening to the rumblings in the bushes and the noises on the ground, I began thinking that with accelerating inflation, we maybe should own some assets that could benefit from inflation. Of course, I had no way of knowing that in just a few years, inflation would go through the roof, no way of predicting that interest rates would hit 20 percent. But I sensed that there was potential trouble for paper assets like stocks and bonds, and looked around for hard assets like oil, gold, silver, and real estate.

Along the way I met a fellow named Dan Krausse at the Young Presidents Organization. I used to go to the meetings to see what I could learn. Dan was president of Champlin Petroleum in Fort Worth. He struck me as the smartest guy in the room. He'd been slated to become CEO of his company, but fell out with the guy he was supposed to succeed, and that ended his career there.

With the huge profits that investors earned owning our UCC stock, I felt they'd be falling all over each other to invest in the next company we took to the public markets. So Charles and I said to Dan, "Let's buy a company for you to manage."

Dan signed up. We started shopping and eventually bought Delta, an oil refinery located on the banks of the Mississippi River in Memphis, Tennessee. Simultaneously, we bought a mining company called Vitro, which had a team of geologists and various exploration prospects in uranium, copper, and silver.

Our game plan was to use Delta as a cash cow to fund minerals exploration. We hocked $25 million worth of our University Computing stock, borrowed $12.5 million, and launched Earth Resources Company.

Then we sold half of Earth Resources to the public. We raised $13.5 million, paid off the debt, had $3.5 million a year in cash flow, and wound up owning our half of the stock for zero net cost.

Over the next decade we developed a copper mine in northern New Mexico, and built a grassroots oil refinery in Alaska, just outside Fairbanks in a city called North Pole, which is where they postmark letters to kids who write to Santa Claus at Christmas.

From the Jimmy Perkins Family we bought a chain of gas stations that we melded with the Memphis refinery and owned and operated gas stations with a private brand called Red Ace. Eventually we had more than 330 gas stations and 2,200 employees in eleven states, and also sold to Texaco and Gulf Oil for their gas stations. We bought a barge fleet on the Mississippi to bring oil from Louisiana up the river. This helped make us a dominant petroleum products supplier in the mid-Mississippi River market.

At the same time, Memphis entrepreneur Fred Smith, who wrote his college thesis on his idea to compete with the U.S. post office with overnight delivery of air mail and small packages, started FedEx, which was growing and expanding in

Memphis (their original hub), and they needed a lot of jet fuel for their fleet. So instead of trucking it to them, we built a pipeline to deliver it.

We also developed the DeLamar Mine up in Idaho, which became the third largest silver mine in the country.

The refinery we built beside the Alaskan pipeline in Fairbanks was about halfway between the giant oil field Prudhoe Bay on the North Sea and the Port of Valdez in the south. So we had a market in the middle of the state where we created the refined products and sold them locally. We also sold jet fuel to the airlines flying over the top of the globe on the way to Asia. The stock and bond markets were getting thrashed daily, but the profits of Earth Resources multiplied unbelievably. All the same, the economic pain in the capital markets of the 1970s had become relentless. We had stagnation. We had inflation. We had unemployment. We had a lot of things that weren't working. America was losing its competitiveness. I would go to Europe in the 1960s and the dollar looked big. I would go to Europe in the 1970s and the dollar wouldn't buy much of anything. People would say, "Don't you have any hard currency? Don't give me these dollars. Give me German marks or Swiss francs or French francs...hard money."

Nobody thought Americans knew how to make cars anymore. All the smarts were in Japan and Germany. America needed a miracle like the German miracle after World War II. America needed to study the Japanese and see what they were doing right. We were fighting a battle we didn't thoroughly understand, even if no one else understood it, either. Companies to the left of us and companies to the right of us were going under.

At the time we started Earth Resources, silver and oil were priced as if they were the last items at a garage sale. Silver was $2 an ounce and oil was less than $3 a barrel. But I believed that economic factors were going to change and send those prices up.

President Nixon, a Republican, stood up in 1971 and announced that he was a Keynesian. What? He took the United States off the gold standard and put price controls in place. One of our UCC board members, Jack Grayson, the dean of SMU's Business School, was tapped by Nixon to run his Price Control Administration. I remember saying to Jack, "But you're a classic free-market guy. You don't believe in price controls."

He responded, "Neither does the president, but he feels that we've got to try something."

As if the country weren't already in enough turmoil, when the Israeli-Egyptian War broke out in 1973, and the United States sided with Israel, the Arabs embargoed oil in retaliation and inflation, only a nagging illness in 1968, became a full-blown epidemic, spreading like Kudzu vines in Mississippi and destroying everything in its wake. People were even losing money on Treasury Bonds. Prices skyrocketed from $3 a barrel to $12 almost over night and suddenly we were standing in line for two hours at the gas pumps. And exactly as Texas geologist Hubbard had predicted in 1956, only ten years after we'd won the Second World War, powered by Texas crude, oil production in the USA began its long decline.

By the mid-1970s, the inflation-adjusted crash was deeper than that of 1929, which had triggered the Great Depression. We didn't know it at the time, but things were only going to get worse. When the Ayatollah toppled the Shah of Iran in 1979, oil prices jumped even higher, to $36 a barrel. In the frenzy to acquire hard assets, the price of silver also skyrocketed.

There are two ways a business owner gets rewarded: either through appreciation of the company's market value or with increasing dividends, and dividends are fine with me. Our tax laws actually motivate you to borrow in a company and pay dividends to owners because pretax profits that go to paying interest are tax-deductible, but dividends to pay the cost of equity capital are not. During the Great Depression, lots of companies went bust, but Ma Bell paid nine bucks and the widows and orphans had food. Dividends constitute what the shareholder has for sure. Everything else is an extrapolation and a guess about the future. You hope prices move higher. But for fourteen years, from the last year of Lyndon Johnson's presidency to the first years of Ronald Reagan's, the average stock price was down.

118

I used to call the dividends we got from Earth Resources "grocery money." It kept my family in food while we sort of prayed that someday the price of our Bonanza steakhouses and the price of UCC would come back to where they were in 1969.

But in the colder light of global macroeconomic change, I started thinking that there was a big gap between the value at which Earth Resources was trading in the market and the value of its assets.

I learned from Benjamin Graham, who wrote about investing and also taught at Columbia University in New York, where his most famous student was Warren Buffett. The only student who ever got an A+ from Graham, Buffett swears he never did anything new; he just did what he learned from Benjamin Graham.

Graham made everything especially clear to me when he described the stock market as manic-depressive. He wrote that when Mr. Market was manic, he'd buy anything from you at any price. But when Mr. Market was depressed, he wouldn't buy anything from you, no matter how low you priced it.

Believing Graham, I reckoned that while Mr. Market might have a manic appetite for oil and silver, for whatever reason his mania didn't extend to the share price of Earth Resources. So there was a gap between the market value of the assets the company owned and the market value of the company's stock. The way to close the gap was to sell the company's assets or the company itself.

Furthermore, I could not imagine any scenario in which the oil scarcity would not ultimately become a glut and prices would come tumbling down. That's what commodity markets do, and I remembered stories of oil dropping from $1 to 10¢ when the giant East Texas field was discovered.

Over the next several months, conventional wisdom had it that oil would go to $90 a barrel. But my gut was telling me no.

When I first came to Dallas, the tallest structure downtown was the Magnolia Petroleum building, with its double-sided, neon-red Pegasus towering over the skyline. Now there were so many skyscrapers you couldn't even see Pegasus anymore. The economy seemed out of sync to me. One-third of all corporate profits made in the United States were coming from oil companies. Exxon was betting $1 billion on Colorado oil shale, and the number of rigs actively drilling in the United States had climbed from 700 to 4,000.

As I see it, conventional wisdom takes you only so far. At a certain point it becomes like a hall of mirrors in a fun house: Everyone stands around reflecting back the same belief to each other, until reality gets warped and bent out of shape. The reason people hang around too long is that they don't want to be caught standing outside the fun house all by themselves.

Don't get me wrong: Trends can go on for a long time. But you can't get caught up in the mood of the market. You need to step outside the situation, to turn around and look back with a more objective gaze. You need to filter out the hysteria in order to come to some sort of real analysis of the bigger picture.

The big picture was screaming "Sell Earth Resources." To me, that was an inescapable conclusion. We'd had a dozen years of building management depth, reinvesting for growth, and solid operating performance. The time had come to get out while the getting was good. Dan Krausse took a different view. Earth Resources had been as low as $5 a share but was now up to $17. He thought we ought to be celebrating. To me, celebrating that share price under the prevailing market conditions was like playing in the band on the Titanic.

And, while all this was going on, a couple of good old Texas boys were falling in love with silver.

Their daddy, Haroldson Lafayette Hunt, Jr., was a wildcatter who hit it so big in East Texas oil that by the 1950s, *Fortune* said he was the richest man in the world. Supposedly the model for Jock Ewing in the popular television soap opera *Dallas,* HL had six kids in his first family, including Lamar—whose trust portfolio was one of those projects I first worked on when I was stationed in Fort Worth with IBM—and four kids in his second family, including my friend Ray Hunt.

HL's boys, Herbert and Bunker, were a pair of the greatest characters ever to come out of Texas. Especially Bunker. He followed his old man into the wildcatting business, looked for oil all over the world (even in Afghanistan), and partnered up with British Petroleum when he discovered a big field in Libya. Unfortunately for Bunker and BP, Colonel Quaddafi came along, overthrew the King of Libya, and confiscated Bunker's oil. Still, for a fleeting moment, Bunker had taken over his daddy's title as world's richest man.

The brothers understood inflationary assets like oil, and in the '70s they started collecting hard assets, or "real money." One of these hard assets was silver. Somehow Bunker and Herbert got it into their heads that if they played their cards right, they could corner the world's silver market.

They borrowed money from the First National Bank in Dallas, plus more from any brokers who would give them margin loans, and started buying silver futures. When they came into the market in December 1973, the price of silver was $2.90 an ounce. They bought contracts for 35 million ounces, and in just two months ran the price up to $6.70. Unbeknownst to them, the Mexican government was sitting on 50 million ounces of silver and decided that $6.70 was a good price. Mexico sold and dumped the price back to $4. Undeterred, Bunker and Herbert spent the next four years in partnership with some folks in Saudi Arabia, buying several hundred million ounces. In 1979, with the price hovering around $6, they picked up 25 percent of all the silver on the New York Commodity Exchange and five out of every eight silver shares on the Chicago Board of Trade. The price shot up to $19.

They had more than tripled their money, but that wasn't enough for Bunker and Herbert, so they borrowed $1.3 billion—which was said to be around 9 percent of all the borrowing in America during that period—sank it into silver, and drop-kicked the price up to $49 an ounce.

The way these futures markets work, they would buy a contract for 5,000 ounces and only have to put down 10 percent. At $6 an ounce, that meant $3,000. But at $49 an ounce, they needed to put a lot of money on the table. The board of governors at the New York Commodity Exchange got so worried about the Hunts that they raised the margin on 5,000-ounce contracts to

$60,000. That set up a massive roadblock, which forced the brothers to sell assets.

In the middle of all this, Bunker and Herbert grew very worried that their silver hoard wasn't safe sitting in the U.S. So they loaded around $100 million worth of silver—actual silver ingots—onto a commercial flight to London, and with that much money in the hold, bought themselves two cheap economy seats on the same flight.

With Bunker seated on the aisle and Herbert in the middle seat, they spent the night crammed in the back of the crowded plane. Just after takeoff, the stewardesses came around selling headsets for the movie. In those days, if you wanted to watch the film, it cost you two bucks. Bunker said no, but Herbert forked over $2. As soon as the film started, Bunker had second thoughts and, with $100 million worth of silver in the hold, he simply took one of the plugs out of Herbert's ear so he could watch the film for free.

I knew what the Hunt brothers were doing in silver, not only because their attempted cornering of the market made for regular reading in all the papers, but also because I was a director of the First National Bank and sat on the review committee, overseeing the Hunt loans. As they borrowed more to buy more, we were asking ourselves, "Should the bank be worried?"

The lending officer kept telling us, "This is the biggest and most profitable loan account we've got. This is great." But I wasn't convinced. I worried that this might be Tulipmania all over again. The bank already had a huge exposure to Texas oil and Texas real estate, and adding silver speculation into the mix at these prices carried the same sort of risk. I started wondering if maybe the bank should sell some of these loans to the New York banks.

And while I was having these doubts, there I was, owning Earth Resources with our DeLamar silver mine up in Idaho, and making big profits on silver. My gut told me it might be time to go see Bunker.

He was a big, round, mellow guy who was fun, a happy guy, and if he was frugal, at least he came by it naturally because his dad could be pretty tight with a buck, too. HL, with his unmatched wealth, brought his lunch to work in a brown paper bag.

When Bunker's kid brother, Lamar, started up the Dallas Texans Football team, which later became the Kansas City Chiefs, a reporter named Richard Hanlon called up HL and asked him, "What do you think about your boy losing a million dollars a year on football?" HL responded, "Well, at that rate Lamar will go broke in a hundred years."

I sold Jimmy Ling's house to Lamar. Jimmy, the "L" in LTV, owed me $5 million, and wanted to give me his mansion in payment—a beautiful French château that was easily the most famous house in Dallas because of Jimmy—but I already had a house and didn't want it. Jimmy said that Lamar wanted to buy it, so I took it and sold it to Lamar. He was very concerned that his daddy would read about the sale in the papers and wanted us to keep it a secret. We tried, but it was like hiding an elephant, and the *Dallas Morning News* knows how to find elephants.

I didn't really know Bunker all that well, although I'd bumped into him around town on nonbusiness occasions. He raced horses and I have a painting in my living room of a white horse in a stable that he once owned. He was a pretty good businessman who just sometimes got it wrong. But then, we all get it wrong sometimes.

As I walked into Bunker's office, Herbert came in and so did Bunker's assistant, carrying a birthday cake. It was Bunker's fifty-sixth birthday and we sang Happy Birthday to him.

After the cake, I said to Bunker and Herbert, "Would you guys like to buy our silver mine?"

Herbert decided quickly and said, "We will make you an offer to buy the total output of your mine for the next twenty years. We will pay you a minimum of fifteen dollars an ounce, plus half of any higher market price for the life of the mine."

That sounded good to me because when we started the mine, silver was under $3 an ounce. I told them, "I want to make the deal, but I've got to get approval from my Earth Resources board. Don't worry, though, because they're gonna love this deal, too."

So I went back to Dan Krausse and told him we were going

to sell out to the Hunt Brothers and he said, "No, we're silver miners. This is our business. We don't want to sell the silver mine."

I couldn't believe it. He was turning his back on a pile of money. So I thought for a minute and suggested, "How about going to the futures market and just selling some silver there?"

He wasn't having it. "That would be speculating on the price. We don't do that. We're managers. This is what we do. We manage silver."

When Dan and I couldn't come to any agreement, I called the whole board together and explained the situation to them. We took a vote. Charles and director Jay Taylor voted yes with me. Dan and the other three directors voted no. I had to go back to Bunker and Herbert and tell them that we couldn't sell them the mine.

I wondered if I could get some cheap money by selling silver-backed bonds. The idea was that in a market fearful of inflation, we'd give investors the option of taking silver or dollars when the bond came to be paid. But Dan didn't want to do silver-backed bonds. In fact, he didn't want to do anything that would reduce our risk of a collapse in silver prices, or oil prices.

At that point, *The Economist* in London ran a story agreeing with me, screaming on its cover, "The Coming Glut in Oil." Inflationary asset prices were going to crash, but Dan and his pals didn't care. They were in their own illusory world, caught in the grip of the madness of crowds, not unlike the dot-com boom.

It is possible to corner a market, but only for a fleeting moment. What happens when a price skyrockets is exactly what they tell you will happen in freshman economics: High prices bring forth more supply, and that increased supply drives the price back down. At $49 an ounce, ladies in America were cleaning up the family silverware for sale.

All it took was a simple reading of history and current economic indicators to know that selling oil and silver assets was common sense. The facts were screaming "This is a bubble." You simply cannot lock horns with one of the unalterable laws of the universe: the supply-and-demand curve. But I couldn't convince Dan, even though every rational argument said he was wrong and I was right. The only thing I could do was go back to the board and say, "If you won't tell the chief when he's wrong, then the owners have to tell the board that they are wrong. Charles and I are the big owners and the owners are going to have to replace the board."

It was now a proxy fight I didn't want to get into, but one I wasn't going to shy away from. I felt betrayed by Dan and was going to throw him and his cronies off the board and sell the company. In my mind, Dan had become infected by the Terrible P's: Power, Perks, Press, and Prestige. I had concluded that, consciously or unconsciously, Dan was making decisions based on what he perceived was best for him rather than what was best for the owners of the company. Charles and I had gone to great lengths to give Dan and other executives generous stock options that aligned their economic interest with ours and those of the public stockholders, and had provided generous severance packages in the event of a change in control. But when the Terrible P's take over, rational thinking goes out the window.

Dan and his managers made robust projections of future cash flows and hired the most prestigious of all consulting firms, McKinsey, to back up their projections. I looked at those forecasts and said, "I don't believe it."

Dan and his buddies continued to insist, "This is what we do. We're oil people. We're silver miners."

That carried no water with me. You can have the best managers and the best equipment and the best strategy, but if it's not the right business to be in, you've got to get out. People in my native South used to say, "We're cotton pickers, that's what we do." But all the cotton-picking jobs disappeared with the rise of the mechanical cotton picker. Instead of saying, "This is what we do," Dan should have been saying to himself, "I'm doing things right, but am I doing the right thing?"

My mistake with Earth Resources was to let Dan put two of his personal friends on the board. And right there, as soon as I realized the mistake I'd made, I was off and running on my first experience in good corporate governance. This issue of good corporate governance would eventually lead me to challenge the corrupt management at Computer Associates with proxy fights in 2001 and 2002, to expose their management team's abuse of power, ultimately to remove the top officers and see eight of them go to jail for the fraud they perpetrated on me and on the other investors in their public stock. It was during my pro bono proxy fight with CA that *Grant's Investor* wrote, "Anyone who owns a share of a publicly traded company anywhere in the world should pay homage to Sam Wyly."

But it was in fighting Dan that I concluded that the most important job of any board member is to decide every year whether or not to rehire the chief.

If I had been merely a passive investor, I would have just sold my Earth Resources stock at the $17 price it was then trading for. But that's not the way I am. For a calm and quiet guy, I can get as aggressive as I need to be. I signed up for the fight and there was no way I was going to lose. I nominated a new board and went to work convincing the shareholders to vote for them. Dan got to work trying to keep his job. I spent my own money running ads saying, in effect, "Throw the bums out." Dan spent the company's money running ads saying, in effect, what a bad guy I was to propose such an awful notion.

The advantage incumbents have, besides the use of company money, is that many shareholders are passive and don't devote any serious thought to who's on the board. It's hard for an investor to do that because the bundle of legal papers you get in the mail from the company is lawyerized and homogenized for compliance with government regulations, and written in corporate-speak, rather than in simple statements in the King's English. Dan and his guys had only 2 percent of the total stock, compared with the 20 percent that Charles and I were holding. People could see how much of our own money we had at stake, and that made us trustworthy in their eyes. Knowing that only 80 percent of shareholders usually ever bother to vote, my guess was that we needed only an additional 21 percent to win.

The key guy we needed was our single biggest institutional investor, Marc Yamada of Manufacturer's Life in Canada. I went to see him and explained the situation. He reminded me, "Institutions usually support the management."

I asked, "But in this case, who's the management? Is it the board? The CEO? Or the entrepreneur who invented the company and really made it work?"

When Dan went to see him in Canada, Mark told him, "Sam was here first and Sam is right. You had better do what he wants to do."

Understanding that they were going to lose the proxy fight and find themselves out on the street, Dan and his cronies engaged Bear Stearns to find competitive buyers. We closed the deal with Tulsa-based Mapco in November 1980. Dan had favored the losing bidder, Huffington Oil (run by Arianna's then husband and father-in-law), where he would have become chief executive of the combined company.

By then our Earth Resources shares were at $56, up from $17. That same month, oil prices peaked at $40 a barrel. After we sold the company, both prices headed down. Silver prices crashed, too. It took a while for oil to reach the bottom at $9 in the mid-1980s, by which time 90 percent of the Texas oil and real estate millionaires were bankrupt and nine out of the ten biggest banks in our state were wiped out. Only after the epidemic spread to other parts of America, wiping out big banks like Continental Illinois, did the Federal Reserve open up the money pumps with a flow of liquidity and save the big banks in the Northeast and on the West Coast.

Ironically, Dan's fighting me turned out to be a good thing. If he hadn't, I would have sold out sooner and for less. But to me, he was fighting for his own personal reasons, against what was so clearly and so rationally the right thing to do for all the shareholders. Not just for the Wylys, but for everyone holding Earth Resources shares. And for the employees, too. His way, they all would have lost their wealth. My way, all the workers still had a job. My way, the public shareholders maintained their wealth. Had our positions been reversed, I would have known where my loyalties lay.

The number of drilling rigs working dropped from 4,000 back to 700. Workers who had moved from Flint, Michigan, to Midland, Texas, moved back to Flint. The Dallas skyline was fuller than it had ever been before, but many of the new office buildings were tenantless.

The cities of the Southwest were filled with "see-through skyscrapers."

Chapter 14

Bonanza

W HEN YOU'RE RIDING HIGH, everyone in town with a deal calls to convince you that they're doing you a great big favor by letting you in on something special. During those times when UCC was king of the hill, my phone never stopped ringing with people looking to become my new best friend.

I learned to say "no" very fast.

But early in 1969, when "Little Red Arrow" Jerry Mann called one day out of the blue, it was a different story. He'd helped me get UCC launched through his company, Diversa, and he came right to the point. Diversa's bankers were demanding immediate repayment of a note, and he wanted me to guarantee the debt so he could hold the bankers off a while longer. He went on to explain that, as collateral, Diversa had put up a troubled chain of steakhouses called Bonanza. Jerry said he was trying to unload the chain, but he needed another six months to get his deal done.

Ironically, this money-losing business had taken its name from what at the time was the most popular television series in the country. The story of a father and his three grown sons, it was set in Nevada after the Civil War and ran for fourteen seasons, from 1959 until 1973. This was a time when everyone, the world over, loved going to see Westerns, and almost every big male and female actor wanted to star in at least one of them. Bonanza was the first television series to be filmed outdoors in color. It's still in reruns, and I still watch it.

Jerry needed a million dollars for six months, which he felt certain would give him time enough to sell Bonanza to Herman

129

1000 DOLLARS AND AN IDEA

Lay over at PepsiCo. PepsiCo had just acquired Herman's company, Frito-Lay, and was getting into the restaurant business. Our offices were actually on the 13th floor of the Frito-Lay Building, whose landlord also was Diversa, so this was kind of a neighborhood thing.

I told Jerry I was already working too many hours a day running UCC and that I didn't know anything about the steakhouse business, and I really didn't want to get involved. Sorry, Jerry, but no, I said.

That night, however, I got into bed and thought about the dire consequences to Jerry if the bank foreclosed, which would trigger defaults on his other debt. I got up the next morning, phoned him, and said, "I owe you. You helped me, now I'm going to help you."

I signed the note and didn't think anything more about it until six months later, when Jerry's bank phoned to tell me that Bonanza hadn't been sold, Jerry couldn't pay, and I now had to come up with $1 million to pay off the debt.

Just like that, I was out a million bucks. Just like that, I became the proud owner of a business I'd never wanted to begin with.

There were all sorts of good reasons Jerry couldn't pay the note, and the banker was perfectly right not to let him have any more money. Right away I could see that if I didn't pump another $1 million (which I didn't have) into the business, the whole thing was going to go belly-up.

There were only three things I could do.

I could say, Oh well, no sense throwing good money after bad. I'll fold my hand and walk away.

I could sit around lamenting the state I was in, and wind up wasting time.

Or I could perceive that the game was not just about the cards I was holding, but about how I played those cards.

Staying in the game to win is as natural and obvious a condition for me as the dirt on the ground and the sun in the sky. So I focused on learning everything I could about Bonanza, faced up to the fact that I had to pay the note, and then I had to create more capital somehow to avoid taking Bonanza into bankruptcy.

Running a steakhouse chain had just never, ever been on my list of things to do. But when I started thinking about it, the idea of a standardized meal—something a step above McDonald's but still cheap enough to appeal to the average family—didn't seem like a bad idea.

Remember, this was the late '60s, right when the country was going through massive social and economic change. A lot more women were entering the workforce, and if they didn't get home until long after the kids arrived from school, that might mean fewer home-cooked meals. The recession also meant that people weren't going on expensive vacations or buying new cars but were, instead, treating themselves to little things, like a good meal out.

Once I'd thought it through, I went for it whole hog. Because the best results come when you treat your ventures like missions, I told myself, "If I can get through this crisis and get good managers in there, this Bonanza might just be a good diversification move for us."

I hocked some other assets—but not our homestead, which I promised myself I would keep debt-free and never put at risk. I never forgot Mama and Daddy selling our painted house in town when I was five and moving into the clapboard cabin with no electricity to pay down the crop loans, and later my mother-in-law's story about losing their house in Dallas during the Great Depression.

Then I set about trying to figure out exactly what the heck it was that I owned, so that I could make a real business out of it. This wasn't going to be easy. Bonanza was bleeding. The franchisees were outraged to the point of not paying their bills, and top managers were simply inept.

I went to see Bonanza's chairman, who turned out to be an old crony of Jerry Mann's from the advertising trade. He didn't know the first thing about running a restaurant chain, so I fired him. Then I went to see the president and he, too, hadn't a clue about the business. I fired him, too. Eventually, I found one of the vice presidents who seemed like a good manager and, although he didn't have a lot of Bonanza experience, he had learned a few things along the way. What he said made sense. So I told him he was now running the company.

Then we began visiting the restaurants together and talking to people. In the Army they say that good intelligence will tell you "How?" and "Why?" Same thing holds true in business. You need to know the truth and you find it on the ground, so we spoke with customers eating steaks, stood around observing the way the restaurants operated, and spoke with the folks running them.

We were a fast food chain one level above McDonald's, selling a budget steak and potatoes for $1.28 to a largely blue-collar market, and we had customers. We also had a great brand name. The characters of the Bonanza TV show—Hoss, Little Joe, Adam, and Pa—were instantly recognizable to millions of people. We hired them all, and we paid them each $100,000 a year to make personal appearances at store openings. Lorne Greene, one of the stars of the show, joined our board of directors.

Bonanza had started out as a franchising operation, but we also built and managed company-owned stores. Our franchisees, however, were doing a much better job than we were. When we studied other restaurant chains, we saw that this wasn't unique to Bonanza. It was true of them all, notably McDonald's.

It took us a while, but we converted the business from being partly company-owned and partly franchised to being a totally franchised chain. That quickly took the company's employment down from about 5,000 to no more than 50 people. We spent money on marketing, burnishing our image, running ads, and developing new menu products.

Some of our franchisees were running five or ten restaurants and had good management teams. Others were making a living with one restaurant—they'd have the whole family working there—but were looking to expand to a multiple store operation, except that they couldn't raise the capital.

When we granted a Bonanza franchise, that person needed

to have had experience in running restaurants and had to risk his own net worth in the venture along with us. But there were cases when we saw a real good manager with no money and said, "We'll put you in business, take your note, and capitalize you." We knew that skills as a manager and entrepreneur were more scarce than capital.

Don Thomson, after three great years at UCC, was ready for another challenge. When I told him that Bonanza really needed fixing, he agreed to join the team. First, he upped the quality of the beef so that customers got a better steak for their money. He also put a kid's burger on the menu. It had a smaller amount of meat and was cheaper, but he kept the regular-sized bun so the kids didn't think they were being shorted. We also offered alternatives that even a devout vegetarian would love.

As we grew Bonanza, we saw that certain locations weren't performing. My preference was to shut them down, but we had leases. That meant we'd be paying for another ten years, whether we closed them or not. Well, all his life Don had been the world's greatest manager, but he'd never started anything from scratch. He came to me one day and said he wanted to try his hand at entrepreneuring, because he wanted the challenge of creating something. I told him to go ahead. And he came up with a new restaurant concept for a younger, hipper crowd. He took the Bonanza restaurants out of the locations that weren't working, remodeled them, and opened a chain called Peoples. He wanted it to be a happening place. He had stools at the bar with legs that looked like real legs, and movie star photos on the walls, and stuff hanging off the ceiling. Teenagers liked it a lot.

Especially the salad bar.

Until that point, you never saw salad bars in restaurants, except in a few upscale places. No one was doing them in popular chain restaurants, the way everybody does them today. Don practically invented that. It was his idea to give everyone a bowl and let them help themselves to the lettuce and tomatoes, olives and bacon bits, whatever they liked, and as much as they wanted, too.

It worked so well in Peoples that we put salad bars in all the Bonanzas. This was a winning innovation and it worked even better in Bonanza than it did in Peoples. Just what your average cowboy wanted when he came in for steak and potatoes covered in butter: to help himself to an all-you-can-eat salad.

The first few Peoples were profitable. We continued moving them into old Bonanza locations, but after a while, Peoples slowed down. Bonanza had a brand image that customers recognized, but Peoples turned out to be more of a fad. So we found ourselves with lots of capital tied up in Peoples and no clear way to make productive use of it.

Meanwhile, times were turning against us. American unity behind our "hold the line" policy toward the Russian and Chinese Communists was falling apart with our cost in blood in Vietnam. The country spent heavily on its cold war arms race with the Soviet Union and the hot war against Communist expansion in Vietnam, as well as President Johnson's Great Society programs at home. The defining, and in many ways most excruciating, year for the nation in those times was 1968: Robert Kennedy and Martin Luther King, Jr., were murdered, our inner cities burned. Parents and grandparents—generations raised to be patriotic—stood by in shock as their boys tore up their draft cards, shut down college campuses, and even fled to Canada to avoid going to Vietnam.

Somebody actually invented an economic misery index, by adding unemployment to the inflation rate and coming up with a number to quantify the pain being felt by the average American. Other than the Great Depression years of the 1930s, no decade of the twentieth century had a misery index as painful as that of the 1970s.

President Johnson felt the heat from Eugene McCarthy and abdicated. Hillary Rodham, president of the all-female Wellesley College's Young Republican Club, went to the Miami Nominating Convention to help Nelson Rockefeller, and I was there to help Chuck Percy. When Percy was out of the race, I ended up casting my Texas delegate vote for Richard Nixon, who then asked me to lead his Texas campaign.

Two weeks before Election Day, the polls showed Texas evenly split among Nixon, LBJ's vice president Hubert Humphrey, and George Wallace, the Dixiecrat. Texas went for Humphrey by a hair, as she would for Jimmy Carter and Bill Clinton in later years. Nixon, as we know, won the 1968 presidential election.

The country had paid dearly for Lyndon Johnson's guns-and-butter policy and our much longer affair with cheap oil. A British friend at the time told me, "You Americans are profligate in your use of petrol!"

He was right.

That's even clearer three decades later, as I write this. It was affecting everything and everyone, economically and socially, and continued into the 1970s when Nixon and Gerald Ford served in the White House.

It's true that there are almost always some inflation and higher interest rates during times of war, but we began to experience both at unusually high and rising levels. These were tumultuous times, devastating to some, euphoric to others.

And, when they came, it seemed like everything got crushed, big-time. Our primarily blue-collar Bonanza customer base got slammed with layoffs and unemployment. The capital markets shut down. And, because of inflation, investment-grade bonds were down 40 to 50 percent. The Dow hit 1,000 in the '60s, but then it sank like a stone. It didn't climb back up to 1,000 until after 1980, fourteen years later.

Bonanza wasn't the only budget steakhouse in the country playing off the country's most popular television program. There was another one in the midwestern states called Ponderosa—the name of the ranch in the show. For a while, there was some give-and-take between Ponderosa and us about who was going to buy out whom, and I finally decided we might as well buy them. Even though the names Bonanza and Ponderosa were often confused, there was very little duplication of locations and no real direct competition. I saw the move as a good meld. The Ponderosa share price seemed undervalued, so my plan was to make an offer to their major shareholder for all of his stock. If he said no, we'd do a tender offer. I knew the top price that I wanted to pay for Ponderosa, which was in the low $20s, so I started the ball rolling by offering around $10 a share.

In situations like these, you have to come prepared with your upper limits. You've got to set your target and, no matter what, stick with it. If you get outbid, you get outbid. What you can't do is let your ego take over and chase someone else's winning bid. As long as you don't get caught up in the excitement, you'll still make money, even if you lose the bid. But if you abandon your strategy and start improvising, if you get caught up in the fool's game of "just one more" bid, when you win you'll ultimately lose because you'll have wound up paying too much.

After the fellow who owned Ponderosa said, "Not enough," I pushed the share price into the high teens. That's when someone else got into the game—either he saw something I didn't and decided it must be worth more, or he didn't care what it cost and just wanted to win. So when the share price passed my limit, I backed away. Ponderosa got sold to those guys for $27, which was fine with me because we'd been buying on the way up and we were making a good profit. It then turned out that the fellow who had bought the company couldn't service the debt and had to unload it.

The man who took it off his hands was a great entrepreneur named John Kluge.

Just that year, *Forbes* magazine had designated Kluge the richest man in America. He was in his mid-70s and he'd built himself an empire of radio and television stations called Metromedia.

In those days, the eat-more-vegetables lobby was warning the country about the dangers of red meat, and this was definitely having an effect on the market for steak. But Kluge was willing to bet that worrying about animal fats was only a fad and that people would always eat beef.

At this point, in 1989, we'd owned Bonanza for twenty years, growing it from 20 restaurants to 600.

One of the things I noticed after each recession was that, in hindsight, the recession had been forecast in Bonanza's weekly sales numbers. They were like a six-month leading indicator.

Now I was seeing our weekly numbers starting to turn down again. So when my friend Peter Ackerman at Drexel Burnham called to say John Kluge was in his office and that Kluge loved steakhouses, I was really happy to hear from him.

Peter said, "John has bought Ponderosa and Steak and Ale and now he wants to buy Bonanza."

It took me less than twenty seconds to say, "Sure."

Kluge came to Dallas and I asked him, "Why do you want to own steakhouses?"

He told me, "I used to drive a Frito-Lay truck and sell to these guys. I understand the business. I was a vendor. Besides, I think they're wrong about people not eating beef." Then he asked me, "Why do you want to sell?"

I answered, "I have been through three recessions with painful consequences. I'd rather not do the fourth one."

Chapter 15

Taking My Losses

GENERALLY SPEAKING, there's a good rule that says your first loss is always the cheapest. In other words, take your losses quickly, move on, and don't look back.

That rule works pretty good for investors in public stocks and bonds. But for an entrepreneur, it's a gross oversimplification. If I had followed that rule in the beginning, University Computing would never have been born and I'd have given up on Datran long before the final bell. I guess your average entrepreneur is just a lot more stubborn.

Well, Datran may have been gone forever, but technology in the late 1970s kept moving forward at a breathtaking pace. Now, in place of digital microwave towers, there were commercially available satellites. I found the phoenix that would rise from Datran's ashes, and we named it NetAmerica.

This time, though, I didn't commit to any money of my own for construction. We spent four years engineering the technology we would need to make NetAmerica work and then promoting it while waiting for the eventual bust-up of the telephone monopoly. Wall Street had revived in 1983, but just long enough for us to get Sterling Software capitalized in May. By the time I tried to get to the market with NetAmerica in October of that year, the window had closed again.

There comes a time for investor and entrepreneur alike when you have to say, Enough is enough. There was no way to tell when the equity markets would capitalize such a big project. You've just got to quit watching your money disappear. In my case, it had been $10 million over four years.

I cheered myself up by noting that at least the time and capital loss in NetAmerica was less than the eight years and $100 million I'd lost on Datran. Maybe I was partly smart by learning to lose less on an ultimate economic failure.

Later, in the 1990s, when the digital combination of the computer and the phone line had grabbed the imaginations of investors in the form of the Internet, a lot of companies not only got capitalized but were grossly overcapitalized. The result was the crash of 2000, when the NASDAQ dropped 80 percent.

A BILLION PERSONAL computers were sold in 2007, most of them bought by consumers and connected to the Internet. In the beginning, however, there was only the industrial market for computers and only mainframe systems. And at first there was only IBM and UNIVAC. Then Honeywell showed up, along with General Electric, RCA, NCR, Control Data, and Burroughs coming into a new industry with huge promise. Everybody was chasing the same 5,000 or so commercial customers, the same IT departments.

We built a large and successful business selling customers on the promise that they would get better results and service from UCC than from their own computer departments.

Sam Goodner was a Texan out of Texas A&M and I sent him to Europe for University Computing. Later he left and, together with a programmer friend, created a software program that they started selling around Europe.

The software worked, so he began thinking about selling it in the American market and found a guy who was born in China but raised on Long Island to be his agent. That fellow's name was Charles Wang.

Wang took a commission on whatever he sold, and because he was ambitious he started selling a lot, the U.S. market for IBM-compatible software being more than twice as big as Europe's. The software market seemed to be opening, so Wang found another product he could sell, and brought in his brother, Tony, who was a securities lawyer. Then the two of them merged Wang's sales agency with Goodner's product company, named the new entity Computer Associates (CA), and took the combined company public.

Computer Associates grew through acquisitions, using their stock or cash to buy out others. By the end of the 1980s, they had become one of the big players in the systems software market.

The other big player was our UCC, the one with the most potent products. Wang approached me through Sam Goodner about Computer Associates buying UCC. I'd recapitalized UCC after our huge losses on Datran and the other disasters of the 1970s, swapped stock for debt, and I was gone from UCC's management by the end of that decade.

A recapitalization to reduce debt is how you get back to a viable balance sheet without going through a bankruptcy process. You offer a voluntary exchange. Whoever doesn't want to trade doesn't have to, so some of the bonds stayed out there, but most of them swapped for stock. Then you can afford to pay the interest.

My Swiss friend, Walter Haefner, got a whole lot of stock, because he turned in his debt along with the public bondholders and became the company's largest owner, by far, while our Wyly ownership dropped from 11 percent to 2 percent.

So I told Wang to go see Walter.

By then, just about everything in UCC had been sold off, so that the company could concentrate on its powerful—and highly profitable—enterprise and banking software portfolio. Wang wanted it badly. With it, he'd not only eliminate his toughest competitor, but also realize his ambition of making Computer Associates the dominant market player, meaning he'd pretty much be able to charge customers whatever price he liked for his software. They were locked in.

In May 1987, he came up with an offer that was 50 percent over market and 45 times earnings. The two companies merged that August.

I'm proud to say that the software we developed at UCC is still setting the pace today, and it's still responsible for a hefty share of CA's annual profits. UCC-1, UCC-7, and UCC-11 are hard at work twenty-four hours a day, seven days a week, deeply embedded in the information technology systems of *Fortune* 5000 businesses and government institutions around the world. If you pulled those three programs out of computers right now, much of the industrialized world would grind to a halt.

Charles Wang and I would do business again, billions of dollars' worth. But when I discovered that he was a crook, I would spend a lot of time, energy, and money throwing him off the CA board.

Chapter 16
Sterling Software

WAYNE GRETZKY, the greatest hockey player ever, used to say that his success on the ice came from a simple philosophy: Don't skate to where the puck is—skate to where the puck is going to be.

For entrepreneurs, that means spotting demand a moment before it bursts forth. You position your company to meet people's needs even before they themselves realize they have those needs. Then, when they do realize it, there you are, ready to solve their problems.

The writing had been on the wall for many years. Don Thomson and I had been talking about how important software was going to be, but that notion didn't hit most Americans until 1977, when Steve Jobs underlined it. That's when he unleashed his Apple II computer on the world, and at a price many individuals could afford. It was an instant success, with its printed circuit motherboard, switching power supply, keyboard, and cassette tape game "Breakout." The only logical conclusion was that to become more than just fancy ways of playing games, computers would need software.

Radio Shack tried to compete with its TRS-80, nicknamed the Trash 80. It sold 10,000 units its first month out, which was more than twice what anyone expected it to sell in an entire year. So it was not just Steve Jobs and Apple who would need software, it was everybody else getting into the business, too. And if there was going to be competition in personal computer hardware, then software would also become a battleground.

My theory played out when the world changed forever with

IBM's entry into the microcomputer fray in 1981. The PC was born and set a new standard for all except those special souls who inhabit the world of Apple. *Time* magazine made the first nonperson its Man of the Year and put a robot-looking PC on its cover.

This was about as far away as you could get from the computer of my school days at Michigan, when machines took up entire rooms and required hordes of people to operate them. If you could afford one of these new personal computers, it was now just you and it—and, best of all, you could play with it at home in your pajamas.

No one knew yet how the PC would affect the business world; big business was still relying on the raw power and speed of massive mainframe machines, and I couldn't see that going away. I knew from my UCC and Datran days that distributed computing would get here, with costs driven down by Moore's Law applied to microchips and digital highways. Since UCC-1 and UCC-2 in the 1960s, we believed software could be a product, but we had estimated a five-year product life, not a product life that would still be robust nearly forty years later, as is the case with much of the software we developed and introduced back then. So in 1981, Don and I began poking around, looking for opportunities in mainframe software, all the time thinking that we could create a "born-again UCC," this time focused on software products, not computing services.

Other people around the country were working on the same thing at the same time. Innovation is often a product of an era—software was what you originally got when you hired people by the hour to be professional coders of a unique program for one company. Now we were designing the same program to run on thousands of computers, ultimately millions. At a very early Sterling management meeting, I heard a startled "Wow" when I put up a chart predicting that software revenue would become much bigger than hardware revenue. Today IBM is more of a services and software company in terms of profit than it is a hardware company, and it becomes more profitable as the Japanese and others drive down hardware prices but cannot do so with software.

I was happy to sidestep the much sexier consumer market for this behind-the-scenes industrial market. And in hindsight, this was pretty indicative of where I was in my life. I'd had all the public success of the American dream before I was thirty-five. I was not looking to get my picture in the papers; I wanted to build another great company and not worry about what others thought. I didn't care if the general public never paid attention to me, as long as our customers, our employees, and our shareholders respected what we did. I'd had enough headlines already for one lifetime. Too much fame in Dallas had already motivated me to buy a vacation home in Malibu, about as far from Dallas as you could get while still being in the United States. In Malibu we could be anonymous. All the local gossip in California was about movie stars, rock stars, and other famous Hollywood people who lived there. We were just some uninteresting folks from Texas.

Gearing myself up for another foray into the software business, I spotted so many budding software entrepreneurs suddenly springing up around the country that they were like mushrooms in an untilled field. That told me that "buy, don't build" was the best approach. We began to believe we could create a tightly bound constellation of entrepreneurial ventures operating inside a single company that would allow great managers the autonomy to manage. There was no reason for us to spend years developing a single high-quality product when we could gather very good products and very good talent and bring them into a single company with good managers. As soon as we owned a product, we invested in the technology to enhance it. This is a growth formula, not a cost-cutting concept. It's creating and building an enterprise.

In those earlier days of University Computing when we developed UCC-1, our first software salesman was a fellow named Sterling Williams. He was a small-town boy raised in rural Oklahoma who came to Texas with degrees in math and physics to work as an aerodynamics engineer for Jimmy Ling at LTV Aerospace. We needed somebody to sell our systems software to technical guys, and he answered our ad. In the years he was with UCC, he impressed me in four different jobs.

He left UCC to run a software company up in Ann Arbor, Michigan. At the height of the oil boom, when I was selling out of our oil refining company, Earth Resources, Sterling's company in Ann Arbor got bought by the French oil services behemoth Schlumberger, who paid for Sterling's company with their stock.

One day a short while later, my phone rang and it was Sterling, who said, "I hear you're starting a new software company."

I said, "That's right, and I want you to come down here and run it."

Sterling was concerned about his newly acquired Schlumberger stock options, which were riding high on the oil boom and doing quite well. He wanted to know what to do with them and I said, "Sell! Grab the money and run."

He asked why. I told him, "Go to Value Line—it lists the stock market valuation of all the big companies—and you'll find Schlumberger at number three in the world. They're a good company with a French name and good Texas well logs, but are they worth almost as much as IBM?"

He cashed out in the nick of time. But it really wasn't my economic prediction that got him. We'd already brought in another ex-UCC-er named Phil Moore, who was a great software developer. I told Sterling, "You and me and Don Thomson and my brother, Charles, and Phil are going to figure out how to create a great company. And you're going to be president."

We didn't talk for more than a few minutes because we didn't have to. I knew there were three things he was looking for in a job—he wanted to have fun, he wanted to learn, and he wanted to have the opportunity to get rich—and I told him, "Here, you got all three."

It was, Sterling often said, the shortest job interview of his life.

Sterling and Phil moved into an empty space in our Bonanza offices, just down the hall from Don, Charles, and me. That way we could hobnob whenever we needed to.

Charles and I put $2 million into a bank account to pay Sterling and Phil, plus outside knowledge workers, and just like that we were a software company. Except we were more like a brain trust because we didn't have any product, we didn't have any customers, and we didn't have a name.

I was very straightforward about how I saw this company developing. We were betting our venture money in order to get us to the point where we could raise capital in public or private markets and make this enterprise work mostly with other people's money. We were not just looking for ways to passively invest but for ways to capitalize and grow the business so that I didn't have to keep putting in new cash forever.

Some entrepreneurs are able to use only their own money and get much richer than if they share the equity upside while at the same time reducing their own risk of loss. But most entrepreneurs who use only their own money end up sitting around broke, reading books about entrepreneurs who understood how to create companies at least partly with other people's money.

When you start with a blank slate, the first thing you need to be is somebody who can create a customer. When I started out with University Computing, I knew that I had to sell something. Then I had to get the capital to fund it. I went through a chicken-and-egg process. I had to make about six different things happen, all at the same time.

This time with Sterling Software was different. We had the idea and knew that the customers were out there, and we had enough capital to make it happen. To get it going I had the advantage of choosing people I already knew and had worked with before. Surrounding yourself with people you already know and trust can give you a real head start. They know how you work and you know how they work. You can finish each other's sentences. So you hit the ground running.

IN THIS RESPECT, I've been lucky in my career. First Charles and then Evan, my older son, have been perfect partners for me. We think alike. We have shared values; we share a belief in looking for the good in people; and we share a high level of spirituality. Each is a very good businessperson, has total integrity, and treats people with decency. And both have sometimes supplied a needed stabilizing conservatism to offset my enthusiasm. They are also both highly literate and read a lot.

Charles and I have been working together since it was our job to wash and wax Dad's '52 Ford.

When your businesses grow and you have boards and company managers, you need someone exactly like Charles to run an orderly board, with audit and compensation committees composed of independent directors who testify to the honesty and integrity of the company. Someone like Charles is capable of saying "no" or "yes" to the managers on behalf of any of the constituencies to whom the company owes obligations. Charles is a great judge of people. He is a great chairman. He is rock-solid and a source of strength and comfort. Like me, when he read Kipling's poem "If" in Mrs. McEachern's high school literature class it made a big impact, so when we meet with either triumph or disaster, he treats these two impostors the same. When we have made a heap of our winnings and risked it, and then lost, he has never breathed a word about his loss.

I can't think of a time when he and I have ever really disagreed. We think along the same lines. While it is important in any company that everyone express his or her own ideas, having a partner who constantly disagrees with you doesn't necessarily create good checks and balances. It means you often check the good stuff. While you are avoiding doing something bad, you may never do anything good.

It's easy to surround yourself with people who will tell you only what you want to hear. Company people need to be comfortable with being honest, with telling you the truth as they see it. Even if you think they're wrong, you need to know. You need to be a simple seeker of truth.

But Charles and I, and later Evan and I, don't believe in running companies autocratically. We believe that enabling people to do good work and giving them the freedom to make their own decisions is the best way to run a company. Trust, but inspect.

Our style in a nutshell is to pick the right people, get in agreement on company goals, pay them well, give them a shot at doing very well, then get out of the way.

We start with trust. If you look for it, you'll nearly always find it, because most people are trustworthy. I've had a couple of disappointments, but that does not change my conviction. Most people want to do the right thing. We all need openness and information and verification in an enterprise, just as in a marriage. People at all levels need to know they're dealing with integrity. Integrity is the single most important quality in a boss. If a boss is not honest, people know it very soon. And they won't be comfortable.

President Franklin Roosevelt said, "The way to make a man trustworthy is to trust him."

THE FIRST CHALLENGE for our Sterling Software brain trust was to put together a shopping list of potential acquisitions. But we weren't going to do anything until we knew exactly why we were doing it, so I asked everybody to take their time, thinking it through: "Don't just do something, sit there."

With UCC, I'd gotten myself into juggling too many plates in the air, and they had all come crashing down when the macroeconomic climate changed. We had bitten off more than we could chew. I preferred not making the same mistake again. I wanted best-of-breed products, talent, and growth potential. If what we had at the point of acquisition was not yet best-of-breed, then at the very least I wanted it to have the potential to be the best once we had invested in the technology and in the marketing innovations to raise it to that level.

It is a rare luxury in business to have guaranteed funding for however long it takes to figure out exactly what you want to be. But without this advantage, would we ever have achieved such companywide excellence? So Sterling and Phil and a few consultants spent a year planning and replanning before we actually acquired anything. Our approach was just like writing and rewriting a book until the author finally has the story and the prose just right. When we did finally make an acquisition, it was one of those best-laid plans of mice and men moments.

We knew what had worked before and what hadn't, and we remembered the struggles we had had at UCC whenever we opted for applications software instead of systems software. Applications software was not as crisply defined, which committed us to the customer to make his accounting, payroll, or human resources system work under unique circumstances. Ultimately, the margins and the growth were less than with systems software. So we said we were going to focus on systems software. But our very first acquisition was a company called Directions—which was banking software—and buying it violated all our carefully laid-out plans. It was in the first bucket on our forbidden list—application software—but we did it anyway.

Eddie Lott owned it, and he and I had a history. University Computing had acquired Eddie's first company; that, too, was banking software. Eddie was a great innovator and manager, his product was fine-tuned, and I knew he would be a good addition to our brain trust. Our agreement with Eddie set the stage for us in many ways. We did not want to use too much of our cash reserves on the first of several buys, so we offered to buy 40 percent for $800,000. We would then have an option to buy the remaining 60 percent out of the proceeds of a public offering. If, after two years, we decided not to buy 60 percent, the 40 percent we had bought would come back to him free.

Eddie jumped at it, saying, "That's the best of both worlds." The financial transactions we used to buy Eddie's company became the model for several acquisition deals.

I love a win-win situation. Because if you figure out a way for everybody to win, you get the best results with the least amount of struggle. It doesn't always work out. But it's a great starting place. Bill Gates did something similar in buying the "digital operating system" (DOS) that was integral to the software he sold to the IBM PC team. It was this product that ultimately gave Microsoft its monopoly power. DOS became the defining operating system and everyone else's software had to sit on Microsoft's DOS, just as mainframes sat on IBM's operating system. In that trade, IBM gave away the crown jewels. IBM's "hardware-centric" mentality blinded them. Owning the operating system and then copying Apple's graphics made Bill Gates the greatest PC interface (Windows) salesman, dominant until Google came along.

Of course, we had yet to name the company. Sterling was getting ready to go to an industry conference in Las Vegas looking for potential acquisitions when he suddenly realized that he could not register for the conference without a company name to put on his badge ("Hi, my name is Sterling Williams, and I'm from... blank"). He went to Don and the two of them settled on Wyly Software. I said, "No; make it Sterling Software." This name flattered Sterling Williams, and the word "sterling" meant something to me.

When I was growing up, my mother never bought plated silver. She explained that we Wylys only bought the highest-quality sterling, even if that meant not buying very much of it. I also knew from reading the history of the British Empire that sterling was a name respected worldwide in currency. If sterling implied "high quality" in silver and in money, then it would easily carry over to our company name as a brand meaning high quality in computer software.

Meanwhile, Sterling and Phil continued to cull through more than 6,000 software products that had suddenly proliferated in the market. We were looking all over the country for companies that might be a good fit. We spotted one in California that had a million in revenue—it turned out to be Oracle. Then there was another one running at a million and a half in Bellevue, Washington, and it turned out to be Microsoft. At least it shows we had good taste! We also looked at the only notable software company on Long Island, Computer Associates, then a $15 million company.

Our intellectual approach to decision making was what we came to call Grad's Grid, a matrix devised by a former IBM-er turned consultant named Burt Grad. While at IBM he had fathered CICS—IBM's great data communications software link to the telephone network, still a vital tool today. Burt was the kind of person who could find order in any amount of chaos. That's how his brain worked.

He had been at General Electric for twenty years making decision tables. Burt saw the world in rows and columns. Grad's Grid showed product types, hardware platforms, required operating systems, industry applicability, product features, and more. By coloring in the squares in the matrix and overlaying that on a strategic model, potential acquisitions

150

could be quickly weeded out or emphasized. It didn't replace the process of due diligence or personal investigation that has to be part of an acquisition, but it was a powerful tool for analysis and synthesis.

It helped us cull our list of 6,000 software products down to 103. We then prioritized the companies making that software into four categories: very high interest, high interest, medium interest, and low interest. We then contacted each company and asked outright if they were interested in selling to us. This was a first. No one had ever come up with a list of companies they wanted to acquire and gone out to ask politely if the company wanted to come along for the ride—before the potential buyers could even afford the prospective company.

After Eddie Lott's company, there were three more we liked. At Software Module Marketing, we bought a convertible debenture that we could convert to equity when we bought 100 percent. Another was Dialacore, but we couldn't afford to buy even a piece of it upfront. Instead, we paid owner Bill Newcomb $20,000 a month for a two-year option to buy the company, exercisable at Bill's price of $12 million.

In the oil world there's something called a "roll-up," in which smaller owners of wells exchange for ownership in a larger partnership that ultimately trades in the public markets. I decided this would work in software. In the end, we did the exact opposite of what is conventionally done. We should have bought the four companies, merged them, and created a new company, written a prospectus for it, and taken it public. "Should," however, has never been a big stumbling block for us. Being "in the box" didn't fit what we wanted to do, so we got it done "outside the box."

We hired a Wall Street underwriter to go to the public equity markets, basically saying, "When we exercise all these options, we will have a company that looks like this." We compiled all that into a prospectus for an IPO of Sterling Software stock to raise the cash to exercise the options.

On May 3, 1983, all we owned was 40 percent of Eddie Lott's company and some options to buy the other three. We didn't own anything else, not one single business. On May 4, we were a company with 100 percent ownership of four businesses, and enough cash in the bank plus the currency of a public stock to keep rolling.

As part of this unusual and innovative way of getting capitalized, we listed the shares on the American Stock Exchange directly, without going over the counter first, as was done by IPOs up until then. Listing on the American gave us an exemption, a loophole, relieving us of having to spend time filing under the "Blue Sky" laws in fifty states. Not only did we break new ground with our software company roll-up; we also broke new ground with the instant exchange listing.

The market loved all this and, within one week, took our share price up from the initial $9 to $15. From there it headed to $30. Along the way, we raised more cash at $17 in what's called a secondary offering. But in June, only thirty days after we'd gone public, the markets ran out of gas and lost their enthusiasm for technology. Prices dropped dramatically and the IPO market was as dry as a pumped-out oil field.

We were one of eighty-five companies on the Morgan Stanley list of technology IPOs in 1983. The next year there were only eight. One of them was Microsoft, but no market was going to stop a battleship like Microsoft from going public. If we hadn't hit the market when we did, we would have suffered during the following seven-year IPO equity drought along with a lot of other wanna-be technology start-ups that never got off the ground. Our timing was perfect.

We had caught the train just as it was leaving the station.

I STEERED Sterling Williams into Peter Drucker's teachings on the practice of management. We admired the decentralized approach of companies like Hewlett-Packard and Minnesota Mining: not top-down but bottom-up. We watched the increasing centralization of IBM. We saw other companies following a centralized approach—like the Seven Dwarfs—and one by one, they were getting blown away. We concluded that everything needed focus.

One of the best preachers of "focus" was Pat Haggerty at Texas Instruments. He built his business entirely on a product-customer focus. While his was a different world of semiconductors and microchips, the same management concepts that worked for Texas Instruments also worked for Hewlett-Packard and for Minnesota Mining.

·We knew this same management model would work for Sterling Software.

To be successful in any enterprise, you need good managers at all levels. Whether you grow through mergers and acquisitions or not, you need good management at all levels. You can't have the attitude in acquisitions that you are the buyer and your job is to fire those people you just bought. You've got to find the best talent that you can, wherever you find it. That means that some of your best people will be found in the companies you're acquiring. How else did a company get to the point where you'd want to own it?

One of the things Sterling and I agreed on right from the beginning was that to follow a business building and growing concept, we couldn't be just a cost-cutting operation. We always had to choose the best products and the best people going forward. We had to be very honest about that. If we were not, it would have become known, and we would not have been a good place to work.

We were a niche business that made money by achieving excellence in our chosen niches. We never tried to be all things to all people, like IBM and Computer Associates, the two really big players in the systems software world at the time. I saw what they were doing, and, for us, it would have been a mistake. Considering that we soon counted 95 of the top 100 banks as customers for our banking software, I think it's fair to say that our strategy was a good one.

We aggressively looked for software companies with two criteria: They were, or could become, important to managers of information technology across all industries, and their products were IBM-compatible. IBM compatibility was paramount in 75 percent of the *Forbes* 5000 companies around the world. So when we saw one we wanted, we moved quickly. To grow a business by acquisition, you need to do several things.

First, you need to integrate quickly and smoothly.

Second, you need to find a way to keep your new employees as passionate about their work as they were before you acquired their company.

Third, you need to clarify your vision, which is central to the first and second things.

Sometimes this vision meant that we sold parts of the companies we acquired. The businesses we had to sell were quickly sold, and the people who didn't have a job any longer were told this as quickly as we determined it, and were then given generous severance packages. There was honesty, no hemming and hawing, no dragged-out decision making, no people wandering around in extended limbo, wondering if they had a job, wondering if their division was going to be dismantled, waiting to be told what to do. Nobody was making water-cooler jokes like, "How green is your parachute?"

We developed a unique collaborative acquisition process. The acquisition team would meet in our Crescent Court offices, owned by Caroline Hunt, one of H. L. Hunt's nine children. Across the street is Caroline's hotel, where we housed company managers from all over the world for as long as a month. We took the company apart and put it back together again with a wary eye on competitors and the strengths and weaknesses of their products versus ours, trying hard to see that the right person was in the right job. Once, when I was on a break with one of our best and brightest—Caroline Rook, with her British accent—she told me that the sessions were so grueling that she had not eaten or slept outside the building for a month. But never, ever had she had a more exhilarating experience.

By interviewing and really listening to the folks coming in, we settled beforehand on what needed to be done once the deal was final. From day one, we wanted all our employees, including those from the newly acquired company, to know that being a Sterling Software employee was something special. And right down to "Sterling Software, Inc.," signs on all our "new" offices worldwide, new business cards with new titles for all our sales and management teams, and every office phone answered with a professional "Sterling Software," we presented a new, fully integrated company to our customers on the first day following the close of the acquisition.

Then we got on with the work of selling software. There was no deadwood at Sterling Software. Every division really belonged, and most of us there really wanted to be there.

Because human capital is what's vital to any business, you need to give your key players a lot of independence. I've noticed over the years that people who are really good at what they do want to be left alone to do it, and that if you start mucking with their ability to do their thing, you're going to kill their enthusiasm.

We built a structure and a culture that allowed key players plenty of autonomy to make their own decisions and do their jobs. When they accomplished that, they felt appreciated and had solid economic rewards. Good pay for good work.

Right from the start, I was insistent that Sterling Software headquarters should be small, lean, and mean. We pushed all the corporate functions as far down in the organization as possible, except for treasury, cash management, investor relations, and auditing. We wanted to think of ourselves as individual teams of entrepreneurs rather than one big herd of businesspeople. I wanted focused teams running individual units as if they were owners. Each unit had its own computer support system and its own personnel officer. Each unit made decisions almost totally independently of other units in the company.

Managers of acquired companies even had a charter to pursue their own acquisitions. We centralized accountability, performance, strategy, and financial planning, but tactical and operational decisions were made on the basis of who was closest to the customer and what was best for the customer.

In the age of "synergy," we erred on the side of entrepreneurial structure and autonomy.

We kept track of what was going on, without micromanaging, partly by setting up a sophisticated centralized monthly reporting system. Profit and loss responsibility was decentralized but had headquarters' oversight.

The one area where we ruled from the top was strategic planning. Every quarter, we dragged all the independent business unit managers kicking and screaming into a room to present their performance against their plan. Sterling and his team would force managers to justify, rethink, and refine every line of their presentation. There was no place to hide. Those sessions were pretty intense and, at times, seemed brutal. You could feel the angst in the room, especially on the part of the presenters. Anyone who had a smooth story with no substance never tried that twice because Sterling refused to listen to any managerial bull from anyone. He insisted that managers do their homework, and he made them justify each route they were taking. When a manager proved that he knew what he was doing, Sterling congratulated him and sent him back to Boston or Frankfurt. If a manager failed to convince Sterling of the logic of his actions, if his numbers were off, with no believable get-well plan, well, that wasn't so pretty.

This managerial approach was a great training ground for executives. Men and women walked out of that room with ownership. Almost no one who was part of those sessions, no matter how temporarily bruised and battered, wasn't glad afterward, because once you'd been raked over the coals and forced to really sign up for your own plan, you had ownership.

In a way, Sterling was like some old-fashioned mother ladling cod liver oil down her coughing children's throats. It may not have been fun for the kids, but it sure improved their health.

He brought out the best in everyone.

Then, too, being brutally honest with yourself about what you're doing and why you're doing it is important in all areas of life.

PROOF THAT WE were doing a good job was the way companies in our industry saw us when we came knocking on their doors.

Eddie Lott became our ambassador to potential acquisitions and he traveled the country, reassuring key people at these places that Sterling Software was different. More and more small software companies were facing the dilemma of selling out or remaining private and taking their chances at not being blown away by the likes of IBM or Microsoft or, later, Google. Eddie would explain to them our entrepreneurial model, set out the risks of going public by themselves, and clarify the new roles they would find themselves playing as part of our company.

In many different ways, we asked, "Is it a fit?" We developed a set of simple principles to follow. It had to fit strategically. We looked closely at their products and services to see how they worked together and how they would work with what we already had. We asked questions like, "What's the future for them in products and marketing? Who is or will be the competition?" Our competitive surveillance was good. Some announced products were really phantoms, just false fears of competitors' breakthroughs that never materialized.

Mostly we saw each company as a separate entity and tried to keep their key personnel in place if we could. Our deal would nearly always make the top folks rich, and we wanted the key players to stay motivated even if they were now millionaires and didn't have to work. Most did stay motivated because they loved the work.

We were looking for synergy, but we were not buying for synergy. We were buying for coverage. We were trying to find areas of opportunity and occupy them.

We weren't crusaders. We weren't techy execs who could write simultaneous equations in machine language. We understood the technology, but we weren't obsessed with the most elegant computer code. As Burt Grad put it, "We were the first computer software company that was planned, started, and run by business managers." We could see with precision and clarity how to steer our company without having egos clash. We were focused on creating customers through marketing and innovation.

It became clear to the companies we wanted to buy who we were and what we wanted to do. They could also see that we knew where we wanted to go and knew how to get there. So most of them were happy to come along. Over a period of eighteen years, Sterling Software acquired thirty-five companies. Only one was hostile.

But that was the big one.

Chapter 17

Money's Not Scarce

B Y THE MID-1980s, the computer boom was taking the country by storm. Sterling Software was doing so well—providing businesses with strong storage management and data communications products—that we were among the top fifty software makers in the country. Three years after start-up, we had $12 million cash in the bank and $20 million in revenue, and the stock market valued us at around $30 million. The brokers and the analysts were saying that we were respectable.

Who wants to be respectable?

I never liked being just one of the crowd, even a small crowd. In the competitive marketplace, if you're going to pour your heart and soul into a company, then you want that company to rise to the top, because being an entrepreneur isn't about making money. There are easier ways to make money. Being an entrepreneur is about creating an enterprise, it's about building, it's about winning, and it's about the quality of the journey—my definition of success.

We wanted to be one of America's fastest-growing companies, to be one of the best investments, and to be a good place to work. I wanted to create more millionaires. I wanted people to whistle when they thought of Sterling Software, the way you whistle when you see flawless design. I wanted the feeling of quality that Mama exuded when she held up a cherished piece of her silverware and said, "It's sterling silver."

To make that happen, you first have to see the opportunities. And they don't always have "opportunity" written across the front of them, like a college sweatshirt—sometimes you need to be "bodacious." That is what Texas oil wildcatters call it—"bold" and "audacious" put together—and, of course, it has to be said with a Southern drawl. Bodacious ain't easy, and it needs to be accompanied by a lack of fear because sometimes creating companies can get real scary.

In 1982, Sterling Williams was wandering through the crowded halls of the annual computer convention in San Diego when he ran into Werner Frank. Werner was then about sixty years old and thought of himself as semi-retired, but he knew software well, having earned his stripes working with the legendary computer scientist John von Neumann, a refugee from Nazi Germany. A mathematical genius, Werner worked on secret U.S. Army "command and control" computer projects and was one of the founders of Informatics, in California's San Fernando Valley. They had about $200 million in annual revenues—enough to make them one of the three biggest software companies in the country. Running into each other at the convention, Sterling and Werner talked for a long time about the good old days, and what was going on in the industry, and about their mutual discomfort with Werner's partner, Walter Bauer, the CEO of Informatics.

Bauer was a man with white hair brushed back impeccably and large-framed glasses, a few years older than Werner, who looked more like an actor sent from Central Casting to play the part of elder statesman. He was difficult, having earned the reputation both inside and out, for autocratic and stingy management. To most, he broadcasted an air of intellectual superiority, but his insecurity quickly surfaced when in the company of someone as amazingly brilliant as Werner Frank. Disenchanted with Bauer, Werner told Sterling that he was leaving Informatics to become a consultant. Instantly, Sterling said, "I want to be your first customer."

Informatics was founded as a computer outsourcing firm but expanded into software products. They had done an IPO, then sold the company to the insurance giant Equitable Life in what proved to be a dysfunctional marriage, and then IPO'ed again.

159

As a result, the company had lots of cash in the bank and no debt. But Informatics' stock price was not only depressed, it was also erratic—something shareholders hate. The closer I looked at it, I could see good businesses buried inside. For example, they had an excellent report writer for the IBM/360 called Mark IV. It was legendary software, the first independent IBM product to reach $100 million of cumulative revenue, but they had never followed it with the next software product. There was no encore. I wanted to own Informatics, but they were ten times bigger than us. No one in the industry could imagine a takeover of a company ten times their own size. Bauer knew that Werner was working with us, so he called him to see if we would be interested in buying a software product that he wanted to divest. Sterling agreed to meet Bauer over dinner in Los Angeles.

The two sat and talked like old friends for a while, until Bauer shifted the conversation. He asked Sterling, "What would you boys think if Informatics was interested in taking over your company?"

Sterling's first thought was, "Not a hell of a lot," because here was a guy we were looking at, who was looking back at us, and now is getting ready to buy this $20 million company out from under us before we even had a chance to get going. His second thought was more to the point: "Bullshit!" That is when Bauer upped the ante. He told Sterling, "The best thing about us taking over your company would be that you'd run it, plus the rest of Informatics, reporting only to me." Sterling was ambitious and loved being captain of his own ship, but he kept thinking that this wasn't very ethical.

As soon as he got back to his hotel room, he faxed me this handwritten note: "Sam, I met with Walter and here is what he said: It turned out he didn't want us to buy his products. He wanted to buy our products. Then he really wanted to buy our company. But he also said that he would have me run all of it, and I'm not even sure he wanted to buy the company. I think he was really recruiting at the end of the day. So what do you think we ought to do? Sterling."

I resented Bauer's bad behavior, while cherishing Sterling's loyalty. Where I grew up, they used to hang horse thieves. I wrote three words on the same memo and faxed it back to Sterling: "Let's buy them!"

The phone rang. Sterling said, "Are you serious?"

I said, "Absolutely."

Bauer had declared war, so instead of retreating, or mounting a hasty defense—everyone who ever played football knows that sometimes the best defense is a good offense—we were going to take the war right back to him.

The next morning, in the cold light of day, it seemed like an impulsive decision. Over the years, people have commented that my decisions often seem instantaneous. I will admit that sometimes once they pop out of my head and go into the world, they take me by surprise, too. In reality, they are not instantaneous. They are the result of a lot of internal brewing and information retrieval. I analyze and synthesize large amounts of data. I look for alternative visions. Everyone can relate to walking along, daydreaming, without knowing how much you have been mulling over something—how many ideas and bits of data you have been absorbing—and suddenly there's a precipitous "That's it."

Bauer's words served as the kick in the butt to push me down a path I had been hankering to take anyway. I had been impatient to move Sterling Software up the food chain. I believed Informatics was ripe for picking, and that we could make it into an extraordinarily good fit. What's more, I was beginning to realize that the two factors that made such an acquisition appear impossible—their whopping size advantage over us and the conventional wisdom on Wall Street that hostile takeovers did not apply to the computer software industry—were not insurmountable.

Bodacious? Yes.

Impossible? No.

I knew this was going to get nasty. Hostile takeovers were simply not done in the software industry because the conventional wisdom was that such a takeover would drive away all the talented and knowledgeable people, leaving nothing but an empty corporate shell of a company. Software developers were a rare breed, and if you had a good group, you were dependent on them. It had never been done, so the law according to Wall Street went, "You can't go hostile to a company where the assets go down the elevator and out the front door every day."

I agreed on who the assets were, but saw that Wall Street missed something big. From the first time I heard the term "hostile takeover," my reaction was, "Hostile to whom?" The way I saw it, most often it's hostile only to the entrenched powers, the top executives and board members. I kept asking myself, "What if you treat the employees well? What if you create a better work environment? What if you build a better business? Can you be a conqueror and a liberator at the same time?" Both roles appealed to me, so we started putting together an army to do battle.

The first thing to do was buy some Informatics stock. This meant, even if we lost the bid, we would still make money off the run-up of the share price—which would likely happen as soon as news got out and another buyer proposed to pay a higher price. We began by buying stock quietly on the open market. Going after a company ten times your size means you need a lot of leverage. We did not have enough equity, so no bank lender was going to back us. I knew the one and only place that would appreciate what we were trying to do, and could assemble the leverage we needed, was Drexel Burnham. I phoned Peter Ackerman and set up an appointment with him and his boss, Mike Milken.

By the time Mike hit forty, in 1986, he was being called every name under the sun, from "economic genius" to "the most powerful man since J. P. Morgan himself" to "the man who epitomizes the decade of greed," but most of all he was being called "The Junk Bond King."

A brilliant guy who had graduated summa cum laude from Berkeley, Mike, while getting an MBA from the Wharton School at the University of Pennsylvania, took the bus to Manhattan to work for a Wall Street brokerage that eventually became Drexel Burnham. By 1973, he had created their non-investment-grade bond department. His ability to bring in 100 percent returns on investment made him a multimillionaire by his thirtieth birthday.

Over the next ten years, he and a small team literally invented a new class of high-yield debt, and with it Mike and his team almost single-handedly fueled the leveraged-buyout boom during the 1980s. That wasn't what Mike had set out to do in the 1970s, however. His bonds paid very high returns because of the perception of a very high risk of default.

Although these bonds eventually became known as a favored tool for leveraged-buyout specialists in the 1980s, Mike's original goal was different. He wanted to provide access to capital for growing companies that needed financing to expand and create jobs. Most of these companies lacked the "investment-grade" bond ratings required before the big financial institutions would back them. Mike knew that non-investment-grade (a k a "junk") companies create virtually all new jobs, and he believed that helping these companies grow strengthened the American economy and created good jobs for American workers.

It was by studying credit history at Berkeley in the 1960s that Mike developed his first great insight. He found that while there could be significant risk in any one high-yield bond, a carefully constructed portfolio of these assets produced a consistently better return over the long run than supposedly "safe" investment-grade debt. This was proved during the two decades of the 1970s and '80s when returns on high-yield bonds topped all other asset classes. Mike saw a great opportunity when he realized that the perception of default risk far exceeded the reality. In fact, these bonds had a surprisingly low-risk profile when adjusted for the potential returns.

After twenty years of superior gains, the high-yield bond market finally fell in 1990. Actually, it didn't fall—it was pushed by unwise government regulation that forced institutions to sell their bonds. The dip only lasted a year, however, with the market roaring back 46 percent in 1991.

Mike's competitors—Goldman Sachs, Morgan Stanley, and Credit Suisse First Boston, the old oligopolies of the syndication business—labeled them "junk bonds" to disparage Mike's brainchild. He was not a member of their white-shoe club and they were not going to take his act lying down. Of course, today Goldman, Morgan, and Credit Suisse make much of their money off the same kind of bonds, and Mike's former protégés run most of that business for them. Actually, this stuff was nothing new. This "less than investment-grade debt" not only had been floating around the markets since the Great Depression but had served way back when to finance George Washington's canals and Abraham Lincoln's railroads. In truth, at the time Mike reintroduced them, they were perceived to be below the quality standard of the big pension and mutual fund portfolios. Mike just did his homework better than anyone else, and found real bargains in these bonds. He then created, as an entrepreneur within Drexel, a fabulous business with underwriting fees by finding companies that could usually pay back the interest and the debt.

The first time I walked in his door, Mike was just getting started and had only twelve people working for him. Once he got rolling, the fees he brought into Drexel grew from $1.2 million to over $4 billion. Mike moved his high-yield bond business from New York to California so his kids could know their ailing grandfather, who was battling cancer. But his team was a shop within a shop; they were still at Drexel, sort of, just taking a bigger chunk for themselves. Then Rudy Giuliani, the United States Attorney for the Southern District of New York in 1989, charged Mike with racketeering and fraud and indicted him.

Most of the activities they charged Mike with had not previously been considered crimes, and prosecutions of that kind are no longer done. Giuliani loved the high-profile case because he saw it as his ticket to becoming mayor of New York and eventually a presidential candidate. Mike agreed in a plea bargain to six securities and reporting violations and was sentenced to ten years in prison. He served twenty-two months.

Mike had supported education and medical research through his philanthropies ever since the 1970s. But once he got out of prison, in addition to resuming his charitable work he started investing in for-profit educational programs. We Wylys invested in "K–12," his online tools for "virtual schooling," a self-learning system used for home schooling and in public schools. This passion grew out of his days at Drexel, when he taught math at a disadvantaged urban school. His conviction, then and now, is that the involvement of a parent (or a grandmother or aunt or neighbor) gets kids started on the right path. As a productivity tool for kids, K–12's mission helps them do just that.

I'd watched over the years as Mike and others put deals together, first for $20 million, then for $100 million, then for $1 billion. They were brilliant entrepreneurs who completely changed the playing field for us smaller guys. Mike was the one who enabled the Davids to beat the Goliaths; he developed financial leveraging tools for them, just like David's slingshot. He said, "Money's not scarce; good managers are scarce." He got us the capital to take on the big boys. Just like my Texas friend T. Boone Pickens, who shattered the "unshatterable" market rule that you can't take over a company with a capitalization of more than $1 billion. Until then, Mike had made headlines by coming up with $20 million for George Griffin, who was Jimmy Ling's CEO. Mike and his team made headlines again when they got Bill McGowan $100 million to build MCI. As Peter Ackerman told me, "Our world changed when Boone walked in."

No one had ever raised $1 billion before, or even dared to do with it what Boone was trying to do with his tiny company, Mesa Petroleum. Boone was going to buy Gulf Oil, one of the "seven sisters." Brilliant Boone had discerned that it was cheaper to buy a barrel of oil on Wall Street than to drill a barrel.

Like the ghost of Jimmy Ling, Boone was an independent oil guy out of Amarillo, Texas, whose company was sometimes pretty good at exploration. But in the early 1970s, when oil was $12 a barrel, Boone had himself a whole mess of dry holes and some wells that weren't coming in fast enough and it was costing him $15 a barrel just to bring it in. He had all this debt and all the financial measures of a company on its way to bankruptcy court. He came to Charles and me pitching a partnership investment. We said, "Boone, you've got to go to Drexel. Only they can do it for you." So he went to see Mike Milken and Peter Ackerman in Beverly Hills and told them he needed money to buy Gulf Oil.

Here was a guy struggling to survive, and now he wanted to go for one of the famous "seven sisters" of the oil business. Nothing was impossible anymore.

Mike put together an underwriting syndicate for Boone. My brother, Charles, and I subscribed as equity investors. Boone started buying, the top managers at Gulf started panicking, and eventually sold to another of the seven sisters, Chevron. In the meantime, Boone, Mike, and the rest of us made good money on the higher share price. I was amused and delighted that Mike was thumbing his nose at the banking and Wall Street establishment. White-shoe firms like First Boston and Morgan Stanley wouldn't do such a disruptive thing for fear of losing their historic place in the Goliath syndicates that gave the Wall Street partners annuities without having to do much work. They envied Drexel's big fees for boldly venturing where they feared to tread.

Of course, today that's how Morgan Stanley and J. P. Morgan make their big fees. They sold $4 billion in junk bonds so that our Michaels Arts and Crafts store chain could suddenly get $6 billion in an October 2006 buyout. The debt proceeds were added to the heft of two giant firms in private equity, Steve Schwartzman's Blackstone and Mitt Romney's Bain, who came up with $1 billion each. So Milken's original sin is now the Morgan's and Goldman's holy grail.

Boone, Mike, and Peter rewrote the rulebooks and made room for people like Jimmy Goldsmith in London and the Bass brothers in Ft. Worth to take on the corporate giants. The Bass brothers (Sid, Perry, Robert, and Lee) inherited the fortune of their wildcatter uncle, Sid Richardson. They hired a gun-slinger named Richard Rainwater, having seen what Boone did, and went after another of the seven sisters, Texaco.

I loved it when Rainwater walked around Ft. Worth wearing his Texaco baseball hat, the one with the star on the front, just like the guys who pumped gas at the station, singing their

TV ad jingle: "You can trust your car to the man who wears the star."

The Basses worked a technique called "greenmail." So did Jimmy Goldsmith. The term derives from the word "black-mail," and is yet another Wall Street–lawyer created word intended to have a negative labeling effect, but to me there is nothing wrong with greenmail. It's just another small part of Adam Smith's free markets, but so is the defense lawyer's effort to attach a negative label to it. The Bass brothers bought Marathon and then Texaco shares and announced that they were going to take over the companies and that when they did, they were going to fire the senior managers and the board. The senior managers and the board panicked and found someone else to buy the shares from the Bass brothers at a premium over the market price. Academic economists think this financial stratagem is a good thing, but some institutional investors have a knee-jerk negative reaction to it. But that's the way markets work. The Bass family made a $478 million profit on their "failed" bid.

The world owes a debt of gratitude to Mike Milken and his creative team. Did some people go too far? Yes. Did some of them take advantage of the freer flow of capital and end up doing more damage than good? Sure. But markets are messy. Major shifts in the flow of capital often lead to periods of excess before the pendulum swings back and equilibrium is restored. Mike Milken and his team made a major contribution to today's market atmosphere of high liquidity, which in turn has also helped lift the world's poor out of poverty. Today the Grameen Bank in Bangladesh has created microloans for mothers living on $2 a day. And that won Grameen the Nobel Prize. The Nobel Committee didn't call microloans "junk" debt.

I PERSONALLY FOUND the anything-is-possible business mood created in the '80s exhilarating, similar to what my pioneer corn-farmer, cotton-planter grandfathers must have felt when their covered wagons reached the deep, rich soil of the Mississippi River Delta land.

And I was hankering to own Informatics.

Being outgunned 10 to 1 meant I needed an army of my own. The minute that Mike and Peter got on board (Drexel signed up for $140 million), the fight was on. In five days, we bought enough shares to put us at just under 10 percent.

Later, when this battle was all over and I was visiting with the woman who had been Walter Bauer's secretary, she said that the day she walked into his inner office and told him, "Sam Wyly is calling," he looked up and said, "This is it!"

The day we published to the world what we were doing, I explained it face-to-face to Bauer. I'd heard the expression "pale behind his suntan" but I'd never really known what it meant until that moment. I saw the blood drain from Bauer's face. "We own 9.9 percent as of yesterday," I told him, "and we're gonna buy the whole company, so why don't you and I work out doing it in a 'friendly' way?"

That was at the end of breakfast. Bauer was not going to let these *poco loco* upstarts from Texas have his very own company, and so things turned nasty quick.

In fact, the software industry (the old hands, not the young bucks) was in an uproar. The industry was very insular in those days—everyone at the top knew everyone else at the top—and many people thought what we were doing was just terrible. Not the gentlemanly thing to do. Some were afraid of change and did not understand that a takeover could mean liberation. Hand-in-hand with being audacious means you can't get paralyzed about what other people say about you, so we moved our executives from Dallas to a hotel in Los Angeles and set up a war room. We brought in computers and multiple phone and fax lines.

Mounting a takeover, I wasn't always sure what to expect, and it surprised me when people came out of the woodwork with some service to provide in exchange for a fee. It became a feeding frenzy of the professional classes. We had to hire lawyers, accountants, and press relations folks, and they would all cost a lot whether we won or lost. I figured that if some competitor outbid us, at least we'd make enough profit on our 9.9 percent to pay the expenses. The same thing happened when I had bid to take over Western Union with University Computing, and you'll remember we ultimately lost that contest because of a monopoly-protecting law passed by the State of New York. But we were able to recover our out-of-pocket costs by selling our toehold shares into a higher market. It was the very market we created by pointing out to the world the hidden digital values in Western Union's ancient copper wires, which had been laid along the railroad tracks from New York to San Francisco. The oldest hardware displayed in the computer exhibit at the Smithsonian is a telegraph. These copper wire rights-of-way would ultimately become fiber-optics-bearing data pipelines.

The halls outside our rooms were a constant blur of people coming and going, rushing in with new data, rushing out with messages to deliver. Room service trays piled up outside the door. Coffee cups accumulated on every available surface and crumpled pieces of paper and soda cans collected on the carpeting. The maids would come in and clean every evening, and then the piles would build up all over again the next morning.

To fight back, Bauer ran full-page ads in the *New York Times* saying what a bad guy I was.

In the middle of this, Bauer and a few Informatics executives tried to put together a management buyout. They tried to find another company to come in as a white knight, to save the company from us Genghis Khans.

We made our first bid when Informatics' shares were hovering around $17, and invited the Informatics incumbents to discuss their own attempted buyout. Bauer led them into the room, thinking he could walk away with the company. But when Peter Ackerman spelled out to them how ironclad our financing was, and it sank in for them that no one had committed that kind of capital to them, or would commit it, they gave up.

No sooner had that happened when an investment company, Maxxam, announced that they had been buying Informatics shares. Whether they were really interested in owning the company or just trying to make a quick buck as arbitragers, I couldn't tell. But it definitely added to the drama.

Maxxam filed the day after Informatics rejected our bid, and now the share price was up to $24 and they announced their bid for Informatics.

What I didn't know was that Maxxam's bid was an illusion. They were just trading the stock.

That only served to up the ante for Bauer, since we could sell our 9.9 percent toehold for profit. If we went away and nobody else came in to buy the company, the price would drop from $24 to $17 or $15 or $12, or maybe even lower. No one knew where the bottom would be.

Bauer had a couple of independent directors on his board, and one of them, Fred Carr, kept saying to Bauer, "I don't hear any other bids. Are you going to buy it yourself? If so, do it."

He couldn't do it, because capital seeks good managers and avoids the opposite.

Bauer called in his top managers and told them, "I want everybody to put in some of your savings." One of his best managers thought to himself, "Under this leadership? You've got to be kidding."

From start to finish, this whole drama took about six months. We wrote the checks and only then realized that we had done what no one else had ever done in the software industry. Little Sterling Software had gobbled up a giant and was now a major player.

Informatics had been run from the top down. Here's a story typical of the way the company worked. They had a trainer at headquarters who was told to educate the troops at the Federal Systems Division in northern California, which was run by Geno Tolari, a tough-minded football player from Pittsburgh. When the trainer arrived and announced, "I'm here to train your people," Geno shot back, "You can't train my people."

The trainer got haughty. After all, he was from headquarters. "I'm the education department. I train your people."

But Geno insisted, "You can't train my people because you don't know what they do."

So now the trainer asked, "Okay, what do they do?"

Geno answered, "I don't know."

The trainer thought Geno was joking with him, and insisted, "I'm the trainer; I need to know what they do."

That's when Geno confessed, "I can't tell you because I don't know. They're under a mountain in Omaha, and it's a military secret, and the Air Force won't tell us what they do."

We put a stop to that headquarters attitude by running the company from the bottom up. Only three out of the eighty-five headquarters employees ended up at our Dallas headquarters. One who stayed, Jeanette Meier, was later written up in the *Dallas Morning News* as the highest-paid woman in town. After a few years of our ownership and growth-oriented management, I went to Columbus, Ohio, where many of the electronic commerce software developers worked. One fellow riding the elevator with me asked, "Do you know how many people worked here when you bought us?"

"Nope."

"About thirty," he said. "And do you know how many people we hired this year alone?"

"Nope."

"Three hundred."

So much for a mass exodus.

Of the 400 people in Informatics' Military Division, not a single person was laid off. Manager Geno Tolari gave us a good laugh when we asked him, "What would help your business?" and he answered, "A good war!" We pushed work functions down into the divisions where the customer and product creation happened and then oversaw the operations of these independent divisions from our very skinny headquarters in Dallas. We now had 2,500 people and 87 products, and we combined them neatly into divisions.

In five months, we sold off three divisions for $34 million, which we used to help pay down our takeover debt. We paid off the rest of the debt, which had originally had a 17 percent cost, by replacing it with new convertible debt at 8 percent.

As I had been convinced it would, our Sterling Software stock was being bid up on the public markets. Equity market players began to see the growth potential and to believe in the quality of our team of managers and the simple beauty of the way our enterprise was working. These very conservative folks, none of whom would have bet that we could pull this off, began to smile secretly at our audaciousness and cheer for us. In two major moves, we managed to save $10 million in annual carrying costs and double our cash reserves.

By the end of the following summer, in 1986, we were reorganized and refinanced.

I look back in wonder at how smoothly that all went. To this day, it still serves as a lesson for me in thinking ahead, in being organized, and in anticipating employees' and customers' anxiety before they've even had a chance to surface.

We knew that Informatics customers had been watching this deal with as much concern as Informatics employees. We also knew from the beginning that we would have to allay their fears. So, for months before the deal closed, we made elaborate plans for a seamless transition.

I knew what those customers and those employees were thinking: Who are these guys? How could that runt of a company possibly acquire an industry giant, absorb it, and make it all work?

Their concerns were legitimate, all the more so when you understand that 60 percent of all acquisitions fail.

I made sure we were ready for them.

Instead of waiting for people to come to us with their fears and their complaints, we went to them with outstretched hands and big smiles. We ran full-page ads in the industry journals introducing our vision and ourselves. We sought out and talked to all the key people. We explained who we were and what we were doing.

The moment we took control of Informatics, we already had new business cards and stationery printed. Then we left each business unit where it was geographically, and made sure the same people were there answering the same phones, their voices radiating genuine Sterling Software confidence in their new leadership.

In other words, we stopped problems before they could start.

Sterling Software became famous for its ability to digest an acquisition smoothly. We bought a total of thirty-five small and large companies over seventeen years, and Informatics was our template. It was a lesson in being proactive rather than being reactive.

My initial investment was less than $2 million. We sold out in March 2000, at the very peak of the tech and telecom stock market boom, for a price per share that was 30 percent over the market. The total sale package was $8 billion. A fruitful journey.

Fearless got us into the game.

Bodacious won it.

Chapter 18

Never Let Your Pocketbook Tell You What You Can Do

M AMA USED TO SAY, "I am firm. You are stubborn. She is pigheaded."

I can be stubborn, real stubborn, and somebody else might see that as being pigheaded. I claim that I come by it naturally because some of my backcountry Scots-Irish relatives were known for their sheer cussedness. Stubborn can be either a blessing or a curse. When you are an entrepreneur, you need to be a more blessed stubborn than a cussed stubborn. As the gambler sings, you've got to know when to hold 'em and that can be a really tough call when all around you are saying, fold 'em.

Knowing when to go and when to stay is one way you win big. If you know when to get out of the game, you can usually avoid disaster and, maybe sometimes, even destitution. In entrepreneurship, in investing, and for that matter, in much of life, you have to accentuate the upside while still defending against the downside, and try to do it in an unemotional way. When emotions creep into decisions, it is easy to confuse good decision making with sweet dreams of being a hero, or alternately, bad dreams of being a quitter.

Of course, we all love to win and acknowledging defeat ain't fun. I can still hear Winston Churchill, *Time's* Man of the Century, urging the British, who were suffering from the Nazis' nightly bombings: "Never give in, never give in, never, never, never!" The thing is that winning requires hard, clear thinking, and not losing requires exactly the same; and neither has anything to do with becoming a hero or being a quitter. Sometimes, though, both have to do with being stubborn, and being stubborn when I'm running into a brick wall has more than once been bruising.

The first time I tried to create that sweet spot where the computer marries the telephone, we lost $100 million of my own and other people's money and eight years of hard work. The second time, with the same goal in mind, we lost only $10 million and four years. The third time we turned $1 million into $2 billion.

We knew the marriage of the telephone and the computer would happen eventually and that we would be instrumental in making it happen. I was thinking, "We're gonna change the world." We ultimately did. But by then I'd been banging into brick walls and seeking an economic reward for a quarter of a century.

By the mid-1980s, there was still no way for most businesses to marry their computers and their telephones in a really effective and efficient manner. The demand for that marriage was accelerating because the march of technology had moved us generations ahead from the mainframe computer at a $3 million cost, to the minicomputer at a $100,000 cost, to the personal computer at a $1,000 cost. By 1986, more than 300,000 new computers were landing on people's desks every week; not only was this happening in offices, but now they were showing up in homes, set up in living rooms and dens and kids' rooms. That weekly rate of new computer proliferation would increase every year for the next fifteen years, until by 2001 there were more computers in American homes than there were televisions. As I write, in 2007, a billion new personal computers and cell phones will be added worldwide in the next year. The beat goes on.

My personal design engineering or programming contribution to the history of the computer is virtually zero. For the most part, I have been a blunt pencil architect. Which happens to be a pretty good definition of what an entrepreneur does. A blunt pencil architect sees all the way to the horizon, finds the people who have the technical and marketing skills to get there, encourages them, and, as quickly as possible, gets out of their way. The more successful blunt pencil architects in this game play to win. They have a genuine talent for simplifying complexity and a gut sense for where the puck is going to be. And they are stubborn when they feel they know something for sure.

That's why, when we set out to buy Informatics, I started poking around. Informatics was a data conglomerate composed of ten different divisions, each strategically unrelated to any other. Like a kid finding ten old trunks in an attic, I couldn't believe my luck when deep in a dark corner, I spotted a tiny but flawless jewel named OrderNet.

The biggest division, which was also the cleanest fit with our Sterling Software products strategy and the one that got all the publicity, was the Mark IV. I'm not sure CEO Bauer even knew that OrderNet existed. It was a small division focused on supply chain technology; primarily, it was a service business that facilitated online purchase orders and invoices, mainly for the pharmaceutical industry. Financially, it was insignificant. It had grown bottom up and was buried inside the much larger wholesale data-processing business in Columbus, Ohio, run by Warner Blow. Out of Informatics' yearly revenue of $200 million, OrderNet accounted for less than a million. It was the runt of the litter.

But I looked at OrderNet and saw Datran and NetAmerica all over again. I saw a massive opportunity that married the telephone and the computer.

Up in Ohio, Warner Blow seemed resigned to wait for the ax to drop from his new owner, figuring that his whole Columbus operation did not fit into our company's software product focus and that we'd sell it off to pay down the Drexel debt. Normally, he would have been right, because software products were our focus.

OrderNet converted standard business documents—purchase orders and invoices—into digital images, sent them over telecommunications networks to trading partners, then converted the images back into standard documents at the other end. Known in those days as "electronic data interchange" (EDI), this was software aimed right at my sweet spot.

Unknown and unloved, OrderNet was my one pearl of great price hidden deep inside the Informatics oyster shell.

With $140 million worth of Mike Milken and Peter Acker-man–placed debt, Peter was all over us. It was his mission to see that Sterling Williams and I got this job done, because our enormous interest costs left little room for error. After all, the Drexel bond buyers needed to know that their money would make a safe round trip.

We were constantly analyzing which parts of Informatics we were going to sell off, but OrderNet was never on that list. I had quickly decided I wanted to make it grow exponentially, even if we had to sell all nine of the other divisions to own it. So we met with our new team in Columbus, Ohio, and committed to back OrderNet's rapid growth in the big, wide world. We were sure that what was already working would grease the skids for our entrance into multiple industries, and that's exactly what happened. At the top of our "must-do" list of objectives was to write industry-specific software protocols and to hire and train industry-knowledgeable sales reps.

Our first contract outside the pharmaceutical industry was with a supermarket chain called Topco. That was a big break-through because almost immediately after, we signed up the much bigger Kroger Supermarket chain, with 1,500 stores in thirty-eight states.

We then bought a software program called Gentran, which translated documents into EDI-standard formats, so our customers could buy a software product from us and do it for themselves. They could now choose between buying our service or buying our software product to run their own computers. We adapted it for both IBM mainframes and midrange computers, and added database and network services.

Next, taking a page out of Ray Kroc's playbook at McDonald's, we created "EDI University" to teach customers how to form better relationships with their trading partners. Once our customers became thoroughly educated in our technology, they were with us forever.

We spent the rest of the 1980s signing up customers all over America.

Our biggest day was the day Wal-Mart signed up. We now had as a customer the greatest retailing entrepreneurial creation of the twentieth century. Soon thereafter JC Penney became our one-thousandth Sterling Commerce EDI partner, transmitting a million documents a month.

This was back around 1986. We'd hardly finished digesting Informatics and were busy getting OrderNet up and running when we set out to scour the nation for start-up software outfits. As I mentioned earlier, one in particular that interested us was a little outfit in Seattle that didn't return phone calls. That was Microsoft.

There was, however, a really big fish that got away, one that would have made us a genuine giant, instantly.

Based on our success in the battle for Informatics, I was thinking that if we could successfully take over a company ten times bigger than we were, why not just add another zero and go after a company a hundred times bigger? I couldn't think of a single reason not to, so we started toying with the idea of taking over Control Data.

Based in St. Paul, Minnesota, Control Data was not a start-up. It was a computer industry pioneer, founded by Bill Norris, the man who built the UNIVAC One, the first really commercial computer, the one that shocked IBM out of the electronic accounting machine world and into the computer age. Once Bill decided to go out on his own, he took his team of engineers and moved across the street to compete with his former employers at UNIVAC.

They had their mainframe hardware business and also a supercomputer venture. I had no interest in either. Neither did I have any interest in some miscellaneous divisions of theirs with no big future that we could immediately sell off. What I did want were some very good software products and services they owned. Then, the more I looked at their intrinsic internal value versus the price the stock market was putting on the company, the more I felt that Control Data could be a bargain. If we could buy it for not too much over its market price, we could build value by growing the parts we loved and cashing out the parts we didn't want.

We calculated the liquidating values of the pieces at about $3 billion. That was well above the market price for the whole company. My guess was that after paying a 30 percent premium, I could buy them for $2 billion, unload the mainframe and supercomputer assets and the miscellaneous divisions for $2 billion, get all our money back, and still wind up with the software and services part at a net cost of zero.

Sure looked like fun to me.

Don Thomson's take on it was to buy it and then sell everything. He said we can have a quick war, declare victory, and leave. But not me. One of the companies inside Control Data was IBM's old Service Bureau Corporation.

Charles and I were enchanted at the prospect of reuniting with this legacy of Tom Watson's IBM. For both of us, that had been our first job out of college. IBM was like our kindergarten, grade school, and Sunday school teachers, except that we were over twenty-one by the time we got there. We felt a certain spiritual brotherhood.

Control Data had picked up SBC in a lawsuit settlement, after suing IBM for abusing its monopoly power in mainframe hardware. I would have kept SBC, partly for its nostalgia value but also because they were a potent payroll data processor, second only to Automatic Data Processing. We knew it well and knew it was a reliable growth business with good gross margins and crackerjack sales reps.

Of course, Sterling Software did not have $2 billion cash. But as my late father-in-law, Len Acton, used to lecture me in his combination British/Texas accent: "Never let your pocketbook tell you what you can do."

HAVING NO MONEY didn't stop us. We went at it with a very determined plan. While we were still doing our homework analyzing Control Data, we started buying their shares. We approached the market slowly so that no one would notice what we were doing, lined up banking (not the total, but enough), and kept on buying as Control Data shares climbed from around $18 to $20 to over $30.

To accentuate our upside, we put a big team to work on Control Data, code-named Project T, and our meetings went on night and day for months. We broke their business down into specific sections and analyzed each section minutely. To help us sort it out, we hired the best brains: hardware experts, computer services experts, and software analysts.

We had a lot of mental horsepower. Yet wanting to win, and even doing everything you can to win, is sometimes not enough. It's like sitting at the dinner table famished, looking at a juicy steak, then biting off more than you can chew. That's what happened.

The deeper we got into the game, the more circumstances changed and the less confident I became that we could pull it off. Initially it looked so good on paper, but in the real world, circumstances were changing rapidly. The cost of our risky Mike Milken debt went from 13 percent to 16 percent, and because we were borrowing a mountain of money, those extra three points added a lot to our already high interest costs. On top of that, Control Data's share price was climbing past $35 and heading toward $40. That was too much. I knew for sure that the deal couldn't work at $50, and might not work at $45. I was no longer sure it would even work at $40. So the price of what we wanted to buy was going up, and our cost of capital was also going up. The quickly changing markets were squeezing all the value out of our big idea.

This was now a bet-the-ranch move. Talk about bodacious! There came a time when I felt it was wise to go, but I had not yet given that order. I hesitated because I was still stewing on it. Just then, Charles, sensing my misery, sat down quietly and said, "Sam, you know that we don't have to do anything!"

That's all I needed. Misery turned to a sense of peace and serenity. I pulled the plug and abandoned our big idea. We started selling our shares in June 1987—sneaking away into the night, taking a profit without anybody figuring out what we'd been up to—and were totally cashed out by October. The last of our shares sold at $35.

If you judge the adventure by the money we made selling the shares on the way up, it worked out okay. We earned enough to pay our expenses. If you judge it by what might have happened, well, we were saved from total disaster.

As the Control Data shares were being sold, I flew to Milan, Italy, to be with my son Andrew and my daughter Christiana, and to mellow out for a few weeks. Every morning I would wander down to the local café and sit there with my cappuccino reading the *International Herald Tribune.* It was idyllic.

Three days after I came back to the United States, the market imploded. It was October 19, 1987—Black Monday.

Control Data plunged from $36 1/4 to $13 and never came back. This really gave me sobering thoughts. If we'd still owned those shares when the crash hit, Sterling Software would have been badly crippled, maybe even wiped out.

Some say timing is everything, but I don't. That's overly simple thinking. But, every now and then, you catch the rising tide or you avoid catching a falling knife.

This time, I felt accidentally smart.

STERLING SOFTWARE survived and the 1980s became the 1990s. EDI was our fastest-growing division. We had expanded into seaports, banking, automotive, chemical, petroleum, and paper. Our 1991 revenues were $224.4 million. That same year, EDI reached that elevated status of "fundamental technology," meaning it had become an integral part of the way retail, wholesale, and most manufacturing businesses functioned. Software developers began building around our programs. I would never forget Datran, and I would never forget NetAmerica. They were steps along the way to the World Wide Web. OrderNet and Sterling Commerce were also part of that continuing journey, but OrderNet, especially, was a constant reminder that you should never mistake a single battle for the whole war.

As EDI became more and more ubiquitous, I began to wonder if we ought to change our name to better describe our changing markets and technology. We were no longer just about software; we were about solving people's problems. Our computer tools were becoming more widely distributed as Moore's Law relentlessly drove down costs. Wherever I looked, our managers were putting transaction automation into every aspect of their product. I wanted to show the world that EDI was just one aspect of how we solved customers' problems. So after a lot of discussion, we came up with "electronic commerce" to describe what we did and, based on that, we created Electronic Commerce Group (ECG). This before IBM began running full-page ads saying, "IBM means e-commerce" and well before "Internet" became a household term.

As growth in electronic commerce appeared to be unlimited, I began to wonder if Electronic Commerce Group ought to be something more. We felt the push of IBM's "Big Blue" and, more important, of the brand-new entrepreneurial ventures bred in the silicon alleys of California and Texas, whose every growth forecast topped the last one.

The idea of spinning off a new company from an already existing one was not new to me. I had done it before. I see opportunities like clusters of blossoms on a tree in springtime. You cut yourself off by seeing only a single tree rather than a living organism capable of growing new blossoms when cared for correctly. In 1984, our Electronic Commerce Group accounted for less than 1 percent of our total corporate revenue. Nine years later, the group had 40 software products and services, 13,000 customers, and 640 employees. It was growing at a rate of 26 percent a year and accounting for 27 percent of our total corporate revenue. It seemed to me that another bud might be ready to burst.

Market timing does matter. In 1995, the first Web browser, Netscape (a commercial copy of Tim Berners-Lee's Mosaic), went public, its shares priced at $28. It jumped to $75, valued at more than the country's biggest defense contractor, General Dynamics. The response was unbelievably euphoric. Netscape launched an "irrational exuberance" in the markets that was to grip the country for more than five years. For me, as Yogi Berra used to say, it was déjà vu all over again.

I remembered the IPOs of University Computing and then Sterling Software and how exuberance—part rational, part not—added to the upward movement in the valuations. This time it was the dot-coms and the fiber optics–based telecommunications. They led this latest version of the 1849 Gold

Rush to California. I saw no rationality to these dot-com companies going public and instantly reaching such astronomical heights when they consisted of little more than a Web site and a few computer kids pecking away at their keyboards. To me, this was nothing more than the old Wall Street broker rationale: "When the ducks are quacking, you feed the ducks."

That wasn't us. We were a real company, operating and growing steadily in the real world, not in the illusionary world of this new market mania.

And we were adding real-world companies to our business. We bought Bob Cook's Systems Center, which was a good networking fit. Thinking we could do no wrong, next we acquired KnowledgeWare, Fran Tarkenton's company. A Georgia boy with a soft Southern drawl, Fran was "the scrambler," one of football's great quarterbacks, who took the Minnesota Vikings to the Super Bowl three times. Outside football, he'd become a late-night infomercial pitchman selling inspirational tapes and a software entrepreneur by founding KnowledgeWare. Unfortunately, Fran's managerial skills didn't match his football skills, and KnowledgeWare was in deep trouble. We thought we could pull off something good by using the same approach we did with Informatics and Systems Center, but this time it didn't work so well.

It wasn't a total disaster, however, and it led us to the opportunity to go after the much larger Texas Instruments Software (TI), and we snapped it up. This enabled us to combine it with KnowledgeWare as twin building blocks in that segment of the business. In terms of revenue, TI was our biggest acquisition ever, but it was a very troubled software business, created and run by the world's smartest microchip people who just happened to be clueless in computer software.

There was a time when TI had been the hottest stock in America. Originally, they were in the oil patch doodlebug business. That's when you blow up dynamite in an underground hole and record the sound waves bouncing back from the various layers of sandstone or limestone or other geological structures miles below the earth's surface to determine if there's oil down there. These original TI guys were geophysical engineers who became adept in electrics and electronics during the war against Hitler and stayed in that field after the war. After Bell Labs invented the transistor, TI engineers were perceptive enough to look for opportunities and invented integrated circuits. But along the way they got into a few disasters, just as I did. Their bad ones included personal calculators and personal computers and also computer software. For a while they lost their way before finally returning to their semiconductor roots. Today, they are the #1 chip manufacturer for cell phones, which are now being shipped by the hundreds of millions.

By then, thanks to strong internal growth and thirty acquisitions, Sterling Software had more than 20,000 customers and employed 3,500 people in 95 offices around the planet, and OrderNet was the world's leading electronic commerce software. Of all the assets Sterling had to offer, e-commerce was valued at the highest price/earnings ratio, and I knew that the market would receive us enthusiastically. In its then "new economy" mood, it didn't give a rat's tail about intrinsic value. At the end of the day, in its increasing madness, the market was saying, "Are you part of the New Economy? The World Wide Web? The dot-coms? No more 'Old Economy' companies for us. The Web renders brick and mortar obsolete."

Our answer was to recapitalize into two separate public companies, one of which the market would value emotionally, while the other it would value rationally.

Sterling Williams and I went back and forth on this. I would come to him with all the reasons I thought we ought to spin off e-commerce, and he would give me all the reasons we shouldn't. He'd talk me out of it, and then I would go away and reconvince myself. I'd come back and we'd discuss it all over again. The two of us kept talking about it, searching for the truth. Of course, he knew full well how stubborn I can be, especially when I know I'm right. So he finally admitted to himself that this was inevitable. Then he got enthusiastically on board, galvanized his team, and made my idea a whole lot better.

In March 1996, we split Sterling Software into two companies, Sterling Software and Sterling Commerce. Then we did an initial public offering of 18.4 percent of Sterling Commerce, and paid a dividend to our owners. That dividend was the other 81.6 percent of Sterling Commerce. We listed both companies on the New York Stock Exchange. We raised $267 million in cash for Sterling Software, while its market cap remained stable at $2 billion. The Sterling Commerce stock was valued by the market at ten times revenue. A home run.

Sterling Commerce was a big hit in this new thing coming to be termed e-commerce. We were discovered by those recently benighted intellectual Wall Streeters, the Internet analysts. We didn't fit the analysts' mental model of dot-com companies because we had real products and customers, real revenue, and real profits.

But we would do.

THE '90s WERE A TIME of great change introduced by the Internet. It was easy to get caught up in the excitement. But the disciplined part of being an entrepreneur is keeping your head when all around you are losing theirs.

As a student of history, I recognized the growing insanity of the dot-com boom—not unlike that Dutch tulip bulb–buying mania of the 1630s I discussed earlier. The dot-com boom was a similar feeding frenzy, where anything and everything that had to do with "www" created more and more exuberance, which was certainly becoming irrational.

Few who lived through it have forgotten the giddiness. The party was in full swing with the punch bowl constantly refilled. Seldom in two hundred years of history has Wall Street been so manic. There were e-commerce start-ups like Arriba, with no customers, priced in the market at $12 billion. Commerce One had six customers and was priced at $10 billion. Crazy.

A lot of years had gone by since Henry Ford built his first car, or even, for that matter, since the 1960s, when there'd been two automotive monsters with big tin tail fins in every garage in America. And old Henry had to wait many, many years before having 13 million of his Model-Ts on the roads, partly because somebody had to build those roads first. So I figured it would be the same for the Internet to take full effect. It would, I figured, require a process many years long.

Could a company's plants and offices, I wondered, simply disappear to be replaced by a home page?

I thought not.

History told me that while this new technology was truly a big thing, there was simply too much excitement. The dance only lasts until midnight and when that time comes, the music stops. Who would be where when the music stopped?

By 1999, Sterling Commerce had penetrated all the industries first served by EDI. I was delighted yet uneasy. I felt big trouble coming. Experience was telling me that it was getting late, and while the tech and telecom band played on, I remembered that so had the band on the Titanic as it steamed its way toward the fatal iceberg.

I remembered studying one of the great builders of the investment business, Ned Johnson of Fidelity Investments. His father had founded the company, and it was still relatively small when Ned came along. He was savvy and did a great job in the early mutual fund business, managing what became the biggest fund of them all, Magellan.

Back in the terrible '70s when managing stocks was a lousy job, Ned, a natural-born marketeer, saw Fidelity's original business of mutual funds disappearing and came up with another way not only to survive but to hit a home run. People had begun to hate stocks and were pulling their savings out of mutual funds because Lyndon Johnson's guns-and-butter policy had sent interest rates skyrocketing; bond and stock prices had plummeted. You could also do better then by just leaving your money in the bank. Recognizing an opportunity, Ned reinvented Fidelity by becoming the first to sell a money market fund that paid interest above that paid by the banks or Treasury notes.

Ned's dad taught him that to understand the market, you had to be able to sort the pragmatic from the emotional. The tech stocks were sexy. That fit Arriba, Commerce One, and the dotcom boom. Emotion was running much too high. As always, bust follows boom. As we approached the millennium, I saw the market as emotionally overpriced, with the technology and telecom part getting more and more outlandish. By the summer

186

of 1999, I knew that the dance was coming to its end. The music was going to stop.

We were earning profits hand over fist, we had no debt and $700 million cash in the bank. Sterling Commerce was intrinsically good, but still didn't have the full mystery and magic of a dot-com. We were never totally accepted as an Internet play by the gods of Wall Street.

So we hired Goldman Sachs to find a buyer for Sterling Commerce. We got a lot of tire kickers, including the big telephone companies in Europe, but our best deal came from our Texas neighbors, the former Texas Bell, part of the original AT&T nationwide telephone monopoly—the same monopoly I'd fought with Datran and NetAmerica and had helped to bust up. What irony that we at Sterling Commerce should arrive there as part of Southwestern Bell Corporation, who would soon buy up the biggest pieces of the old Bell system, including their former long-line parent company, and then retake the name AT&T as its new global brand.

Simultaneously as we were selling Sterling Commerce, we decided we ought to sell Sterling Software, too. We had come a long way, but now was the time. We had a strong product line, consistent quarter-to-quarter revenue growth, and impressive profit margins. My worry was that this would be a harder sell because we did not have the sexy cachet of electronic commerce, and the best fit for Sterling Software, IBM itself, was shut out of the buying market by U.S. anti-monopoly laws.

Morgan Stanley lost out to Goldman for the job of representing us, but I came up with a way that they could still help get a good deal done. I asked the disappointed banker at Morgan Stanley to whisper in Charles Wang's or Sanjay Kumar's ear—the top two guys at Computer Associates—that Sterling Software just might be available.

My Morgan Stanley friend laughed. "CA hates investment bankers and won't pay a fee to anybody," he said.

It was true that Wang and his trained-from-a-pup president, Sanjay Kumar, were tightfisted—except, of course, in paying themselves. But I knew that they needed a deal to keep Computer Associates' acquisition machine growing. What I didn't yet understand was that they really, really needed a big deal simply to keep an illusion alive. So I said to my friend at Morgan, "You talk to Computer Associates, and if they end up buying Sterling Software, I'll see that you guys get a $10 million fee as part of the total cost that CA pays. I will not let them renege on you."

The Morgan team went off to do their thing, while the folks at Goldman were finding other buyers, and in one amazing week, we sold both companies for $8 billion, effective March 30, 2000.

Sterling Commerce went to AT&T for $4 billion cash, which felt particularly good because we were getting all that money from the same people who had killed Datran. And Sterling Software went to Computer Associates for $4 billion in stock. It turned out that Computer Associates was the only buyer for Sterling Software.

Selling the company to Charles Wang would not provide the ideal home for our company because of Computer Associates' negative culture, just the opposite of our own. Before finalizing the deal, we agonized over that, but our overriding duty was to maximize value for our shareholders.

The $8 billion total was more than a 30 percent premium to the two blended share prices. The shareholders of both companies walked away happy. All the more so because, amazingly, we hit the very last month of the long bull market. The tech-heavy NASDAQ Index would drop 80 percent over the next two years.

I had met Charles Wang only briefly and had no personal feel for him one way or the other, but after CA bought University Computing, at a 50 percent premium over the market, their behavior made CA the most hated company in the software industry. They were notorious for their hard-hearted bloodletting. "ABC" became our prayer: "Anybody but CA." But there were no other buyers. Goldman searched, and if anyone could have found another suitor, it would have been Goldman. To minimize the pain, we provided very generous termination pay for everyone at risk of losing his or her job, which rankled the control-freak instincts of CA's top two, but there was nothing they could do about it.

Back at the very beginning of the negotiations for this sale, Kumar arrived at my house on a sunny Sunday afternoon and sat in my backyard gazebo. I kept saying, "We want cash," but Kumar kept repeating that he could only do a deal for CA stock. He also kept trying to convince me that CA stock was as good as cash. The company books were, of course, in the public domain, so I could see for myself CA's revenue and balance sheets and other financial book ratios, which all seemed fairly reasonable for a $6 billion software company ranked the fourth largest in our industry. The market would see that in this deal they were getting solid products from us that fit easily into their sales network, and that there would be positive synergies from the merger. We had $800 million in revenue and they were closing the year with $6.5 billion of revenue.

So I decided it was okay to do the stock swap.

In fact, I was a true believer in the future of CA. That's why, along with many family members and the like, we chose to keep our shares and options after the sale of Sterling to Computer Associates. Every senior corporate executive at Sterling cashed out their options at the sale, but we Wylys held on to CA, believing the company would be a good long-term investment.

What I could not know at the time was that Wang, Kumar, and their CA board were telling a big lie to me and to all the other public shareholders. Four years later, after the wrongdoers used company money to protect themselves by settling certain class actions, it finally came out that there had been a huge conspiracy and fraud by executives and board members.

At that point, Ranger Governance, a company we formed to pursue the two proxy contests against CA's board in 2001 and 2002, offered to work as co-plaintiffs with CA to pursue the wrongdoers. But the leadership of CA told Ranger and me that there was no interest. That's when we filed a derivative case, in behalf of the company itself, to pursue individuals, like Charles Wang, who personally benefited at the expense of shareholders to the tune of billions of dollars by their breaches of faith, and had cost the company hundreds of millions of dollars.

Of course, everything we did has proved to be insightful now that numerous executives have pleaded guilty to exactly the type of conduct we were alleging. Even the board has concluded that there's at least half a billion dollars in claims for CA against Charles Wang. Yet the company has given no support to anyone going after Wang and others who fleeced the true owners of the company, its shareholders, in the open market.

And now a federal judge has said that CA did not move quickly enough in pursuing its claims. In fact, that same judge has concluded that the only ones who took action in a timely manner to save those claims for Computer Associates were Ranger and Sam Wyly!

At the end of the day, I believe that we will be successful in curing some major damage for myself, my family, and others. I also believe that we have done a great good for Computer Associates and its other shareholders.

Chapter 19

The Crafty Woman

W HEN I CREATED University Computing, I knew I'd found my calling. At the same time, I don't believe there's a single moment in life when you wake up and, once and for all, know that's who you are. I thought of myself as a computer guy in the beginning. But as I climbed higher mountains and saw farther along the horizon, I saw myself as an entrepreneur. What I didn't understand until many years after I started UCC was how much I would continue to evolve.

That's why, when a small arts-and-crafts chain called Michaels Stores came my way, I didn't ask myself what yarn, quilts, and scrapbooks had to do with me. Instead I thought about Sam Walton, and I admired what he'd done. I took a good look at the balance sheet, and I liked what I saw.

Until then, my whole exposure to arts and crafts consisted of taking family pictures to be framed and buying witches' hats and coal-black cat costumes for the kids at Halloween. If I had held on rigidly to that "computer guy" perception of myself, I would never have been able to take advantage of a huge opportunity. The key to thinking like an entrepreneur is to focus on the positive: When you do, you start seeing opportunities. Sometimes they come knocking on the door. But you have to open the door and then respond quickly and effectively. Sometimes they're disguised. Rather than carrying a big sign on their backs that says, "Here I am," they form a hidden pattern in a long series of seemingly unrelated events. You have to be able to connect the dots and discern the pattern.

In the late '70s, Don Thomson had taken some of those underperforming Bonanza locations and turned them into Peoples, and we found ourselves struggling to keep the concept afloat. We needed to invent or buy a new business for Peoples, or liquidate the company. Right around that time, an old friend from the Jimmy Ling LTV days, George Griffin, came around, frustrated by his difficulty in unloading a small chain of stores that sold arts and crafts. He said no potential buyer could figure out how to "unscramble the eggs."

The problem, George explained, was that the father and son who owned the company were so constantly at each other's throats that they were scaring away prospective buyers. And the father was determined to cash out and move from Dallas to Miami Beach. The chain was called Michaels. I'd never heard of it but, as George related its ancestry, I became more and more intrigued. You see, once upon a time it had been a Ben Franklin store, and therein lies a story.

Back in 1877, Edward and George Butler, brothers from Boston, came up with a new concept for retailing. Instead of setting up a specialty shop to sell one line of items—like shoes or dresses or kitchen supplies—they set up a store where they could sell all sorts of stuff. This was the very beginning of department stores, except that they weren't yet called that. They were called variety stores, and they carried a large assortment of low-cost goods. Then the Butlers set up a "five-cent counter," where everything cost a nickel. It worked in Boston, so they expanded westward and called it Ben Franklin Stores.

Three-quarters of a century later, in the days when America was just starting to move westward with the automobile, there were no shopping malls or big national retail chains. What you found in every town, especially in small-town America, was a variety store, like Ben Franklin's. In Lake Providence, we had Morgan and Lindsey's, where you could buy everything from paper napkins to thimbles, birthday cards, curtain hooks, and boxes of chocolates. The Butlers' idea of a nickel counter became so popular and widespread that these places came to be nicknamed "five-and-dimes" or "five- and ten-cent" stores.

While some of them became the heart of Main Street America, others grew to become legendary department stores, like Macy's in New York, Wanamaker's in Philadelphia, and Lehman's in Chicago. Still others merged into chains to compete with Ben Franklin Stores. That's how JC Penney's was born.

One fellow from Missouri who worked as a trainee at Penney's just before World War II loved retailing so much that when he came home from the war, he borrowed $20,000 from his father-in-law and bought himself a Ben Franklin's franchise in Newport, Arkansas. Leading from the front, and spending most of his time on the store floor listening to his customers, he pioneered many of the notions that are the basis for great retailing today: The shelves must always be fully stocked with a wide array of goods at low prices; the store should be open later than the competition because that was in the customers' best interest; the more you sold, the easier it was to negotiate volume discounts with your suppliers and then, when you've got those discounts, you passed them on to your customers because everyone loves a discount.

Within a year, that one store led six states' worth of Ben Franklin's in sales and profits. But the young retailer's success was his undoing. The landlord decided he could have it all for himself, so he demanded more rent and a share of the sales. The young retailer shut down in Newport and moved to nearby Bentonville, where he started all over again.

His name was Sam Walton.

He'd grown up in the same type of Missouri culture, heavily influenced by the Scots-Irish traits of my own Bubba Country and described in Senator James Webb's book *Born Fighting.*

He called his new place Walton's Five and Dime and made it as successful as the one in Newport had been. He soon expanded into new markets and grew the size of his stores. By 1962, he had sixteen stores in Arkansas, Missouri, and Kansas. That turned out to be a good year for new retail chains. Target started in Minneapolis and Kmart in Garden City, Michigan. And Sam Walton opened a new store in Bentonville, which he named Wal-Mart. Presto! Big-box retailing was born, and the world would never be the same.

Sam Walton is my pick for America's greatest entrepreneur of the twentieth century.

He not only built the world's largest retailing empire and the single most valuable company in America, he created the institution with the greatest muscle to do good today. He changed the world with his concept of retailing, and his managerial heirs are changing it again because Wal-Mart has gone green. It's not just a million and a half employees who will have an effect on energy conservation, saving the planet, and climate change, which is huge all by itself. But, more than that, they've got tens of thousands of vendors all over the world who will be expected to do their part. They're going to demand that vendors conform to green practices, at the risk of losing Wal-Mart's business.

Inevitably, this means Wal-Mart will be a force pushing China to accelerate its own greening-up. If the Chinese want to keep Wal-Mart's orders, they will start to green up voluntarily or risk losing out to other countries in selling to the American market. In moving our small planet toward cleaner air, I'd say that Wal-Mart could eventually matter more than our State Department.

But that's only one of the reasons I pick Walton as the twentieth century's outstanding entrepreneur. Another is because Walton himself was totally positive. He was a fabulous salesman, a great buyer, and a diligent researcher.

Michael Rouleau, who ran our Michaels chain, had been a merchandise manager for Target for twenty years. One morning on a buying trip to Hong Kong, he bumped into Sam Walton in the hotel elevator and invited him for a cup of coffee. They were competitors and he was looking to pick Walton's brain. He wound up spending the whole day with Walton. But by the time it was over, Michael says he realized he'd learned nothing. "Instead, Walton emptied me of everything I knew."

Target is thriving because they learned the lessons of the discount business. Kmart is gone because they didn't. And Wal-Mart is Wal-Mart because Walton built it. Kmart got to be nationwide first by focusing on the big cities. Wal-Mart learned how to be profitable in towns of 5,000 and, gradually, surrounded the big cities. Walton closed in on the city centers and Kmart got killed.

Walton knew everything there was to know about retailing and made a point of teaching the people who worked for him. As Peter Drucker taught, Sam Walton demonstrated, "The purpose of a business is to create a customer."

"There is only one boss," Walton used to preach: "the customer. And she can fire everyone in the company from the chairman on down, simply by spending her money somewhere else."

He also knew where to find out what the customer was thinking: from the folks on the front line. "They're the ones who actually talk to the customer, the only ones who really know what's going on out there."

Best of all, Walton was a man after my own heart when he said, "Ignore conventional wisdom. If everybody else is doing it one way, there's a good chance you can find your niche by going in exactly the opposite direction."

So there was Sam Walton turning his Ben Franklin stores into Wal-Marts, and here was a banker telling us about Michaels, which had started out as a Ben Franklin's.

That would make us first cousins.

I looked at the balance sheet: Michaels had $4 million in cash and no debt. Every store had double-digit increases in same-store sales, and the asking price was $8 million. I decided to buy it without even walking into a store. In fact, had I done that, I probably would have walked right out again, because there was no way I could have had any real understanding of Michaels' 35,000 products. Even today, I find that most men don't know anything about Michaels, especially men in suits and ties. But the crafty women do. And there are tens of millions of them.

We did a rights offering on the Michaels' stock to the Peoples' shareholders. Some of them took it up, but no underwriters wanted it. Even though we had a solid track record, the underwriters looked at Michaels as a dinky little retailing chain and, at 67 cents a share, they just weren't interested. So Charles and I became the underwriters. We bought our own pro rata shares, plus any not bought by the other shareholders. Everyone who passed up the opportunity to buy the stock at 67 cents missed riding with us to $44 over the next twenty-two years, a 99th percentile performance. That's one in a hundred.

The father half of Michaels' original owners had been a Ben Franklin franchisee when his son came along and created the concept. The son was a college dropout whose first store was in a big shopping mall in north Dallas. The father, who owned the stock, wanted to sell, but the son, who had a profits interest in some of the individual stores and also ran the warehouse, wanted sole ownership and control of the company for himself.

George Griffin told me, "The son's the merchandising genius. He's got the vendors, and he controls the buying and the distribution center. But the father and the son are at war."

Don Thomson and I figured there had to be a way to make this work, so we negotiated a deal where, initially, we split the assets. We owned the business, but the son owned outright some of the most profitable stores and continued to run the warehouse for both his stores and ours. He got a royalty-free franchise on the Michaels name for the Dallas/Ft. Worth metropolitan area, all the way down to Waco in the south and up to Plano in the north. We looked at this as a win-win situation.

Then the son psychologically substituted us for his father as the available enemy. No matter who we had as managers, there was no getting along with him. But we kept trying. During the course of the next several years, he and our team got divorced and remarried three times. He started another chain to compete with us and actually built it up to fifty stores before going bust. When he did, we bought up some of his better locations from the bankruptcy sale.

Serendipity led us to Michaels while we were trying to solve our restaurant real estate problem, but retailing was new to me, so I become a student of the great entrepreneurial retailers. I studied Sam Walton first and foremost. Then I studied James Cash Penney, Ray Kroc of McDonald's, and Mary Kay Ash of Mary Kay Cosmetics. I knew her personally. She was a Texas gal from Mineral Wells, and I really admired the way she had built such a fantastic selling organization. She took the old

Fuller Brush method, sending sales reps door-to-door, turning zillions of women into entrepreneurs. And building a business that is still thriving today. If you were one of Mary Kay's top saleswomen, everybody knew it because she rewarded you with a pink Cadillac.

We all stand on the shoulders of giants who came before, which is why I read everything I could about retailing and the entrepreneurs who had built great retailing empires. My favorite book about retailing is Stanley Marcus's *Minding the Store*. He became an American retailing legend, building the Neiman Marcus department store into one of the country's most outstanding, and highest-quality, brands.

Reading is one of the keys to success, because if you won't admit what you don't know, you'll never discover what you need to know. I read to conceptualize challenges. I read to know what I'm getting into. I read for ideas. I wanted to know how Sam Walton kept prices so low. Ray Kroc insisted that every McDonald's keep the restrooms clean and drove that message home by first inspecting the restrooms each time he visited a McDonald's. And what led Kmart into bankruptcy? And how did JC Penney and Sears become dinosaurs? When I was a kid, Sears & Roebuck had the market position that Wal-Mart has today. Mamas wanted their girls and boys to grow up to be Sears people. I wanted to find out what changed. I read thousands of pages on retailing, like a gold miner panning every inch of his claim, searching for just a few precious nuggets that would give me real insight into what is vital.

Then something terrifying happened.

Sam Walton started an arts-and-crafts chain just like ours. He named it after his wife, Helen, and planted his first Helen's stores in the heart of Michaels' territory: Monroe, Louisiana; Fort Smith, Arkansas; and Springfield, Missouri.

Our top guys wanted to go toe-to-toe with him by opening a Michaels across the street from each Helen's, but I said no way. We must not awaken a sleeping giant. I said, "We're going to leave him alone and pray that he loses interest."

About a year later we got a call from Wal-Mart's chief financial officer saying, "This isn't us. We're a high-volume, low-margin business. Are you interested in buying Helen's three stores at book value?"

The Bentonville Battleship in Arkansas no longer had our little chain in its crosshairs, and with barely a pause I said yes.

In separating the vital from the trivial for Michaels, I concluded that good real estate was absolutely vital to our success. We'd grown from 6 stores to 105 stores, and we set out to find one of the best and brightest in the field. We stole Doug Sullivan from Family Dollar Stores in 1988 to run real estate for us.

As we expanded across the country, we opened new Michaels stores and bought some existing independent arts-and-crafts stores, which pretty much discouraged our competitors from opening up next door. We bought the Monteil chain, with thirteen stores, mostly in Colorado and Arizona, and the Moscatel chain, with twenty stores in California. Cross the Continental Divide today and there still isn't anybody out there but us. There are some one-store operators who do a great job and have a fine business, but in terms of a chain west of the Rocky Mountains, it's just Michaels.

Years later, Doug told me that his bosses warned him against coming to work for me. They didn't want him to leave and tried to persuade him to stay by claiming that Michaels was a high-risk proposition and that "this Sam Wyly is just a wild man. He lives on the edge."

I had heard this "wild man" bit before, and I assumed it came from my tendency to move quickly and aggressively. But I have to laugh because I rarely make a big move without really thinking about it, even if sometimes the answer seems to arrive in a blink. Perhaps having the audacity to think I could bust up AT&T, where Doug's dad had spent his career, with forty patents to his credit (including the little bird that stands on a cup of water and keeps drinking when you dip its beak), may seem like living on the edge. To me, though, it was just good entrepreneurship. Only much later did Doug tell me that his dad had worked for Bell Labs, and that what I did to bust up Ma Bell's monopoly was viewed by some there as almost sacrilegious.

Therein lies another lesson. You can't spend your time

obsessed with what other people say about you. The world was littered with garbage gossip long before there were bloggers. I guess the reason the "wild man" tag seems particularly funny in regards to Michaels is that, while we were aggressive as all get-out in expanding as fast as we could, Michaels is really a story of perseverance and patience.

Sam Walton used to joke that people thought he was an overnight success. "No," he'd say, "they just heard of me last night."

It's easy now to look at Michaels' more than 900 stores and think, "What a beautiful economic engine." But it took us over twenty years. Successful entrepreneuring is as much about being willing to reinvent as you go along—and about having the patience to do so—as it is about grand visions. What was it old Thomas Alva Edison said? One percent inspiration, 99 percent perspiration.

Having studied Walton carefully, we copied him closely. I talked to the people on the ground and watched the customers. I'm a strong believer in roaming halls and hanging around stores, because that's the best way to find out what you've got. There is simply no substitute for seeing how things work. The early years of company building are the creative years, and when you're trying to figure out what you're going to be, you need to see it on the ground.

Early on, hanging out at a Michaels store, I became fascinated watching the fellow who did the picture framing. I saw what he did and how he dealt with customers, and I had an epiphany. Until that moment, in my mind, picture frames were simply another product. But as I observed people bringing in their cherished photographs and pictures, it dawned on me that this was very different from the rest of what we sold. It was light manufacturing to order. This was a service, a deeply personal and highly emotional one.

So we decided to look for someone to run the custom framing division and run it right. We hired Mike Greenwood, who walked into my office one morning and said that we ought to be making our frame molding ourselves. He wanted to cut out suppliers and distributors and acquire a company to take the raw ash and oak and make all our frame sides. When he had pitched his ideas in other companies, he'd been told, "That's not what we do." If I hadn't spent time in the stores, I never would have caught on to just what a bold idea this was. I immediately told him, "Go find us a factory."

We acquired a company in North Carolina that supplied us with framing materials. We also bought and built up a free-standing framing services and art supplies company named Aaron Brothers. Before long, there were 168 Aaron Brothers stores in eleven states, along with 930 Michaels across the country.

No one in retailing had done anything like this before. We named our framing business Artistree and, by vertically integrating light manufacturing into our mass retailing concept, when Michaels hit 10 percent pretax operating profits for the fiscal year, it was in no small part thanks to Artistree.

That was because Mike Greenwood believed, "If you can dream it, you can do it." And one of the hallmarks of all really good companies is that managers are free to innovate. Mike dreamed it, I backed him, and we did it.

By design Michaels is a merchandise-driven, "Let's have a perfect store" business. But one important aspect of Michaels' success is their newspaper advertising strategy. It doesn't sound very entrepreneurial, and certainly it isn't "wild," but it's crucial. On any given day, there's something marked 40 percent off. A Michaels craftswoman wants to know what and when. They aren't like Wal-Mart, with the same prices week after week; they use price promotions to drive business to the stores and need a regular way to get their unique coupons to their customers.

Michaels spends about $140 million a year inserting coupon sheets in local newspapers, spending nothing on television. The customer opens her newspaper and there's the Michaels ad, so buying something on sale at Michaels becomes part of her weekly routine. One of the first things a new top executive would suggest is that we get rid of the old-fashioned, low-tech ads. And every guy who tried it had to take his punishment as same-store sales dropped dramatically that week.

Our competitive stimulus and huge volume purchasing

forced vendors to innovate better products and to bring down prices. We created thousands of jobs in our stores and in our distribution centers, and over a thousand new jobs in our head-quarters. For every new job on our payroll, probably more than ten were created on the payrolls of vendors and customers and other service providers.

From 1984 to 1994, we opened new stores at a rate of 35 percent a year. We made big regional moves, like our acquisition of Leeward's Creative Crafts, which brought us into the Northeast and added 184 more stores. It was a costly and risky strategy, required a lot of capital, and caused some organizational nightmares. I'd bet the farm on my vision of consolidation in a traditional mom-and-pop and small-chain market. Clearly, we were pursuing aggressive growth, which came with higher risks. But we were doing so because I firmly believed that the key to long-term success was establishing Michaels in local markets before anyone else got too strong.

In 1994, ten years after we Wylys got involved with Michaels, the business recorded a fabulous year. We'd grown to 380 stores, and our stock price had hit $11, up from that 67-cent starting point. We were inching up to the $1 billion mark in revenues. Where competitors were already present, we rolled into town and took them on. A few were such good merchandisers and managers that we nodded with respect and admiration at a job well done and moved a few miles beyond their firing range.

But by the mid-1990s, we had also developed a severe case of indigestion. We had bitter pills to swallow and were appropriately punished by Wall Street. Yet I believe the pain was worth it because our aggressive growth is what put Michaels in the enviable place it now enjoys. Today Michaels opens a new store almost every week. The store count growth rate is about 4 percent, and if you add in a same-store sales increase of 4 percent, you get 8 percent sales growth. This is not only healthy, it's more than twice the annual growth in America's total economy.

When it came time to stop acquiring and start building an efficient, well-planned, well-controlled company out of what we'd assembled, we had to reinvent the nature of the company. We had 442 stores by 1995, and we were bigger than all our competitors combined in terms of outlets, square footage, and revenues. Michaels had captured the hearts of craftswomen all over America. But operationally, we still had a lot of hard work to do.

Michael Rouleau grew up in northern Minnesota in the 1930s with parents who had never made it past high school, and he was the first in his family to go to college. My first interview with Michael in 1996 took all day. Like me, he has a story from his rural childhood of seeing an executive—in his case, a man from Honeywell wearing a camel hair coat—and thinking that man was the incarnation of everything he wanted in life. Later he told me that the first thing he did when he got a job was to buy himself a camel hair coat.

In 1962, he'd been part of the original group of twenty-six people who created Target. Over the next twenty years, he gained valuable experience in retail's two basic line functions: store operations and merchandising. Michael was then recruited to run a start-up office supply business. He built it up and ultimately sold it to one of today's three survivors in office supply chains.

Earlier I'd interviewed several possible candidates for the president's job at Michaels, but he was far and away the most impressive. He told me he'd spent a week at his local Michaels, looking and listening. The store was always busy, which he liked, but the registers were backed up, customers waited in long lines, and they were getting lousy service, which he didn't like at all. Seeing that Michaels' customers were mostly women, he phoned five women in his family who lived in five different parts of the country and asked them if they'd ever heard of Michaels. Not only did they know us, but all five told him emphatically, "I love Michaels."

Then and there, he decided we had great potential, that he knew exactly how to make the best of it, and that this was the right place for him. Later he confessed that he'd come to Dallas absolutely determined to get our offer.

When we first met, Michael got right to the point. "You've got great real estate, but everything else needs fixing." He was tough, tenacious, and straight-talking. He wasn't a financial man or an entrepreneur, but that's not what I was looking for. I agreed that our operating, merchandising, supply chain, and information technology systems needed either fixing or building, and I could see that Rouleau was the guy to do it.

His style was to bulletproof everything. Before he made any changes, he'd call buyers, vendors, and local store managers and run his ideas by them. He was meticulous about detail, and always testing things to make sure they were right.

We were struggling when Michael came on board, because our regular Dallas bank had been bought and we found ourselves dealing with new bankers from North Carolina. They didn't understand us and simply redlined our company, along with all the other Texas retailers who didn't have investment-grade credit. I decided to raise a war chest to create a margin of safety so we could build Michaels without fear of a cash crunch.

I liked the high-yield bond market: Mike Milken's so-called junk bonds. Even though you paid a price for your money, you got long- rather than short-term capital. Some businessmen looked at the debt and thought, "This is too expensive," but I didn't blink. What I saw was how much we could do with the money. At Sterling Software, Mike's junk bonds multiplied our $20 million into $140 million and saw us through the world's first hostile takeover in software. The bond buyer was out of risk in one year. So I knew my credit was good in Milken's market.

During the early years of fast store growth, we had a highly decentralized structure, which fit with my belief that local managers can often make better decisions than a heavily staffed central office.

I happen to like very flat organizational structures. I don't like lots of layers. I want the people at the top, the ones who have the most responsibility, to be as close as possible to the people who have the most contact with the customers. And the more I can shrink that distance, the more I can assure myself that top managers know what's going on.

So in our early days at Michaels, each manager had a lot of authority over his or her store, including the P&L, bank account, and bookkeeper. Each store paid its own rent and payroll, and bought its own inventory. Each manager was rewarded with a percentage of profits, and some managers ended up making more than top headquarters officers, which was fine with me.

I knew that the greatest company presidents brag when great incentive-based sales reps or P&L managers earn more than they do, and rightfully so. Sam Walton and J. C. Penney originally got their chains launched in the same way.

But size changes things. When you pass a certain point and you have hundreds of different managers all doing their own thing, it becomes impossible to maintain consistency and control. You can't run an efficient, profitable business. You have to go instead for greater economies of scale and purchasing power. Tight merchandising plans and controls become absolutely necessary to maintain standards for your customers and to create margins so that you can pay your costs of infrastructure and capital. The competitive world of retailing is brutal. Failed retail concepts litter the landscape of American business.

Michaels needed to change into a company with a strong centralized system and top-notch technology to back it up. As much as I liked the highly entrepreneurial spirit of the decentralized structure, we couldn't stick with it any longer.

We took comfort in knowing that Sam Walton had gone through the same emotional calamity. Some fifteen years into building Wal-Mart, old Sam had to centralize, too, investing heavily in highly sophisticated technology. His managers had to pull teeth to get him to pay for it, but that technology ultimately was vital to Wal-Mart becoming what it is today. Walton originally was something of a technophobe. Me, I'm a bit of a centralization-phobe. It's hard when something goes against your nature.

It was Artistree, created not long before I brought in Michael Rouleau, that helped me appreciate the beauty of a centralized system run with great technology. Our framing division serviced the entire chain with five chop shops. We had installed software that allowed a framer to punch in the dimensions of the picture to be framed, then the computer would calculate the dimensions of the frame and send the information to the appropriate chop shop. This not only cut down on the margin of error in the business—which had been hovering around 50 percent— but also guaranteed that people's treasured goods stayed safe in the store waiting for their frames, rather than being driven back and forth to the chop shops.

Finished custom frames would then be packed so UPS could ship them from the chop shops straight to the store, instead of us having to operate a fleet of vans. We no longer had to train every new employee in manual frame making, which took time and cost money. Instead, the managers could teach each new employee how to input to the computer system. When you're scaling up in size like this, you've got to find a few killer opportunities, like Artistree, and then relentlessly execute them.

Another example. Before we moved to a centralized system, each store manager was essentially the buyer for his store. That raised two issues.

The first was purchasing power. When you've got 500 different managers all placing their own orders and getting the orders shipped directly to them, you're not going to have a great relationship with your vendors; you're certainly not going to be able to command the best negotiation on quality, price, and service. It was easier and more cost-efficient for Michaels to place one big order, have it all sent to any one of the regional distribution centers, and then ship the goods weekly from there to the stores. That's the difference between 500 managers each calling up Crayola and saying, "I need six boxes of green crayons," and one centralized buyer e-mailing to say, "We need three thousand boxes of crayons shipped to our Texas distribution center."

The second big issue was inventory. Before we adopted a centralized system, we had store workers all over the country walking around their stores trying to eyeball 35,000 different items, to determine what was selling and what wasn't. As a result, we had hundreds of people making hundreds of different buying decisions, which led to bad choices and either overbuying, which subsequently meant big inventory writeoffs, or underbuying, which meant lost sales. Changing that brought our inventory-in-stock percentage up from 80 percent to 96 percent. That freed up about $400 million in cash for us to invest in opening new stores.

Michaels may well be the only retailer in history that grew to 500 stores without point-of-sale (POS) registers and related data systems. We were so busy building and acquiring stores and gaining market share that we ended up maybe twenty years behind the rest of the world. As an entrepreneur who pioneered online computing and software, I felt like the shoemaker whose children had no shoes. The beauty of POS is that you know immediately what's going out of the store. The register feeds that information to a central computer in the store, which in turn feeds the information to a centralized computer at headquarters. So if I always have 100 red pens in my store and a woman comes in and buys 90 red pens, our computer system knows to reorder the pens. It sees what the historical data on red pens is, sees what was bought, determines what is needed, and places the order. POS registers involve much less human grunt work and free up more time to deal directly with customers.

Knowing what's leaving the store is only half the equation. The other half is knowing what's on the shelves. Perpetual inventory and automatic replenishment are the big words. Until the early 1990s, our local managers were in charge of their own inventory replenishment and had to do it without radio frequency guns, those gadgets you wave at the shelves to read bar codes. That was because we didn't always have enough bar codes.

Now, bar coding has been around for thirty or forty years, and if you're Wal-Mart or Target, using them is as natural as breathing. The items you're selling are bar-coded by a big vendor before they arrive in the store. No toothpaste has left Proctor & Gamble without a bar code in at least a generation. At Michaels, however, we had more than a thousand vendors, and some of them were originally moms-and-pops who started making little wooden footstools in their garage or seasonal lawn art in a small shop with their kids as employees. For many, bar coding was too much added cost or just too much bother for true-blue craftspeople like themselves, so for Michaels, getting inventory bar-coded was like pulling teeth.

When Michael Rouleau arrived, we'd already been working on these changes for a handful of years. With his Marine mentality, Michael promptly went from store to store and vendor to vendor, shouting "Ten-hup!" and demanding that these changes happen and happen fast.

I challenged Michael when he wanted to take authority away from the store managers because I loved the way decentralization made customers feel that this was their store. But that's part of company building, too: giving in to someone who has a better solution to a problem. You have to reach outside your own tendencies, your own preferences, and do what's right for the company, even if it collides with your instinctive philosophy or your educated rhythm.

Today our systems and processes give Michaels the ability to withstand competition from any big box retailer, because Michaels is better at its niche than they are. Wal-Mart might carry paint, but they're not going to carry 100 choices of artists' materials. They will have a deep stack of a very few colors, and none of the rest, which amounts to an end-of-the-conversation moment for the American woman crafter who is our core customer.

We maximize strengths by always carrying a complete stock of everything the artist or hobbyist needs. Top-of-the-line centralized purchasing and distribution further maximize that core strength, ensuring that the customer never walks out of Michaels and goes somewhere else for, say, a glue gun or any other vital crafting tool. Wal-Mart can't compete with that.

After ten terrific years, Michael turned sixty-seven and decided it was time to start working seriously on his golf game. He'd brought perfect order to the chaos, put a strong management team in place, and paved the way for his successors. By 2005, the Internet was becoming a major force in retail, and we needed someone at the top who could take us there. We made Jeff Boyer President and CFO, and Greg Sandfort President and COO, and then we hired JP Morgan to make sure we weren't missing any new opportunities to create value for the shareholders. Essentially, we created an auction and, by late 2006, there were something like twenty private equity firms bidding for Michaels. As I've said, the initial public investor paid 67 cents a share for the company. We ended up selling Michaels for 44 bucks to Blackstone and Bain, two Wall Street private equity firms who obviously agreed with us that the business was worth $6 billion in cash.

It was a great journey over twenty-two years, and Michaels will always hold a special place in my heart. I love the company. And, naturally, I still get my pictures framed there.

Today there are 30 million American women spread across the country who shop at Michaels at least once a month. My Louisiana cousins drive 60 miles to get to a Michaels store in Monroe. And the woman who installed my phone in Pitkin County, Colorado, drives almost 100 miles to shop at one.

I'll always remember how Mama used to go to Main Street in Delhi to buy her thread for sewing, and her wool for knitting, and her fabric for making slipcovers for our sofa and chairs. When I think about that, I tell myself, "If Mama were here today, she'd shop at Michaels."

Chapter 20

Maverick Investor

I HAVE GONE through four phases in my investment life.

First, I was a Saturday-morning investor. There have always been a whole bunch of information services and stock newsletters that will send you a ninety-day free trial, so I signed up for loads of them—because being a good reader makes you a better investor—and I read everything I could before deciding what to buy to build my portfolio. I liked *Value Line*, newsletters from brokers, *Bank Credit Analyst,* and John S. Herold's *America's Fastest Growing Companies.* I have also always read the *Christian Science Monitor,* the *Dallas Morning News,* and the *New York Times.* Occasionally I read *The Economist,* the *International Herald Tribune,* and the Asian edition of *The Wall Street Journal.*

I moved up a gear, into my second phase, when I started University Computing in the mid-1960s. In our first four years of public ownership, during a time when both Dow Jones stocks and treasury bonds lost value, our UCC stock multiplied by a factor of 100 to 1. In the entire history of Wall Street, that has not happened very often for public investors.

Next, as I entrepreneured new businesses and diversified my portfolio, I became what I call an active investor-owner in several companies, including Sterling, Bonanza, and Michaels.

But it was not until I founded Maverick, partnering with my elder son Evan, that I moved into the truly "hedged fund" world. Today Maverick manages $10 billion for my family and 700 other investors, including a lot of pension funds for American workers.

Of all the investment vehicles around the markets these days, hedge funds are probably the least understood and the most maligned. One reason for that probably stems from the fact that they are private partnerships open only to "accredited investors"—which usually means guys with a lot of money— who can lose their own money in their own way without the protection and help of federal security regulators. In fact, in all my years of being an entrepreneur, I have rarely run across any financial vehicle as little understood, as shrouded in mystery and controversy, or as feared, by the general investing public as hedge funds are.

Yet, while a few of the financial tricks some hedge fund managers use can be complicated—and some super-smart managers outsmart themselves and lose all their investors' money in a week or even a day—Maverick's basic concept is barber-shop simple: Invest in great companies that will likely increase in value and, at the same time, reduce risk of loss by selling weak or badly managed companies that are likely to decrease in value. That requires homework, a lot of homework. And the teams at Maverick do their homework because the goal of the company, as Evan articulated right from the beginning, is "to preserve and grow capital."

The man who created the first hedge fund was Alfred Winslow Jones, an American born in Australia in 1901, who went to Harvard, got himself a Ph.D. in sociology from Columbia, and eventually found a job writing for *Fortune* magazine. Except Jones called it a "hedged" fund. Somewhere along the way the press dropped the "d." Put it down to bad editing and shoddy lexicography, but this is how our version of the English language was created and is now being expanded and modified thanks to phenomena like Wikipedia.

While working on a story for *Fortune* called "Fashion in Forecasting," Jones decided it was impossible to know when the market would move in any particular direction. So whenever brokers or money managers said the market would go up or go down—and they nearly always said up, so their customers would buy and generate commissions—Jones reckoned, "They don't know what they're talking about."

Confucius says, "Forecasting difficult, especially the future."

Jones theorized that if you buy good companies and simultaneously sell short bad companies, you reduce your worry about which way the market is going to move. Volatility—ups and downs—is neutralized by shifting risk away from market timing decisions and toward stock selection.

Next he realized that his "hedged" idea became even more potent if you borrowed money from your broker, called "margin," to leverage the long and short positions. That can radically increase profits or losses.

Now, there are three schools of thought about borrowing money to invest: Never do it. Always do it. Sometimes do it.

There are times when you should do it, the argument against it being the Crash of 1929, when borrowing was worse than otherwise because of a 1,000 percent exposure to loss or gain. Banks then loaned against stocks with only 10 percent down. There was no hedging of risk, so that when the market crashed, the banks called their loans and the investors were bust. This is how my Granddaddy Evans, the town doctor, my mother's father, lost his savings.

A. W. Jones & Co. invited the public to invest in the first hedge fund in 1949. Seventeen years later, Carol Loomis at *Fortune* magazine saw that Jones's fund had outperformed every mutual fund on the market over the previous five- and ten-year periods, and wrote about him in an article called "The Jones Nobody Keeps Up With."

That sparked a rush of copycat funds. Today there are probably 10,000 hedge funds available to investors, with possibly more than a thousand coming and going every year. And many of them are not "hedged" at all because they do no hedging. Some are long only, some are short only, and some have become famous for leveraging at more than 30 to 1. There are hedge funds that bet on cotton futures or the price per barrel of oil. My Amarillo, Texas, friend Boone Pickens made a killing on oil and natural gas in 2006, after losing 91 percent of his and his investors' money in an earlier year. Some hedge funds bet on commodities, bonds, or interest rates; others on the Japanese yen versus the American dollar. Some try to time the market, guessing when to jump out of retail stocks and into frozen pork bellies. There are quantitative models or "Black Box" funds, which rely on computers following software instructions created from complex mathematical models. Such funds make robotic decisions based on statistical trends in things like prices and volumes, totally avoiding any research into the fundamental investment characteristics of the companies the fund is betting on. No doubt, someday someone will try to make a business of guessing the weather and package it up as a hedge fund, although I am sure if he does, Mother Nature will find a way to humble him.

Some hedge funds are well publicized, usually for all the wrong reasons. In 2006 Amaranth Advisors in New York lost $6.5 billion in one week betting on some crazy strategy that the price of March 2007 and March 2008 natural gas futures would be higher than the price of the April 2007 and April 2008 contracts. When it didn't work out, they went straight down the tubes. Their investors would have had a better shot in Las Vegas.

Then there were the hedge-funded, Stockholm-certified geniuses. A bunch of Nobel Prize winners set up a fund to hold money in trust for retired folk and their pension payments. The big pension funds just loved the notion of these bona fide "smartest people on the planet" pooling their intelligence, at least until the gaps in the market—which is where they were betting their money—didn't work out, and all the money in the fund disappeared. I figured they were doomed from Day 1 because hedge funds are not what Nobel Prize winners do. It helps to be smart running a hedge fund, but it takes more than that.

What has happened to Mr. Jones's big idea is that it has become an investment format rather than a strategy. The cynic's definition of a hedge fund is a place where smart young men can make your money disappear very quickly. Caveat emptor!

Many people find the idea of selling short to be something gloomy, sort of distasteful, and lacking faith. Not me. For every buyer, thou shalt have a seller. That's what makes a market.

Common sense says that one of them will be wrong. But the one who is wrong may only be wrong temporarily.

When I was running University Computing, a guy named Jimmy Rogers was shorting our stock. Market enthusiasm had driven our share price up 100 to 1 in four years, which was just too much for this rational man to believe. But his strategy simply encouraged me to find a way to preserve my values. Eventually, he took his losses and gave up. When University Computing stock got walloped by the great crash of 1969–74, Jimmy no longer had his short. He would have been right, but he was too early.

The most famous hedge funds have been built around a lone gunslinger rather than a great team. For example, George Soros and Michael Steinhardt both won big-time, but neither built an investing enterprise. They're good traders, but they're not entrepreneurs. As much as I admire these men—and I especially admire Soros for using his wealth to help the people emerging from seventy-five years behind the Soviet Russian Iron Curtain—I see their management philosophies and investing strategies as cautionary tales.

When I started, I studied how their firms were organized and how they made decisions, and it is undeniable that they have had awe-inspiring track records. But it was obvious that they were not team builders. When *Institutional Investor* magazine asked Soros to tell them about his support staff, he admitted, "There's fifty people back there. I don't know their names or what they do."

Michael Steinhardt, who lasted an extraordinary thirty years, also admitted that his skills as an organization builder were next to nil. His failure to think about standard business questions like teamwork, succession, or how to hold on to good employees meant that when he finally lost his hot hand, he had to close shop. I knew Steinhardt was in trouble in 1993 when I heard that he had just fired all his analysts; he concluded he didn't need them in order to understand companies anymore.

The "gonna do it myself 'cause nobody's as smart as me" attitude is not how companies should be built. It's certainly not the way I build them. So when Evan and I went in search of big investors, we were blessed to have a terrific financial officer, Shari Robertson, who helped us form a small but solid infrastructure. Our philosophical background as company builders separated us from the hedge fund gunslingers.

We started the fund that would ultimately be called Maverick in 1990 with $15 million of family assets, much of it coming after the sale of our Bonanza Steakhouse chain. We gradually added a few wealthy and some not-so-wealthy private investors. If you did the calculations, you would find that the first dollar put at risk was worth $12 fifteen years later.

Our idea was to find big bargains in various asset classes, and one of the first was junk bonds. By 1989, government intervention had turned the boom in them into a bust, forcing Drexel Burnham into bankruptcy. The markets hated Mike Milken and his high-yield bonds with as much passion as they had earlier loved them, and not without cause, because the default rate rose as high as 14 percent. But there was so much negative noise in the press that bonds originally sold with a 12 percent yield were selling to yield 20 to 30 percent. What was already a bargain became a better bargain.

Congress actually blamed the Savings and Loans (S&L) crisis on junk bonds. It is probably not a coincidence that many of those politicians grew up learning about this stuff from black-and-white TV replays of the Christmas movie *It's a Wonderful Life*, where James Stewart saves his hometown from the beady-eyed banker. So they passed a law forcing all S&Ls to rid their portfolios of junk bonds within five years. But Congress made the S&L problem into a huge American disaster by doing this and simultaneously freezing interest rates on savings accounts. The S&Ls had committed themselves to long-term mortgage loans at low fixed rates, and then Congress allowed the rates to float upward, squeezing the S&Ls between fixed income and the rising cost of money. As a result, many of them went belly-up. But as S&Ls were forced out of business, thereby depressing prices, we saw real bargains in busted American junk bonds.

At the same time, we started looking at the sovereign debt out of what were then called "lesser developed countries," now called "emerging markets."

One of my investment heroes, Sir John Templeton—the man who pioneered globally diversified mutual funds—used to tell people, "I never in all my life bought a stock because I liked it. I bought it because it was a better bargain than any similar stock I could buy anywhere in the rest of the world. See the investment world as an ocean, and buy where you get the most value for your money."

The idea of multinational opportunities had intrigued me since my University Computing days, when I built our businesses in more than a dozen countries. I'd found that for every $2 we made in the United States, we made another dollar in Europe, plus about 20 cents in Asia. The calculations were much the same with Sterling Software. Also, by looking overseas, we found bargains in Latin America, too.

The groundwork was laid for investments in sovereign debt in 1973, and again in 1979, with the oil price markups. Banks with lots of "petrodollar" deposits had sought out assets with good returns in odd places. Men like Walter Wriston, then head of Citibank, championed the old theory that sovereign debt would always be safe because any government can tax its people to pay back its debt. I was skeptical, however. In those days, the Shah ruled Iran with an iron hand. But the country never really felt stable to me, especially because I knew there was a high level of corruption. That sordid fact was driven home for me when University Computing's European president told me he wanted to bid on Iranian contracts but needed money for bribes. I said no, we are an American company, and I do not care what other companies are doing, we refuse to do business anywhere with bribes. So we didn't go to Iran.

During my time on the board at First National, the bank bought some of the Shah's sovereign debt because it could "never fail." One night in Tokyo, the Shah's ambassador to Japan beautifully described to me how Iran was such a solid brick in America's wall of containment around the "Reds" of Russia and China. Except the Shah was forced into exile by Ayatollah Khomeini and the Mullahs in 1979, and First National Bank in Dallas got hurt big-time, sovereign and all.

I remained skeptical when sovereign debt regained popularity in the 1980s. Many of these sovereign debt bonds started going sour by the end of the decade. As a reminder, on my office wall I have two framed bonds, one from the regime of Russia's Czar, the other from America's Confederate government. Both are worthless. Both confirm my sense of perspective about things that can "never fail."

The World Bank and the International Monetary Fund soon came up with a new idea to attract investors to bad debt: Brady Bonds. Named after Nicholas Brady, Secretary of the Treasury under President Bush the elder, the idea underpinning these bonds was to give each $1,000 bond a new principal value, say, $600. In theory, even though everyone had already taken a haircut on bad debt, the countries issuing these Brady Bonds would now, for sure, make their future payment. Washington even put in some Treasury Bonds as security. Partially bolstered by the U.S. Treasury, Brady's were priced in the market at around 20 to 50 percent of the face value of the Lesser Developed Countries' bonds, so you knew that even if the bond defaulted, you would still get at least the 20 cents on the dollar inherent in the U.S. Treasury's backing it. I calculated that if the countries did nothing but pay the interest on these bonds for three years, I'd be home free.

So we took big positions in Brazilian, Argentinean, and Mexican debt, and also bought debt in a few Caribbean islands. Just as with American junk bonds, I was convinced with these new sovereign debt Brady Bonds that there was little downside and huge upside potential, just the kind of great risk-reward ratio I like.

A real advantage to this version of foreign debt was that it took a while for the notion to catch on in the general investing community. When we started buying them, the term "Brady Bond" was not even part of most people's vocabulary. Since then, they have been renamed "emerging market debt" and, as they became better known, prices rose dramatically.

Next there was a sort of mutual fund that Wall Street came up with called "closed-end investment funds," which focused on a particular country's stocks. Shares in these funds are bought and sold in public markets at whatever price a willing buyer would pay. If people wanted Indonesian stocks, Merrill Lynch or Goldman Sachs simply created an Indonesian fund. If people wanted Parisian stocks, the investment houses created a French fund. Actually, some of these closed-end country funds had been out there for decades, a few all the way back to the 1920s. But more were created over the last two decades as interest in them became euphoric. The proliferation of these closed-end funds is hardly surprising, seeing as how the mantra of Wall Street investment underwriters is, "When the ducks are quacking, you feed the ducks."

You bought these funds at par, but brokers took a massive 6 percent fee, which instantly reduced your capital to 94 cents on the dollar. Hardly a good start. That said, you could make money as long as that overseas hot rod roared for you. And in the initial euphoria, some did, at least for a while. Then the long, slow disenchantment set in as investors lost interest and moved on to the next new thing.

But as public interest waned, these closed-end funds began trading at big discounts. My interest peaked when the "I want something more fashionable" attitude drove prices down to the super-bargain level, and in the early 1990s there were loads of these closed-end funds trading at 20 to 40 percent discounts from the market value of the stocks and bonds inside the funds.

While scouring the world for bargains, I was not alone in liking Asia. And here, too, you had to do your homework to find bargains. At the end of the 1980s, the place to invest was Japan. But when I looked at Japan, I saw a mature market grossly overpriced.

Japan had sopped up the American-style government and economy based on individual liberty, freedom, and democracy that we had imposed on them after the war, and then they added to that their cultural strengths based on dedicated teamwork. They came to America selling Honda motorcycles, then Sony TVs, then Toyota cars, and they whipped us badly in our own marketplace. Some Americans were outraged that the Japanese were buying sacred monuments like Pebble Beach Golf Course and Rockefeller Center. Since they were paying outrageously high prices, I saw it as a good thing, a wealth

transfer to the USA, with which we would build more Rockefeller Centers.

Consider this as an example of the perils of investing in
Japan in the late 1980s. The Nippon Telephone Company went
public at 240 times earnings, this at a time when AT&T was
trading for 16 times earnings. The land under the Imperial
Palace in Tokyo was valued at a higher price than all the real
estate in California. Hysterical overvaluations, no? For me,
Japan was a huge bubble poised to burst.

More appealing were the "Asian Tigers": Taiwan, Singapore,
and Hong Kong. These three really interested me because they
were a gateway into China, and I saw China as a huge growth
story because it had been held back by a command-and-control
economy for two generations.

When Mao's Red Army took over in 1949, entrepreneurial
families in China fled to Hong Kong, Singapore, and Taiwan
with whatever gold they could stuff in their pockets. As soon as
they could, these "overseas Chinese" then bought "backup"
houses in places like Vancouver, just in case they had to flee all
over again.

By the late 1980s, many of these exiled Chinese families were
second-generation entrepreneurs with successful businesses
abroad in Singapore, Taiwan, and, especially, Hong Kong. I
decided that was a good place to be. Adding to the attraction
there was the constant fear in the air that once China regained
control of Hong Kong, Beijing would confiscate private companies, just as it had in Shanghai in 1949. That kept prices for
these companies low. But the Chinese government had just
made a billion-dollar investment in the Hong Kong Telephone
Company, and I thought to myself, "That's not what we would
do if we were about to confiscate a company with a shot at hundreds of millions of customers." I felt, when you combined the
powerful energy of the Chinese culture with the commercial
stability of English common law—which had been well established in Hong Kong by the British rulers—investments there
would flourish. Jimmy Rogers liked China so much that he was
teaching his little daughter to speak Mandarin, rather than
Spanish or French, as a second language.

The Tiananmen Square Massacre in the spring of 1989 put serious doubts in many investors' minds about China. It was indeed a terrible tragedy, and I certainly never mistook China for the most democratic country in the world. But an old Chinese proverb gave me faith that, regardless of the government, the people would find their way to a free-market system: "The mountains are high and the emperor is far away."

We based our initial interest in Hong Kong on history, but our investment in selected stocks there was based on microeconomics. We did our research. We looked at industries and companies with solid growth prospects. I looked for Hong Kong entrepreneurs whose companies would prosper as China opened its markets. I looked for the best bargains.

There were some early mutual funds specializing in Hong Kong, and I studied what they had in their portfolios. It was the old Sam Walton trick. As he himself used to say, "I borrow other people's ideas."

I also noticed that, unlike exchanges here, the Hong Kong exchange published a list of every company that was buying its own stock. We sorted through that to find companies that were family-controlled. As long as these were good and profitable companies that published honest financial statements, it struck me that these family folks weren't going to be buying their own stock if they knew trouble was heading their way. If the family already owned, say, 20 percent of its own company, and they were buying more, then they were confident of the future. So we kept checking those lists and co-invested in their companies, at the same time and at the same price.

Another trend I followed was "the work."

I wanted to know where the work was being done, when it moved, and what replaced it. My son-in-law David Matthews and I visited a plant on the Chinese mainland where 1,500 young women were hand-painting silk flowers that we imported and sold in our Michaels chain for $5. We couldn't have made that flower in America for $50. Actually, we couldn't have made it at all. What they were doing on the Chinese mainland, they had once done in Hong Kong. The work moved to mainland China because people in Hong Kong could earn more money in the higher value-added tasks that were developing there. Earlier, this same kind of work had moved out of Japan to Hong Kong. If you traced it all the way back, you could see how this work got pushed out of Tennessee and made its way to Japan.

Adam Smith said it all in 1776: "Free markets work."

IN THE NINETEENTH CENTURY, Nathan Mayer Rothschild said, "Buy when there is blood in the streets."

He saw that traumatic events, such as war, lead people to panic and sell their assets at less than their intrinsic value. Remaining clearheaded in the midst of chaos is not easy, and Evan and I soon found ourselves put to the test.

In 1990, Saddam Hussein grabbed Kuwait and made it very clear that he was going after Saudi Arabia next. The market went into panic mode. There was a rush to quality, like Treasury bills and bonds. Buyers for what I owned, which was the opposite, totally disappeared. Bank liquidity dried up. Share prices dropped precipitately. And the price of oil jumped very quickly from $17 a barrel to $40.

It was white-knuckle time. If Saddam were permitted to keep Kuwait and help himself to Saudi Arabia, I could see oil prices easily hitting $200. The big question in my mind was, "Will the president act?"

What I knew for sure came from a briefing on national security given by Bill Clements, who had been Deputy Secretary of Defense for Presidents Nixon and Ford. In that briefing, Bill stated categorically that no American President, Democrat or Republican, liberal or conservative, could ever permit any other power to control the two-thirds of the world's oil in the Persian Gulf.

That meant the President had to act. And once I had decided that, my conclusion was clear: Don't cut and run, buy.

There was nothing written in stone telling me I was right. There never is. Even the most diehard fundamentalist investor is only acting on what he or she believes. But I had a high level of confidence that President Bush would throw Saddam out of Kuwait.

That very week, President Bush and British Prime Minister Margaret Thatcher were scheduled to speak at the Aspen Institute and were bunking at Jessica and Ambassador Henry Cato's house, next door to Charles and Dee Wyly's ranch in Woody Creek, Colorado. While visiting privately with President Bush before their press conference, the clear-thinking, tough-minded, instantly-get-to-the-heart-of-the-matter Margaret told the President, "Not a time to go wobbly, George!"

So while some saw Saddam's move as Doomsday and fled to safe havens, like Treasury bonds, I increased my bets on more speculative investments, like Latin American debt and American junk bonds.

Was it scary? Of course!

The President warned Saddam that Iraqi soldiers had to be out of Kuwait by January 15, 1991, and when they weren't, the counterattack began. Watching television that night, I asked my wife, Cheryl, what she thought the war was going to do to share prices and oil. As most people would, she predicted stocks would go down and oil would go up, which was the very condition that would have made my decision a disaster.

I told her, "Nope. As soon as the market sees there'll be an American victory, the fear factor in the market will go away."

The return on our portfolio that year was 199 percent.

By 1993, the investing landscape was vastly different. Brady Bonds, Hong Kong stocks, and sovereign debt had all become so popular that they were no longer bargains. Good opportunities on entire classes of assets were vanishing right before our eyes, too. It was time for change.

If you want to preserve and grow your wealth, you must think independently. It's either that, or hire an honest and competent manager to think independently for you. Where I was once comfortable with the wide swings in our short-term gains and losses, I started to think that if we wanted institutional investors to take our hedge fund to the next level, we needed to find a way to lessen that volatility. Evan was also convinced that the time for aggressive growth and opportunistic ventures had passed, and that the time for conservative decision making had come.

We were looking to build an investment enterprise. We wanted a portfolio manager with superb stock-selection skills and real shorting experience. So we hired a management-recruiting firm to find candidates for us, and we put the word out to friends that we were looking for someone. In April 1993, Richard Hanlon phoned me. He had been with us at University Computing in the 1980s and stayed with us on the Michaels board. At the time, he was managing investor relations for another software company, Legent, on the way to becoming one of the top people at America Online. He wanted to recommend "the smartest software analyst I've ever met." His name was Lee Ainslie.

Evan and I had long trusted Richard's opinions. And we were especially interested when he mentioned that Lee was working for Julian Robertson at Tiger. Learning at Julian's knee could be no bad thing, especially since Tiger was a hedge fund known for being very savvy when it came to shorting weak companies.

Richard told me one incident in particular that clinched it for me. He described the time Legent's earnings had missed Wall Street expectations by a couple of pennies, and the stock got pummeled. I remembered it well. Knowing the company's fundamental strengths, I'd seen the price drop as a bargain and started buying. Lee, meanwhile, already had a big position in Legent at Tiger, but when his boss saw the price drop, he wanted to sell everything. Lee had called Richard and requested an urgent meeting with the senior management team. He said the meeting would determine whether he'd unload the entire position or double his holdings. He wound up doing the latter. That told me Lee and I had the same basic principles when it came to defining value.

Richard promptly arranged to have dinner with Lee in New York to determine his interest in meeting with me and listening to what we had on our minds.

Over several months and quite a few meetings, I met Lee's parents, and his future wife, Elizabeth. We talked about a lot of things, from colonial history and our shared American heritage of the Virginia backcountry to stock selection. We also got into long discussions about great portfolio managers. I had been reading Warren Buffett's letters to his investors for over twenty years. Lee, who was only twenty-eight at the time, had been reading them, too, if not for as long, but he had dug up all the old Buffett letters to study.

This was a kid who'd been in investment clubs since he was in high school, and all he'd ever dreamed of was becoming a portfolio manager. He had only been with Tiger for three years and didn't yet have an auditable track record of his own; at hedge funds even the best analyst's records are merged into the fund's overall performance. Julian was a fantastic mentor, and Lee was already a managing partner, but at Tiger, it would always be Julian calling the shots. Conventional wisdom told us to find someone with longer experience and a great track record. But I remembered when I was twenty-eight being told I was too young and too inexperienced to run my own company. I remembered how much I yearned to do it, no matter what anyone else thought. I saw that same burning desire in Lee.

As USUAL, I chose to take what I saw plainly before my eyes more seriously than conventional wisdom and invited Lee to join us. These days, when I think about some of my best recruits—Don Thomson, Sterling Williams, Michael Rouleau, Dan Krausse, Lee Ainslie, and Paul Thomas—it strikes me that they all have this in common: They need to be the decision maker.

These guys burned for it. They had to have it. Being captain of the ship was essential to the way they did business. So I gave that to them and, in exchange, I got the best, hardest-working, most dedicated presidents for the companies I had built and owned that any entrepreneur could ever ask for. These managers are definitely not men who suffered from lack of ego, but watching them rise beyond anything that even they imagined themselves capable of has been one of my greatest pleasures as an entrepreneur. Totally aside from anything economic, it's a big, positive quality-of-life thing.

With Lee Ainslie on board, we came up with the name Maverick for our hedge fund. He started out by managing about 30 percent of the portfolio, and over the next two years we kept giving him more. And in the first quarter of 1995, when we had around $100 million in the fund, we made him the sole portfolio manager. When Maverick had grown to $400 million, I left the management and Lee became the major owner of the general partnership, with Lee and Evan as the two managing partners.

Since the beginning, Maverick has taken half the risk of the stock market and earned twice the return of the market. We have never had a down year, not even during the great crash of 2000–2002, when blue chip Dow Jones stocks dropped 40 percent and the more speculative NASDAQ stocks dropped 80 percent.

As I write, in 2007, the bubbles in real estate mortgages and leveraged buyout investing brought on by the very low interest cost of high-risk debt over the last few years are now bursting, with several funds so focused losing all their investors' money. But Maverick has gone through the crises like the Rock of Gibraltar.

Before Lee joined us, Evan and I had been investing mostly in an eclectic collection of high-yield bonds, international stocks, and emerging market debt, using a macroeconomic approach. Lee's strategy is stock-centric and totally bottom-up. This means he does not try to time markets or rotate between sectors that are in and out of favor. He focuses instead on the most fundamental aspects of any particular company. He has a team of about fifty people who spend all their time researching and analyzing stocks.

Maverick continues to focus primarily on medium- and large-cap U.S. companies and, by hedging in every region and every industry, dramatically reduces the casino element of investing. About half the companies are longs, and every investor dollar is leveraged by a dollar and a half of the lowest-cost cash.

When Lee and Evan closed Maverick to new investors, I decided I wanted to do something with my son-in-law Jason Elliott (he's married to my daughter Kelly), so I gave him a portfolio to run and, out of that, we developed our second hedge fund group, Ranger.

Inside Ranger, which manages something like $1.2 billion now, there are two portfolios. One is a long-only growth stock portfolio of America's fastest-growing, highest-quality mid-cap and small-cap companies. This team, led by Conrad Doenges, has persistently performed in the top 10 percent of managers of small- and mid-cap portfolios. The other Ranger strategy is a fund of funds, a portfolio of over thirty hedge funds. The accent is on steady earning with low risk, as measured by volatility. This team, led by Robert Chambers, has a record of lower risk than long-term Treasury bonds, and with a much greater return.

Chapter 21

The Good Earth

W E ARE KILLING the earth with friendly fire.
It has only been a few generations since we humans
moved beyond the basic struggle for survival, but the cost of
winning that fight has been huge. We have used the earth's coal
and oil in such gargantuan quantities that the last three generations have now consumed more of those precious resources
than all the generations that came before us.

The warning signs are clear. We need to understand what we
have done and, more important, radically change what we are
doing. We face serious questions that need to be answered now,
and I believe entrepreneurs are the right people to wrestle with
one question in particular: How do we go forward in a manner
that not only creates value for ourselves and our stakeholders
but is also mindful of the threat to the earth and its inhabitants?

I CAME TO CLEAN AIR first as a child, then as a parent, then as
an owner of an oil refinery, and finally as a veteran of the battles that broke up our nation's telephone and computer monopolies. As a child, I remember when it was time to give the crops
their dose of DDT. "Get out of that cotton patch," Mama would
holler to me and Charles Junior, "we're going to poison the cotton and kill the boll weevils."

My grandfather, who was a doctor, used to say that next to
penicillin, DDT did more than anything else to stop death in
our swampy, mosquito-infested part of Louisiana. Today, we
understand the unintended consequences.

An eye opener was Rachel Carson's terrific book, *Silent*

Spring. She was the canary in the coal mine that triggered today's Green movement. President Jack Kennedy so honored her at the White House.

She warned, "The most alarming of all man's assaults upon the environment is the contamination of air, earth, rivers and sea with dangerous and even lethal materials." She singled out DDT and not only set Congress on the path toward banning it, but all these years later, thanks to that ban, she helped guarantee the survival of the bald eagle, our national bird. Poisonous chemicals in the food chain had so seriously depleted the numbers of our national bird that it was on the endangered species list. Once DDT had worked its way out of the ecosystem, the bald eagle's survival rate increased and today it is no longer endangered. Closer to my home states of Louisiana and Texas on the Gulf Coast, we also saved the Eastern Brown Pelican, the Louisiana state bird.

As a parent, I was faced again with questions of environmental stewardship when my daughter Christiana, as a fifth grader, asked me, "What are we going to do about toxic waste?" I have never forgotten her question, or the Bible story about seeing as a child sees. I firmly believe that education is the most important factor driving environmental awareness, and I'm encouraged that schools across our country are taking up the cause. Our children are learning about the condition of our planet, and they are challenging their parents for answers.

One of the first major problems to confront us at Earth Resources, way back in 1974, was the government mandate to take the lead out of gasoline, which we made from crude oil at our refinery in Memphis. If it had been just a bottom-line decision, there wouldn't have been any discussion, because separating gasoline from lead simply cost too much. But my growing awareness of environmental issues led me to consider more important factors than simple costs. I was convinced that both profitability and sustainability had to be achievable.

Lead had once been considered a terrific modern advancement. But by the early 1970s there was evidence of lead poisoning from both leaded house paint and gasoline, and the Environmental Protection Agency decided that burning lead was to blame for releasing a lot of poisons into the air. The practice had to stop.

When we did the math, it didn't look good. The capital investment required to meet the new gasoline-refining standards equaled our little company's total net worth. Unleaded gasoline was being phased in, but it would cost consumers four cents more a gallon. No one knew if people would pay the extra four cents, or if they would just ride in the old cars longer and keep buying the less expensive leaded gasoline. So, more than thirty years ago, we faced the big environmental question that all entrepreneurs will eventually have to address: Are we willing to bet our businesses on getting the lead out?

Trying to guess how much more consumers were willing to pay back then for environmentally enlightened products was not easy. The thinking was that environmentally friendly products—gasoline, clean electricity, organic cotton, dolphin-free tuna fish, and so on—would always cost more to produce and therefore would always sell at a premium.

We've since learned that cost is not necessarily the only determining factor when it comes to conservation. The first person who decided to save dolphins that were getting caught in tuna fishing nets priced his tuna at 50 cents more a can than anyone else's, and didn't sell very many. Later, after he was able to narrow the price difference to a nickel, consumers responded with a huge grassroots effort to "save the dolphins." People are willing to pay another nickel to do the right thing.

In our case, with leaded gasoline, it still wasn't a sure thing. What would be the right decision, we asked ourselves, for our own Delta Refining Company on the banks of the Mississippi? Our Memphis facility had been producing a lot of "bottom of the barrel" products, such as asphalt. While making our new, legally required capital investment, our engineers recognized that we could change the mix in our refining process and start producing more "top of the barrel" products, like jet fuel. Jet fuel had higher profit margins, and, as another profit multiplier, we could also produce substantially more barrels per day. At a time when other refiners closed up shop rather than bet the money on new equipment, we were rewarded for investing in cleaner technology that produced greater amounts of higher-margin product. That meant that doing the right thing in this case carried an economic bonus. It was a win-win.

Those oil refineries that shut down rather than make the necessary capital investment, seeing only the dangers of change and its initial costs, became progressively more negative, created self-fulfilling prophecies of doom, gloom, and failure. Perceive dead ends and you'll find what you perceive. That's why entrepreneurs are by nature optimists.

FAST-FORWARD three decades and, today, everyone knows that cars create air pollution. Most people do not know, however, that the greatest source of industrial pollution comes from the making of electricity. It accounts for the majority of three major pollutants: 85 percent of nitrogen oxide, which contributes to smog; 97 percent of sulfur dioxide, which contributes to acid rain; and 99 percent of mercury, which is associated with many health problems.

For seventy years, the electricity monopolies in this country had a free ride. This has allowed dirty old coal plants to pump pollution into the air without factoring the environmental damage they do into the cost of doing business. In my mind, this is trespassing on the rights to clean air of all the rest of us who live on this small planet.

And that is why, in 1997, I decided to get to work and become a champion of the clean-air revolution. I began what would become a ten-year investment in a little company called Green Mountain Energy, whose slogan is, "Choose wisely. It's a small planet."

The fundamental concept that brought me to this conviction is an inescapable fact of human behavior, known as "the tragedy of the Commons."

Over two thousand years ago, Aristotle observed, "That which is common to the greatest number has the least care bestowed upon it." The tragedy of the Commons is, simply, that free access and unrestricted demand create abuse. The classic example is a spot of "common" ground owned by the villagers, each of whom has a cow grazing there. Because it is free, one person decides that instead of one cow, he can graze two and then three cows. When he does, everyone else brings more cows to the Commons, and before long there's no grass left for any of them.

The same is happening to our air and water. It's a Commons. There is no charge to use it. There is no ownership. Our market system is based on the idea that somebody owns something, but the Commons is outside the market system.

Consider the amounts of carbon dioxide that we are throwing into our air and atmosphere. Over 70 million tons a day. That is unsustainable. Our small planet cannot cope with this much poisonous gas for much longer.

Al Gore's *An Inconvenient Truth*, and Leonardo DiCaprio's *The 11th Hour* speak the truth. Gore has played a valuable part for over thirty years in educating the public, but his film sells more fear than hope and solutions. Leonardo's lesser known film is one-third diagnosis of the ailment and two-thirds treatment. I like the hope, the solutions, and the answers. Our company motto at IBM was, "Answers are our products."

Our recent presidents and Congress have been hiding behind a false economic argument, saying that protecting the environment is going to hurt the economy. They got it wrong. I've grown convinced that moving toward a carbon-free economy will create good jobs and stimulate economic growth. Entrepreneurs—green entrepreneurs—will lead the charge and find ways to get clean air and water. Their investment in technology will result in economic growth.

It will take not only political consensus but also politicians' courage to put tough caps on emissions—to limit the number of cows that can graze on the Commons. Some European countries have already taken action. Somehow we in America have to come from behind and lead by example and persuasion, to get all the nations of the world to negotiate emissions caps for coal plants, cars, and planes. With only 5 percent of the world's population, America produces 30 percent of its pollution, and yet it still has not signed up for this mission.

Even better than caps on emissions would be a carbon consumption tax. This stops polluters from externalizing their costs and instead imbeds the cost of the carbon dioxide in the cost of goods and services they produce. That cost would translate into higher prices for the consumption of those products produced from oil and coal energy. The tax can be stepped up gradually to require polluters to recognize the costs of their products over time.

A companion tax, a tariff, needs to be applied to imports. This will place American workers and companies in a fair fight with overseas competition. We have incentivized energy-intensive production to move to China and elsewhere overseas. The carbon consumption tariff will give incentive to those foreign producers to generate energy in an earth-friendly way in order to reduce the tariffs on their goods at the borders of the United States, Europe, and Japan.

Global agreements need to be created to standardize tariffs on imports. The Montreal Protocol can be used as a model. "Globalized" success in the control of ozone depletion was achieved under U.S. leadership by Secretary of State George Shultz during the Reagan presidency at a world meeting in Montreal. America now needs to duplicate this on a more grand and noble scale so as to eliminate our addiction to oil, and to cut back enough on the poisonous greenhouse gas all countries are creating to make the world safe and secure for our children and grandchildren.

But I wouldn't stop there.

All the cash that's raised from the carbon consumption tax and tariff would be given back to the people, exclusively to reduce the Social Security taxes paid on up to about $100,000 of earnings. That would keep it from being a regressive tax: You would shield the lowest-paid Americans while those who chose to consume more with big houses and big cars would pay more. In fact, I could argue that a carbon tax and tariff is a *progressive* tax. The definition of "progressive" is "making progress; advancing to something better." This tax would bring with it huge entrepreneurial opportunities, motivating innovation and the marketing of products and services to foster efficiency.

This arrangement would reward every company that

231

reduces its pollution. By cutting their carbon consumption tax, they would simultaneously trim costs and boost profits. By taking advantage of incentives to invest in new technology—to clean up coal plants and make cars run like hybrids—forward-looking companies would become more competitive. Make products with less carbon and the better they will sell, and the more profits you'll earn.

Along the same lines, alternative sources of energy would also enjoy incentives. Not just wind and water and sun, but atomic, too. The French and the Japanese have done a great job cleaning up some of their emissions by going heavily nuclear. Nuclear power is safe and it seems to me to be very low risk. We have never lost a life in America due to nuclear generation. Chernobyl was a result of bad engineering and the Stalinist stupidity of giving their engineers no safety goals, only production goals. Yet the fear generated from Chernobyl and Three Mile Island has resulted in no new nuclear construction since 1973.

Whole Foods is a great example of a company that has positioned itself well to flourish in a carbon-regulated world. Their corporate mission already includes stewardship of the earth. Sustainable agriculture and other wise environmental practices are part of their core values—this means organic, natural, and locally grown products. Whole Foods has found that their customer will pay more for green products and Green values.

A different example of what I mean by forward-looking companies that are making more conservation happen is Wal-Mart. Though Wal-Mart is a low-price retailer, they have found that they can reduce costs by going green. And they have told their suppliers in China, India, and everywhere, "We are going to sell green products in the huge American market"—which, by the way, is 30 percent of China's world market—"but we are only going to buy from suppliers who produce them in a clean way."

I WAS FIRST DRAWN to invest in what became Green Mountain Energy by the Vermont name. Its origins come from Ethan Allen and the cussedly independent militia of settlers in southwestern Vermont. They organized themselves in the 1760s to keep the British in New York from claiming sovereignty over them and that's how their name, the Green Mountain Boys, came to symbolize a fearless stand for right over wrong.

Green Mountain Power was a tiny, four-county electric utility based in Burlington, Vermont. It had been sleepily around for 100 years when Kevin Hartley, a freethinking soul, began promoting the idea that Americans should have the choice to buy "clean" electricity to help save our planet. By 2004, my Green Mountain had joined the Chicago Climate Exchange (CCE), the first global marketplace for trading emissions offsets in all six greenhouse gases. It's a free-market solution, and a simple one at that. Companies that reduce their carbon emissions can sell credits to polluters, who buy them in the open market to offset their greenhouse emissions. In other words, polluters pay for their polluting by rewarding companies that have reduced their carbon emissions. The idea is to create a situation, through the markets, of "carbon-neutral" companies. Green Mountain may have been one of the smallest electric utilities in America, but Kevin's grand vision convinced me that the nation's electric utilities would be deregulated. When that happened, I knew Green Mountain could become a national player.

Back in 1997, their sales pitch to me had been pretty clever. They said, "Sam, because you battled long and hard to bust up the phone monopoly, you may be the only entrepreneur in the country who understands what we hope to do and who isn't afraid to help us do it."

They were talking about selling clean electricity and getting there, first, by monopoly busting. This naturally stirred not just my environmental consciousness but also my David-versus-Goliath competitive juices and my fond memories of surviving against the IBM and AT&T monopolies.

Essentially they were saying, "Now it's time to Beat Dirty Power."

I found myself thinking that if Americans were actually given a choice between buying dirty or clean electricity, many of us would choose clean, even if it cost a bit more. I imagined a future where the price of clean electricity would drop as oil and natural gas became increasingly scarce and more costly, as they recently have. At the same time, we could find cost reductions through increased volume and better technology.

Also, I thought, there would ultimately be a change in the law that would penalize companies externalizing the costs of air pollution and climate degradation. When that happened, the comparative costs of clean versus dirty electricity would change in favor of clean.

I itched to do it.

But my battle with AT&T buzzed before my eyes. Going through that again—working eight years and losing $100 million—was not exactly at the top of my entrepreneurial to-do list. On the other hand, I had helped break up the most powerful monopoly in America, the old AT&T, and if anything I had done in my life had earned me a footnote in America's economic history, surely that was it.

But did I really want to play this monopoly-buster role again? My answer was yes. Whatever the investment outcome, I knew we could at least push the markets forward by helping to educate people about clean electricity and give them the power to choose. It would be a long and risky road ahead, but I was at a place in my life where I could afford to take a loss. Even if that happened economically, I would still win in a very real and spiritually satisfying way. I would just not be using economic success as the way to keep score. I would adopt a different and perhaps more important report card.

So, with ultimately $150 million in investments and a partnership with British Petroleum and Nuon, the Dutch electricity utility, I committed my time, energy, and focus to Green Mountain and started looking for a good chief executive and a capable team of managers. Then we moved the company to Austin, Texas, because, as states decided whether or not to deregulate electricity, Texas went into a free-market mentality and Vermont was still in the monopoly mode.

I believed that as energy markets began opening up, environmental issues would play an increasingly important role in the new players gaining acceptance with consumers. Mind you, this was more than ten years ago, before the *New York Times* was running daily articles on the environment and clean power. Environmental awareness still seemed limited to a few "alarmists" and leftover hippies. So that made Green Mountain unique. We would be the only player in those new markets offering customers a choice. We created demand for cleaner energy by going after customers who valued clean air. We were educating voters who have the power to change national policy from its focus on fossil fuels to a new emphasis on renewables.

Green Mountain's focus was initially only residential. The American electricity market was around $300 billion in annual revenue, with residential accounting for about one-third of that. Our research showed that 20 percent of U.S. consumers were willing to pay a small premium for environmentally friendly electricity. So our potential market was huge.

Originally, we lobbied state governments to write laws to support competitive markets. Then, when those states opened up, we went in to compete with the former monopoly. We thought it would take just a few years to get into the fifty states.

There I was, being the optimistic entrepreneur all over again.

California was the first state to change, and the Sacramento lawmakers did it all wrong. Instead of deregulating, they took one bad law and replaced it with another bad law. Then along came the California price spike, already teed up by California lawmakers who didn't understand Economics 101, the basic law of supply and demand. Then there was the Enron scandal, which was totally irrelevant to the price spike, but got blamed for it by politicians and the media. That threw an old monkey wrench into the process, across the country. Jeff Skilling, Enron's CEO, can be blamed for other things (for which he's now doing twenty-five years), but California got it wrong! Period.

That experience caused us to do some rethinking. We had gotten into some states, as planned. Now we decided to turn to states where the door was still closed but where we could find a way to collaborate with the monopoly utility, partnering with them to bring a green product to market.

For instance, in Oregon, which is a regulated state, our partner today is Portland General Electric. We are also in Florida, another state that prohibits competition, working with Florida Power and Light.

We sell wind, solar, hydro, geothermal, and efficient natural gas power, and everything we sell is cleaner than the monopoly power grid mix. I would love to sell renewable power exclusively, but that's simply not possible yet. The cost of wind power and its transportation to market still varies too much around the country. We do sell wind and sun in Texas—and the wind doesn't blow there all the time and the sun doesn't shine every day—but we are changing the world. And for the average household, buying clean electricity from Green Mountain does as much good for the environment as not driving your car 21,000 miles a year.

We got into Texas by taking on the state monopolies and beating them. George Bush was the governor and, although he wasn't the greenest guy in the state, he was green enough that his door was open. His knowledgeable staff worked step-by-step with Steve Wolens, the Democrat's tiger in the House, who led the charge. Republican Senator David Sibley brought the state Senate along and the result was that Texas got it right.

It wasn't so much that George the Younger wanted to make the state greener, although it was okay with him, in part because the green Wylys were long-term, clannishly loyal backers of his dad and him. More important to him was using deregulation to create a competitive market in electricity. So Texas created the opportunity, and Texas has now passed California in building windmills.

We had suffered through some real financial disasters in California, Pennsylvania, and Ohio before Green Mountain's breakthrough and triumphs in Texas, Oregon, and Florida and on the Internet.

As we'd anticipated, the price of cleaner electricity started coming down. The price of wind, compared to the alternatives, has come down dramatically, but it is still not cheaper than coal. As long as coal can externalize its costs on the rest of us without having to pay for cleaning up the air it pollutes, it will seem the "cheaper" alternative.

Today, Green Mountain is nicely profitable and growing fast, thanks to a few early believers, stubborn persistence, and a ten-year investment in hoped-for clean air through clean energy. The world has changed in those ten years and, in our own small way, we've helped. Green geopolitics is now a rising tide. People I meet tell me how they have just bought a car that gets an extra 5 miles to the gallon, or how they are installing a solar roof on their house, or that they have just put in insulation. We are all learning to conserve.

People have a choice today. Everyone can go to www.Be GreenNow.com and sign up to offset their carbon footprint from their cars, planes, and houses. That represents people taking action and making choices. A recent Gallup poll says 84 percent of Americans want to take action to clean the place up, yet in the U.S. it is still illegal in most states to sell alternative energy to homeowners.

Illegal!

Sweeping deregulation of electricity markets simply has not come to pass. By and large, the state monopolies have held on to their power with real tenacity. Fighting many entrenched electricity monopolies in fifty statehouses across the country has turned out to be harder than beating a single gigantic nationwide telephone monopoly like the old AT&T. And, more important, it is not just a matter of getting people better phone service or data transmission. It is more vital than that. We're talking about giving people clean air so all the world can breathe.

Ever the optimist, I firmly believe a clean energy revolution is starting to gain traction. And I believe that the key is replicating the success of the digital telecommunications revolution. The question is, Will it happen quickly enough to prevent a global climate tragedy?

Despite the fact that deregulation of the U.S. energy markets did not happen as I'd hoped, I am not part of the doom and gloom brigade. I look at the overall positive trends. For starters, I believe that protecting the earth and the life it supports must become a primary goal of every business. "Value" must include the cost of having clean air and clean water. "Profit" must include a protective or restorative component.

We must recognize these essential costs of doing business, of producing and consuming our goods and services.

I find the notion that we ought to use nature itself as our model for creating sustainable enterprises highly compelling. It calls for differentiation between an "extractive economy" and a "restorative economy." In the former, businesses are created to make money. In the latter, a business's ability to grow is determined in part by how well it succeeds in mimicking the cyclical aspect of nature—in other words, how well it manages to avoid waste and provide replenishment.

This is exactly the approach we've been taking with Green Mountain. And today, I am encouraged by the fact that we are not alone.

More and more companies, from Whole Foods to Texas Instruments, are operating this way. British Petroleum is being transmogrified into *Beyond* Petroleum, investing $8 billion over five years in alternative energy. At Starbucks, managers have a triple bottom line of sustainability—people, planet, and profit— and try to deal directly with co-ops and small farmers who produce coffee using sustainable methods, like composting and rotating crops. In 2004, FedEx introduced an environmentally superior delivery truck. And in many of its locations, IBM is investing $1 billion a year to conserve electricity in its data centers and has invented an energy-saving microchip. Like our happy band at Green Mountain, these companies recognize that we do not have enough environmental capital to continue behaving badly. We must make the tough choices.

For us all, the environmental answers are obvious: education, liberty, good government, and making daily decisions to choose wisely. Yet two billion people on the planet still do not have access to any form of electricity. That kind of deprivation reminds me of when I was five and my dad ran a line over the chute to our cabin so we could read at night and listen to the radio. Our house was no longer lit only by fire.

Liberty comes from the freedom to choose and to innovate, and without it there is not much point in having a planet to live on.

Good government accepts the task of setting the standards that the corporations and the individuals within their nations follow. Lawmakers have to lay down good laws. We are fortunate in the United States that our laws often allow us great latitude, and we must—especially now—make personal decisions that are forward-thinking and responsible.

The time has come for tough laws on clean air and clean water and conservation and sustainability. We, the people, must mandate the political will to arrest, reverse, and heal negative climate change. We need to do with CO_2 just what we did with cigarettes. When we came to understand that smoking was bad, we changed, and we no longer see doctors in white coats on TV pitching Lucky Strikes or Camels. Education helped Americans realize that tobacco was one of the ways we can poison ourselves, more addictively self-destructive than alcohol or drugs.

THAT'S ONE OF the reasons we created BeGreenNow.com.

Through this innovative Web site, anyone, anywhere in the world can become "carbon-neutral," by buying renewable energy credits from us. BeGreenNow.com helps consumers anywhere, not just in deregulated electricity markets, to calculate their carbon footprint, then to buy carbon offsets so that any individual or any business can reduce their impact on global warming in a convenient, flexible, and innovative way. Those credits go to fund capital investment that cleans up dirty coal plants and other sources of greenhouse gases that cause global warming.

It's clear to me that the Web can democratize us, educate us, and help bust up monopolies. Utility lobbyists and their bought-and-paid-for state senators prevented us from bringing Green Mountain and clean electricity to all fifty states. But with BeGreenNow.com we've found a way to marry Adam Smith to Rachel Carson, and bring the entire planet to clean energy.

Albert Einstein once said, "The significant problems we have cannot be solved at the same level of thinking with which we created them."

So here's my question to everyone running a business, to all you entrepreneurs and budding entrepreneurs: What does it take to be a great company in this day and age?

Epilogue

IF ANYONE HAD ASKED me whether I wanted a birthday party, I would have said no. So I'm glad no one asked me. As far as I know on that night, I am simply out to dinner with my family. My wife, Cheryl, and I, plus four of my children and three of my grandchildren, drive over to a favorite café in our caravan of Priuses. Some think it's odd that we drive these funny little hybrid cars. But we're clean-air people, and since hybrids came on the market, we Wylys have bought about a half dozen of them. The restaurant is owned by a friend of Cheryl's. It's in an outdoor mall not far from our home in Dallas, where I've lived for the last forty years.

We come through the double swinging doors, chattering to one another about this and that. My head is turned toward my little granddaughter Viola, who is singing some tune of her own invention. Then I look around and, all of a sudden, I realize that this is not a routinely crowded café but one packed with a lot of the people who have made my life what it is.

My mind stills. You know how it is when things slow down? When your perception of time elongates, like slow-motion film? You are taking in the data in front of you, but your feelings and thoughts have downshifted into a much slower gear—they're almost deadlocked for the moment, slowed to a crawl. I see my brother, Charles, and next to him, his lovely wife, Dee. There are my other two children, my twins, Laurie and Lisa, and their families, too. There's Lee Ainslie, the brilliant young investor who has run our Maverick hedge fund, along with my son Evan, better than I myself ever could. Lee is talking to Alan Steelman,

240

who managed the staff of the Presidential Advisory Commission that I chaired during the presidencies of Nixon and Ford. I flash back to the '60s, when our cities were burning and Nixon appointed me to carry out his campaign promise of "Black Capitalism." With Berkeley Burrell and Joe Kirven, I set about defining specific ways this promise could actually be helpful at the local level. Today there are over 1.2 million black-owned businesses, and this number has grown 45 percent over five years.

My cousin Newt's cowboy hat is hovering above and behind Richard Hanlon, a colleague and dear friend for nearly forty years from the early computer days when we were pioneering what has become the software products industry and also what has become the Internet. My cousin Flo Guenard, who still lives in Arlington, the antebellum cotton plantation home our forebears built beside the Mississippi River, has driven all the way from Lake Providence, Louisiana, for my birthday party.

I feel almost overwhelmed, but it's not anxiety that's flooding through me. It's pleasure. It's the result of comprehending suddenly that my family is even bigger than I'd ever realized; and since nothing is more important to me than my family, the good feeling is overwhelming me.

Because I rarely think about the years passing by or growing older, being taken unawares by this surprise seventieth birthday party crystallized a lot of feelings and thoughts. I've been blessed with huge successes that overwhelm a bunch of failures since my earliest days as an entrepreneur. I've been a millionaire since I was thirty, and *Forbes* magazine says I've become one of the 600 richest guys in the world.

Along the way I've been heralded as a genius by the press and the pundits, and decried in their same pages as a scoundrel and an idiot. For philanthropy I've been given more thank-you's and civic awards than I could keep track of, and I've given to more good causes than I can remember. I felt it was the right thing to do, that it was both a duty and an honor to help those in need and to give back to the community, town, church, and nation that had provided such opportunity and bestowed such blessings on me and mine. I've also been both disappointed and vindicated as a backer of candidates in elective politics, an arena

I've been involved in at the local, state, and national levels for as long as I can remember, honoring an old family tradition dating back to the time of our country's founding fathers, up to the days of my dad as editor of the *Delhi Dispatch* opposing abuse of political power by the Huey Long machine in our home state.

But money, power, and fame have never represented my core values. Not that I'm against them; I never bought into that Bible verse about a rich man not being able to get into heaven. But spirituality, family and family history, and the quality of the journey—these have always been more important to me. Becoming wealthy was never my goal; it just happened. I was just doing my work, first as a doer, then as a manager of doers, then as an entrepreneur in all its manifestations. I have always had a deep sense that I would be in the right place for me and, if not, God would show me the way out. When times were tough, there would be a way to overcome them. As a result, by the time I was thirty-five, I had more money, power, and fame than most ever wish for.

As for power, it's of no use unless you do good with it, like create jobs and opportunities for others to enrich their lives and those of their children. As for fame, it initially was a thrill, and I loved it. But after a while, I came to see the joys of anonymity. So I've lived a mostly private life. So why now am I publishing this book, a very public act? Maybe it's partly DNA, having an editor dad, and an attorney granddad and theologians and Bible-reading frontier gunfighters as great granddads.

But also, I realized as I wandered through that party that I'd been mulling over stories from my life and wondering what they had to offer others. Taking stock of everything, I was feeling one overriding emotion: gratitude. The urge to tell my story hit me hard; more than just a distant hum in the background, it was a palpable force pulling at my concentration like a child tugging at your sleeve. Reading perhaps a thousand biographies from the time I was in high school had helped and inspired me. I'd learned so much by reading about the lives and work of people like Andrew Carnegie, Tom Watson, Sam Walton, and Helen Keller. I thought that my story, properly told, might inspire and help others, too.

So the next day, I started to write it.

PEOPLE ARE ALWAYS SURPRISED that I don't dress like the proverbial Texas oil baron, or wear a big gold Rolex. Or that I prefer to eat in diners instead of five-star restaurants. Or that even though I once owned an oil refinery, I am a big advocate of the greening of America and the world.

People are also surprised that I, along with Cheryl, bought the Explore Bookstore and Vegetarian Bistro in Aspen, Colorado, so it would not be shut down, and that the cat at the bookstore came from the Cheryl and Sam Wyly Pitkin County Animal Shelter.

Can this same man be the philanthropist who along with his brother, Charles, recently endowed the new theater, designed by modern architect Rem Koolhaus, at the Dallas Center for Performing Arts? Is it possible that this same man has backed both George Bushes but attends the lectures of Bill Clinton at the Aspen Institute? Is it true that this same guy contributed heavily to the campaign coffers of politicians characterized as staunch conservatives, but has always been a big supporter of Planned Parenthood and an advocate of tolerance on social issues?

Of course he can be the same man. He's me. Now, I don't like labels and have never embraced the characteristics of any single label put on me. Yet people want to plunk you down in whatever bucket it's easiest to assign you to. They do this to avoid thinking much about who you actually are. Sometimes it feels like I've been given every label in the book at one time or another, some flattering, some not. None of them trouble me really. The evening ahead of me at this birthday party gives me many retrospective glimpses of all the Sams who reside under the one label I am comfortable with: me.

AS THE PARTY PROGRESSES, I stand in the entranceway and talk to the lifetime's worth of people streaming past me. I can hear people talking about me, swapping "Sam stories." I hear Sally Bingham explain to someone how she didn't trust me when I first got involved with her faith-based clean energy

243

group because I had just spent $2.5 million bashing John McCain and causing him to lose New York's electoral votes after some of my environmental friends had just done the same to my boy Bush in New Hampshire. I had two goals for the ads: first, to get the issue of clean air through clean energy into the presidential debates of 2000; and, second, to support my candidate, who at the time had opened the Texas market to green electricity. Bush, Jr., had promised at Grand Rapids to regulate CO_2 as a pollutant under the Clean Air Act. Sadly, to me, he reneged on that promise his first year in office. As for Sally Bingham, I flew to San Francisco to look her in the eye and tell her that my interest in the environment was not politically driven. And we've been friends ever since.

Sterling Williams is eating a Caesar salad and recounting the origins of Sterling Software and Sterling Commerce. Selling those two companies in 2000 made everyone around me whisper that I had preternatural timing: The tech bubble would burst the exact same month that we closed on the sales of the two for $8 billion.

Once, when I was asked how I could have a 199 percent return on an investment fund I was managing in a year that was not good in general, I answered, "I read a lot." The questioner laughed. But I wasn't joking. It's true. I do read all the time. What I'm trying to say is that having good timing is a result of paying attention to the ideas and trends floating around out there, studying them, coming to some intellectual conclusions, and then, ultimately, listening to your own gut about how to apply your conclusions to the business ventures you elect to pursue.

I'm a strong believer in instinctual intelligence, the unquantifiable kind. Finding success—in business, in family, in life—comes from somewhere deep inside. You have to work hard, apply yourself fully, do your homework diligently, but you also have to be true to your interests, your ethics, your ideas, your desires, and your passions. You can't breach your core values or your overriding bliss, that deep sense of who you are. If you do breach your values, no amount of so-called success will matter, because it's the quality of the journey in life that really matters, not the destination. It's not about how many things you acquire or how much money you have when you reach the destination, but about how much fun and satisfaction you have along the way.

That's what success is: the quality of the journey. Looking around that party, taking in all the affection and humor, the good will of my friends and family, I knew the quality of my journey had been high. I'd been blessed with abundance, not simply material or earthly abundance, but spiritual abundance, emotional fullness, and intellectual gratification.

BY THE TIME DINNER is ending, the noise level goes up, and my sense of time passing is a little bit back to normal. A lot of the murmuring I hear around me is about what a casual party this is. I have heard that kind of comment all my life, and I am used to it. So this surprise party my family organized for me is, like the rest of my life, down-to-earth.

Once when I was in New York to do an interview at *Fortune* magazine, the editor walked straight into the room, looked right at me, and asked where Sam Wyly was. Looking for a bombastic, forceful fellow from Texas who was making big things happen, he didn't believe that the quiet fellow sitting at the table in the low-key business suit was really me.

After dinner, Cheryl gathers everyone into the main dining hall. She's made a reel of Happy Birthday messages, and watching it and listening to the recorded messages is a bewildering and incredibly moving experience for me. I find myself clenching my jaw, and keeping back tears, and forgetting that there's a room full of people watching this film with me.

Jim Lehrer tells the story of how I backed the beginning of his KERA-TV *Newsroom* in Dallas. Jim has a message that moves me a great deal, stating that's what got him started in public broadcasting. I'm especially proud of that because I believe *The NewsHour with Jim Lehrer* is the most honest TV news in the country today. When Jim finishes, Ross Perot pops onto the screen. Watching him generates a mental flash in my head that I haven't got around to mentioning to him that I was planning to borrow a bit of his fame by writing a book about the two of us opening up the computer industry back in the '60s, him with outsourcing, me online with software computing and products.

Next up comes Michael Rouleau, one of the best CEOs I ever recruited for running our 900 arts-and-crafts stores, Michaels My mind briefly shifts to a memory of Don Thomson, "the best there ever was," helping us out in the early days of Michaels. Don was the best CEO I ever knew. How I wish Don was still with us. To this day, I miss this Bronx Irishman's great heart and friendship.

Quickly, my focus is brought back to Mike Milken, a friend of mine for three decades, speaking on the video. His genius for financial innovation was a good thing for the American entrepreneur and for American business in general, effectively revolutionizing both in the '70s and '80s. Mike tells a story about his first investment in a Sam Wyly company; it makes my heart swell with pride.

Then ex-Cowboys great Roger Staubach talks about coming to my office for the first time after he got into the real estate business. He says I made him walk up fourteen flights of stairs rather than use the elevator. He reveals what he was thinking back then—"Man, this guy is really competitive!"—and the room erupts in laughter.

My brother, Charles, is up next. On the screen, Cheryl has made a montage of the two of us as kids that runs under his voice. There's one old photo of us bundled in our winter gear, and another one of us being presented with our Eagle Scout pins by our parents. A third one shows us playing with two other boys in a little red wagon pulled by a billy goat. I hear Charles's voice on the tape saying, "Sam, this is a long way from our small town in the Louisiana cotton patch."

The last message on the tape comes from George Bush the elder. Despite the fact that I grew up a Democrat and devotee of FDR (for his first two terms only; we Wylys, like most Scots-Irish, take a dim view of kings, czars, and emperors) and despite the fact that on many issues I'm a better fit with the Democrats, I have supported him since he was a freshman Congressman. But again, my love of politics goes way beyond labels like Democrat or Republican.

I've always been involved in politics because of family heritage. Granddaddy Wyly was a key man on the parish police jury, Louisiana's name for county government. He was also on the levee board, which was crucial in trying to avoid or minimize floods. That's why people are startled when they ask me today, as the election of 2008 approaches, which candidate I am going to back and I reply, "I have no horse in the race." I was never involved in politics to meet politicians who could help me out. In fact, one of Cheryl's favorite stories is set at a Camp David event for a small group of President George Bush's most loyal backers. It was a sad event that took place after he lost the '92 election to Bill Clinton. George the elder pulled Cheryl aside and said, "These two Wyly guys backed me in every race I ever ran, and they never asked me for anything."

The Woodrow Wilson ideal of freedom, democracy, and free markets is why I'm involved in American politics. And this is why I love America. The opportunity to make one's destiny based on hard work and good ideas and not based on blood or baccalaureate—as was the case in the Old World from which my ancestors came to America seeking land and freedom and a fair shot at earning their way—that's what I believe in.

PEOPLE GET UP after the film ends and start to mingle, milling around and chatting in clusters. Lee Ainslie takes me over to a corner, and tells me, in a way he never has before, that he feels he owes much of what he is to me. Make no mistake, Lee is a brilliant young man and he would have done just fine if I'd never been born. As with so many guests at the party, I'm the one blessed to have known them and to have benefited from their talents, generosity, and affection.

As I'm reflecting on all these thoughts and emotions, cousin Newt strolls over and tells me that his son Rusty is re-enlisting for his second tour of duty in Iraq. Now, I've had my own mixed emotions about our eighteen years of war in the Persian Gulf, first triggered when Saddam grabbed Kuwait in 1990—my more spiritual nature and my gut are telling me that violence begets violence—but I hug Newt and tell him in no uncertain terms that we all owe Rusty and his fighting buddies a debt of honor.

And I mean it. We Wylys don't drive Priuses just because they lead to cleaner air. We know that we as a nation must cure our addiction to Mideast oil and end the wars fought for its control. People don't often link our energy independence to our national security, but the two are inseparable. Together with my youngest daughter, Christiana, I'm now writing an extended essay, in the great American tradition of pamphleteering, on powerful moves our nation can make that will impact life on this planet, ensuring our national security, climate security, and Social Security for future generations. I intend to publish that extended essay as my next book. It will detail a program by which revenue from an internal carbon consumption tax, paired with a tariff on foreign imports, pro rated for the amount of carbon dioxide generated in products, would be allocated to help reduce the Social Security tax on wages and income for all Americans.

As THE PARTY winds down and people come over to say good-bye—many of them have planes to catch the next day, back to Louisiana, or to San Francisco, or to Houston—I'm suffused with happiness and flooded with gratitude and affection.

I cherish my friends, whose companionship has enriched and enhanced my life beyond my power to describe it. All of them have contributed their individual talents and creativity and charted their own individual journeys. We're a country that allows for self-creation. I especially like that.

To me, that's the great American way. It's certainly my way. And it's certainly at the heart of my story.

Acknowledgments

My dad, publisher of the *Delhi Dispatch*, mentored and motivated me to begin the thinking and writing that resulted, six decades later, in this book. He wrote 2,000-word stories about every game our high school football team played–including our first losing, then winning, the state championship.

A few teachers influenced me profoundly. My first-grade teacher, Mrs. Newman, took our class to Arlington Plantation to see where the Yankee generals occupied the upstairs and left their horses' hoofprints on the living room floor. This class trip reinforced the love for American history that I inherited from my dad, and began my study of the entrepreneurs of cotton farms, from large plantations like Scarlett O'Hara's Tara, to the small yeoman owners and the southern sharecroppers, both black and white, who struggled with 40 acres and a mule.

A couple of my Sunday school teachers deeply influenced me early on by making stories from the King James Bible spiritually uplifting and thereby introducing me to the same Shakespearean cadences that I met again at age fifteen, standing in the Lincoln Memorial, riveted by Abe Lincoln's Bible-based Gettysburg Address.

At Louisiana Tech, Dr. Pennington awoke the debater and thinker in me. He was the professor who taught me during one year to research and honestly debate both sides of whether America should recognize Mao's Red China instead of Chiang Kai-shek. During the following year, we debated whether America should pursue a worldwide policy of free trade. China and free trade are still on the table today. We now call it globalization.

Dr. W. A. Paton, at the Michigan Business School, invited me to apply to become their first Paton Scholar. There I was introduced to the writings of Peter Drucker.

I'm grateful to the researchers and writers who helped me with the early drafts of this book: Dennis Hamilton, Heather Chaplin, and Jeffrey Robinson. The research process, begun 30 years ago by Mary Anne Norman Davidson, has now encompassed interviews with over 100 people, mostly in the companies we created and built, whose recollections and perspectives on our work and life made this book infinitely better.

Richard Hanlon, my business partner and fellow director, read several drafts of this book and advised me wisely on all of them.

At Newmarket Press, President and Publisher Esther Margolis and those on her team contributed so generously to this book's success, especially Executive Editor Keith Hollaman, Associate Publisher Heidi Sachner, Director of Publicity Harry Burton, and Editor Linda Carbone.

On my staff, I'd like to thank Susan Tiholiz, who has enthusiastically overseen this project for the last three years; and Karen Wade, Stacy Huebner, Juanell Lance, and Jeannette Gibson-Walker, who expertly supported my writing and rewriting for years.

Bob Asahina and my next-door neighbor, Jan Miller, helped me focus.

My agent, Ed Breslin, had the energy and literacy to actually get a real book to a real publisher.

My wife, Cheryl, has brought me fun and peace, plus her Texas A&M valedictorian edits to this book helped. She shares my love for sports and attended Texas A&M on a volleyball scholarship, just as my brother, Charles, attended Louisiana Tech on a football scholarship.

I deeply appreciate the early readings and comments of my daughters, Laurie, Lisa, Kelly, and Christiana; and of my sons, Evan and Andrew; and the contributions over the years of Rosemary Wyly and of Charles Wyly, both of whom endlessly supplied wisdom and joy.

Index

About the Author

SAM WYLY, A SELF-MADE BILLIONAIRE of Scottish and Irish descent, grew up in Louisiana and attended local schools before going to Louisiana Tech University to study journalism and accounting. He won a scholarship to the University of Michigan Business School, where he earned his MBA.

Sam has been a working entrepreneur for nearly half a century. He has founded and/or grown successful companies in online computing, computer software products, oil refining, insurance, steakhouse franchising, arts-and-crafts retailing, hedge fund investing, environmentally friendly electricity and Internet carbon offsets. Among the companies he created and grew are University Computing, Sterling Software, Sterling Commerce, Earth Resources, Gulf Insurance, Bonanza Steakhouses, Michaels Stores, Maverick Capital, and Ranger Capital. An active proponent of clean air through clean energy, he created Green Mountain Energy (and BeGreenNow.com) and Green Bull Fund.

Sam and his wife, Cheryl, are generous contributors to countless philanthropic organizations, including the Dallas Center for the Performing Arts and the Aspen-Pitkin County Animal Shelter. Sam has also endowed alma maters Louisiana Tech and the University of Michigan Business School. Sam and Cheryl recently purchased Explore Booksellers and Bistro in Aspen, Colorado.

His autobiography, *1,000 Dollars and an Idea*, is his first book, and he is currently at work with his daughter Christiana on a book about green entrepreneuring. Sam has six children, ten grandchildren, and one great-grandchild. He has lived most of his adult life in Dallas, Texas, and also spends time in Aspen and New York's Greenwich Village.